AF560388

WOMEN AND SOCIETY

WOMEN AND SOCIETY

Shagufta Parveen

ANMOL PUBLICATIONS PVT. LTD.
NEW DELHI - 110 002 (INDIA)

ANMOL PUBLICATIONS PVT. LTD.
H.O.: 4374/4B, Ansari Road, Darya Ganj,
New Delhi - 110 002 (India)
Ph.: 23278000, 23261597
B.O.: No. 1015, Ist Main Road, BSK IIIrd Stage,
IIIrd Phase, IIIrd Block,
Bangalore - 560 085 (India)
Visit us at: www.anmolpublications.com

Women and Society

First Published, 2007

ISBN 978-81-261-3227-0

PRINTED IN INDIA

Printed at Mehra Offset Press, Delhi.

CONTENTS

PREFACE

Social contexts are typically different from other areas. Interestingly, whatever is prevalent in the world of imagery, is not applicable to the real world of society. The harsh truth is that Indian Society has not recognised the woman as its bona fide member. She is still a second grade citizen, inferior to man. Women's social empowerment has been an area of serious debate and concern for several decades. As far as India is concerned, social empowerment of women and their education are being wrangled by many a social taboo.

In fact, in a male dominated society, the women-folk are kept at second fiddle only. Apart from the society, the woman has to play her due role in her family also. She is mother, sister, wife and daughter, all rolled into one. She begins as daughter and ends up as grand mother. She plays all these roles in perfection. In society also, the woman has a defined role. She is a teacher, leader, clerk, typist, nurse and domestic servant. She is also a farm labourer and industrial worker. Now, she is journalist, architect, engineer, doctor, soldier, air-woman and even police officer. She wrestles and participates in races. To precise, she is active in all walks of life. Now women are shining in all arenas and all areas in career and profession. Evidently, they prevail everywhere.

Present book, *Women and Society,* is an effort, in order to fill the gap for a comprehensive and exhaustive book on the subject. The undersigned hopes that, this modest attempt would awaken the people concerned. Expectedly, it would also be beneficial for scholars, students and social activists, alike.

—Editor

1

THE BACKDROP

The woman has been the subject of study, in all ages — from the ancient to the modern times. Comments on the nature of women their ambitions and aspirations, desires and wishes, birth and upbringing, relations with husband, paramour, children and other relatives have been the subject of discussion, comments, conversations and investigations throughout the history of mankind. The woman has been branded as a mysterious creature as well as a devoted mother and self-sacrificing wife during various periods of time through which the human civilization has evolved out from its primitive roots to an advanced scientific and technical culture.

The changing status and position of the woman in different periods and in different civilizations have very greatly influenced her upbringing and education. If during one period of time or in one civilization she was brought up as a prized possession of the parents, in some others she was completely neglected and was accepted only as a provider of sexual pleasure to man and as a producer of his offspring. As a provider of pleasure and producer of children, her education was completely neglected but whenever and wherever she was given high prestige in society, her education became the primary concern of the social order. Thus, the education of the woman has been completely limited to her sociological status and psychological make up. In the present book the focus is on the social psychological dimensions of a women education in India.

For better understanding of the socio-psychological dimensions of women education in India one may look into the background out of which the role, position and education of women have emerged from the past to the present. In the following pages the authors have presented a brief description of women's role, position and education in the religious and historical perspectives. The authors have confined their description mainly to the Indian women but have also focused attention on the women in the West in the context of their struggle for emancipation and empowerment in order to visualize its influence on the Indian womanhood.

Old Age

Ironically, very little information is available about the civilization in pre-Aryan India. However, opinion of some, archaeologists is that the non-Aryans had originated in India as early as around 2500 B.C. and were of mixed origin and diverse ethnic composition. Later, their intellectual bent of mind influenced the Aryan thought process. The law of karma, reincarnation, animal veneration, female or earth-mother goddesses, deity worship and male and female fertility symbols might have been imbibed by the Aryans from them.

It seems that to begin with the Aryans overwhelmed the non-Aryans, suppressed their religion and culture and imposed their own values. However, as time passed the Aryans became progressively Indianized, they absorbed the customs of the original inhabitants and modified their religion assimilating the existing culture. The Aryans' own religious and social customs were fused with theirs and Indianized by the native people. Thus, fusing together of incoming concepts and prevailing customs became the tradition of India and of Hinduism.

The Aryans produced vedic literature. The philosophies of Vedanta and Upanishads are their contributions.

Aryan family life was stable. The society was founded on the institutions of home and family. The women were assigned prestigious position in the social order. The Rig Vedic expression "the wife is the home"-shows how domestic life was woven around the woman.

The prevedic society was basically matriarchal. It worshipped a goddess of earth-mother type. The Aryan society was patriarchal but the worship of the goddess prevailed. Earlier the mother goddess was worshipped in the form of icons but the Aryans almost replaced the icons with matronly women real mothers who were human and humane. The mother was given a high status in all the spheres of life.

There was attached great importance to the goddess Aditi who typified the motherhood. She was considered the ideal mother like Maat of the Egyptians and Themis of the Greeks. Her function has been described to tenderly the living beings.

Rig Vedic Aryans loved their wives and children. They had a desire for male child but the birth of a daughter as potential mother was also accepted and welcomed. However, in Rig Veda no desire for a daughter is expressed, while in Atharva Veda the birth of a daughter is even deprecated. In Upanishads there are prescribed certain rituals to be performed by a man who wants a learned daughter to be born.

In the Rig Vedic period the son and daughter were not discriminated in their upbringing. The son was to take to the profession of the father, while the daughter was to inherit the glory and honour of her mother. The wife as mother was given the dignity and respect in the household. She was expected to perform duties which were both of celestial as well as terrestial in nature. She participated in all sacrifices instituted by her husband.

Women were educated both in the spiritual as well as temporal subjects. They were given training in the religious lore, in the historical tradition and mythology. They were also given training in the fine arts as well as in the military science in certain cases. As a qualification for marriage, the education of a girl was considered as important as that of a boy.

The education of the women mainly centred round the acquisition of language and literature, the fine arts and the military science. The ancient literature records that there were scores of women, eligible to become Rishis and composed very effective poetry. The name of Ghosa, the wife of the great seer Kaksivan can be mentioned. In Rig Veda she has been mentioned many a time. Two long, hymns, 39 and 40 of the tenth mandala stand to her credit. Lopamundra is another lady Rishi who is credited with having composed a hymn jointly with her husband Agastya.

Music was a necessary equipment for women of the period. Songs were sung on all important occasions and functions. Dancing as an art was also learnt by the women. The women were also trained in self-defence. They knew how to use bow and arrow.

The paternal and maternal tie was very strong among the early Aryans. The father was respected as the earner and protector, the mother was loved for providing daily nourishment and maintaining the household. The daughter was caressed and fondled by her parents and brothers who gave her lavish presents at the time of her marriage. She was considered the breath and life of the family.

The women had liberty of movement. There was no Parda.

Indo-Aryans recognized the truth embodied in the dictums, "Ignorance is weakness," "Knowledge is power".

The number of Upanishads is estimated to be around fifty. In most of them, we do not find any reference to women. It is only in Chandogya and Brihadaranyaka Upanishads that we find that women were admitted into philosophical groups and were allowed to discuss the highest spiritual truths of life. They enjoyed a position on a par with men. The men and women were considered as the 'two wheels of the same chariot'.

From the account of this period we find that women were free from social constraints. Girls were free to choose their own husbands. They married only after attaining puberty. The women were even exalted to the position of goddess and given different celestial names like Prithvi, a vague personification of the earth, Usha, the goddess of dawn, Ratri, the spirit of night, etc.

The concept of Ardhanarishwara was propagated. The concept was that of a figure image of half Shiva and the other half as Parvati. This image signified the interdependence of men and women. It conveyed the message that separately men and women are incomplete. Only jointly they are complete. The figure image depicted the masculine and the feminine functions of the Supreme being.

It may be noted that in the Upanishadic texts woman was not eulogized as a person in herself but first and foremost her role as wife and mother was given high status and value. The women were idealized and glorified as mothers. The girl as a potential perpetuator of a family line was valued as much as a son.

Since Rig Vedic age education of women was given much importance. There is evidence that the discipline of brahamacharya was also required to be observed by the girl. The stage of brahamacharya in all probability may be the period of studentship of the girl preceding her married life.

The girls were taught that marriage was not for lust, but for perfect domestic life and for producing illustrious progeny. They were given training in the art of house-keeping and house management. Their education was to prepare them to conduct themselves properly in the married life. They learnt the art of some handicrafts, the elements of hygiene, physiology and nutrition.

The pattern of education in the Upanishadic period became more philosophical in nature. The men and women shifted their attention from Vedic ritualism to more intricate problems of life. The women engaged themselves freely in debates and philosophical symposia. Education helped the women to become more balanced and lead a regulated good life. It was directed towards the development of their natural virtues and latent capabilities and aimed at all round development of their character and personality. Eminent women scholars of this period, like Sulabha, Vadya, Maitreyi and Gargi made significant contributions to the advancement of knowledge.

A description of status, position and education of the women of ancient India is incomplete without the mention of Manu's views. *Manusmriti* (about 200 B.C.) prescribes duties and obligations of a woman. For Manu, woman is a perpetual minor and has to lead whole of her life under the guardianship of either the father, the husband or the son.

Manu prescribes that the wife must always worship her husband as God even if he is debauch, immoral and lacks good qualities. It is the bounden duty of the wife to obey and follow the dictates of her husband. The woman's salvation lies only in the devoted service to her husband. He refers to her duties in the following words:

> "She must always be cheerful, clever in the management of her household affairs, careful in cleaning her utensils, and economical in expenditure"

Manu favoured only the domestic and religious education for women. He also favoured the giving of training in music and dance to the woman in order that she may be able to please her man.

The society in the Epic period was completely patriarchal and patrilineal, so the husband was considered the senior partner in the home. But the wife was also given the dignity in the household because of her vocation of motherhood. Her virtues were recognized. Her abilities in the maintenance of the household were appreciated. She was considered to be a true friend of man given by God. She was man's half, his religious partner, giver of joy and sons.

The epics *Ramayana* and *Mahabharata* contain the description of women who presented ideal conduct and models for the womenhood to be adopted by the lesser mortals. But these models also have ingrained in themselves the subordination of the women. Thus the epics trace the story of the rise and fall of the status of women in Hindu society. Mentioned below are a few highly revered and illustrious ladies who form the central theme of these epics.

The foremost among all the ladies mentioned in epics is Devi Sita. Sita is a paragon of virtue. She is an ideal wife who serves her husband with complete devotion, who is an embodiment of the spiritual sublimity of feminine character. She suffers great hardships but remains unperturbed by them. Her only wish is to serve her husband with all her capabilities. She has to suffer the ordeal of fire but at no occasion she expresses any doubt in her loyalty, fidelity, devotion, love and sacrifice for the well being of her husband. She is learned. She can quote moral tales and smrities. She had religious education.

No doubt the ideal of Sita has inspired Indian women for ages. But in the modern times some are raising doubts about the complete subordination to the husband eulogised in the character of Sita. For educationists, it is a dilemma. Should the women education be directed towards the flowering of the women as devoted as Sita to her husband or teach them for independent outlook. For a proper answer all the aspects of Sita's personality as portrayed in the epic have to be carefully examined. One thing stands out that as Sita had her own will and determination and even when she had to undergo torture her determination did not waver.

She was one of the strong-willed women of the Epic Period. She possessed not only physical charm but also a brilliant mind. She was exposed to the brutalities of men when she was forced to discard her clothes before the men of the Kauravas court. But she did not lose the balance of her mind and reasoning power. The arguments presented by her in the Kaurava court were so perfect that nobody except Vidura and Vikarna possessed the courage to reply to her question. In the midst of her humiliation, she still showed good manners and saluted those Kuru elders who did not dare to check the evil. She was deeply learned and had comprehensive knowledge of old traditions, history and the Puranas. She did not hesitate in condemning her husbands when they failed in the performance of their duties. She did not tolerate her insult and inspired even a peace loving man like Yudhistira to war.

Draupadi presents to us an ideal of womanhood who was learned, iron willed, revengeful, intolerant towards undignified behaviour, loving and affectionate and also forgiving. She was a perfect wife, wise counsellor and dear companion to her husbands.

Among the other learned ladies of the Epic period we may name Gandhari, Kunti, Kaushalya, Sumitra, Kaikeyi, Gautami, Sulabha, Mandodri, Trigata and many others.

Gandhari was the noblest of mothers. She had understanding, judgment, intellect and good sense. She remained attached to the cause of justice and righteousness even when her sons were on the verge of being annihilated and their empire destroyed. She had a high sense of justice, possessed great intellectual qualities and depicted in her conduct both human virtues and frailties. She was jealous of Kunti's motherhood and had a longing for a daughter and son-in-law in order to attain Heaven. She spent her life in penance, self denial and righteousness. But she had weaknesses which make her character real and thus presents ideals which are attainable by ordinary human beings.

Kunti was an ideal wife and mother. She was also of strong will. She taught her sons to die gloriously in war than live in infamy. She was an unwed mother of Karna whom she threw in the river. But her love for her son was irresistible, sublime and pure. Kunti presents an ideal of womanhood which is unflinching in love, righteousness yet not so bold as to face the hostile society for her begetting a son out of wedlock.

The three queens of king Dashratha-Kaushalya, Kaikeyi, Sumitra were well-versed in household affairs but were also involved in the state craft. They had many virtues but also sufferred from human frailties. Kaushalya was the ordinary human being but served her husband, as a slave, friend, sister, wife, and mother. Sumitra was calm, steady and balanced. For her the path of duty and righteousness was more important than any material possession. Kaikeyi was dominating, bold and resourceful. Her life shows that she was over-ambitious and wished, to control the kingdom through her husband, and, later through her son. She is by and large portrayed as a negative character.

There are many other women whose lives and exploits are presented as the ideals of Hindu womanhood. These ladies were highly cultured and were prepared to sacrifice personal good for the social good. The education of the Indian women, particularly the Hindu women has been very greatly influenced by the ideals propagated through the study of their lives and exhortations. However, in the modern times some questions are being asked about the ideals so propagated. In the various chapters of this book we will examine these doubts and try to arrive at some conclusions regarding their validity in the twenty-first century.

Buddha inculcated in his followers a reverence for learning. He conveyed the Dharma or Truth to his first disciples at his teaching sessions at Varanasi. These disciples became the first members of the Sangha. Among his first Upasikas or followers there, were two women. Initially, he was reluctant to incorporate women into the Sangha and this attitude resulted in the subsequent neglect of female education by his followers.

Buddha believed that seven factors lead to wisdom: inner mindfulness, searching of the norms, energy, zest, serenity, concentration, and mental balance. These thoughts were installed in the young Buddhist males but were ignored in the case of sisters of the Sangha. As indicated above Buddha initially was averse to the admission of women into his Sangha system but later on agreed to the formation of the order of the nuns-these nuns were imparted religious and spiritual education. A life of celibacy, austerity and strict mental discipline was expected of them. The education for the women was also introduced at the later stage in order to help them to acquire the knowledge that would enable them to lead a fuller life. But the end of Buddhist era in India also resulted in the end of female education for many generations.

In Jainism, there was given great importance to self-denial, restrains of passion and a life of renunciation. A life of restraint and devoid of passion was expected from men and women. The women were also admitted into monasteries and given full facilities to get the best possible education. The Jaina system of education had depth, was universal in nature and applicable to all alike, irrespective of caste, creed or sex.

The spiritually trained Jaina women attained a high degree of academic education and involved themselves in preaching their faith of universal love and brotherhood. They dedicated themselves to social service.

Jainism was divided into two main sects-Digambaras and Shwetambaras. The Digambaras were of the opinion that women were incapable of attaining salvation and so did not admit them into their order. The Shwetambaras, on the other hand, made no distinction between the sexes and freely admitted aspirants of both the sexes into their order.

Theoretically, Jaina believed that man and women both had the right to attain perfection or perfect liberation of the highest order. But in practice Jaina felt that there were very few women who had the strength of mind and body to endure the hard life of an ascetic. The women were considered weak and so unfit to undertake a course of self-mortification and self-effacement. Thus in the spiritual order women had secondary position.

Sikhism considers woman as worthy of respect as man's helpmate and a partner in his domestic life. Women are not looked upon as evil or perpetrator of sin, nor simply the objects of men's pleasure. A woman's roles as mother, wife, sister and daughter are praised and the qualities which the women are expected to develop are love, obedience, contentment and sweet temper.

Sikhism advocated equality among all the human beings. The social equality of the women is ungrudgingly recognised. The militant brotherhood of the Sikhs, the Khalsa founded by Guru Gobind Singh in the seventeenth century was open to both sexes and all classes. The women were initiated into the Khalsa by taking the name of Kaur and were expected to perform the same duties as men.

Since in Sikhism the equality of sexes was recognized, very few restrictions were put on womens' education.

In Christianity, women are considered as the harbinger of evil. No doubt Catholics give a high respectful place to Virgin

Mary but both Protestants and Catholics feel that the women brought the evil to the earth. The fall of Adam is attributed to the evil design of Eve. Hence the pious and saintly Christians like St. Bernard, St. Antony, St. Bonaventure, St. George the great, all cursed women. The woman was described by them as the organ of the devil', 'a scorpion ever ready to sting', 'the poison of an asp', 'the malice of the dragon' and 'the instrument which the devil uses to get possession of our souls'.

The position of the woman in the Jewish faith was very low but in Christianity it was further lowered. They charge her with the crime of disobeying God, causing the fall of Adam and her guilt being transmitted to the whole mankind so that every child is born in sin. Since God had to send, Jesus to be sacrificed because of the first crime of the woman, so she is considered responsible for the crucification of Jesus. The Christian saints and priests considered women to be unclean and so gave much importance to a life of celibacy. It is because of this attitude that the Christian women were denied those rights and privileges which Christian men enjoyed. It is only in twentieth century that the movements of women liberation have resulted in their recognition as equals to men. The women had to wage a severe and persistent battle to achieve those rights which should have been their on the basis of their recognition as a part of humanity.

It is true that women have now been given rights. But they obtained these by their own struggle and by the slackening of the hold of priests over western societies and laws.

Education, historically, was the sole privilege of the rich and the priestly class. The priests dominated the transmission of knowledge throughout Christiandom. They controlled the access to institutions of learning. In all the Christian countries education was the monopoly of the religious orders. The governing priests did not consider the education of women essential. They were of the view that women were incapable of absorbing the same amount of education or the same in-depth knowledge as men. Besides this they thought that women's minds were weaker than men's and did not require that intellectual exercise which the men needed. They had spread the myth that women should be restrained from speaking in church and from getting education.

The Christian priests' disregard for women education was rooted in their belief in women's inferiority. This disregard was further reinforced by the fear of female emancipation. They were afraid that free education may lead to the deployment of women's full potential.

This in their view was going to upset the natural order between men and women and God and women and the church. They emphatically pointed out that the women are modest, obedient and docile and as such do not require as thorough an education as men do.

Later the missionaries started giving education to women but they segregated boys and girls and prescribed different courses of study to the two sexes. The boys were taught useful subjects in the vocational, mechanical and scientific spheres. The girls were taught domesticity, cooking, knitting, etc. The idea was that boys should be prepared for life outside home and the girls for life inside the home.

As we have already pointed out that the situation has very much changed now in almost all the Christian countries but still the stigma attached of being a woman has not been completely wiped out. And whatever women have achieved in raising their status and position and in attaining prestige has been the fruits of their own struggle for emancipation and empowerment.

Intermediate Age

In Islam straight forward directions regarding the status and the position of the women have been laid down. It is the only religion in which the universal laws for all walks of human life are laid down including that for women. There are directions regarding social and political rights of women. There are laws regarding their claims to property and their privileges for the custody of children and their religious duties.

Islam gives equality to women in relation to men in many respects. It makes a case for the dignity of women. In holy Quran it is mentioned that "women are the twin halves of men". "The world and all things in it are valuable but the most valuable thing in the world is a virtuous wife", God enjoins upon you to treat women well for they are your mothers, daughters and aunts".

There are also many aspects which present seeds of discrimination between men and women. Islam gives rights of inheritance of property to women as a daughter, a wife, a mother, a sister and in some cases even to more distantly related. But when a man has a son and a daughter both, the share of the daughter is, half that of the son.

The inequality between men and women is also evident in Islam when we find that women are put in seclusion in Islam. They are put behind parda and debarred from any male company besides their immediate and near relations. Other areas of discrimination are man's right of divorce, the right of men to practice polygamy, have four wives at a time and similar other provisions like "the testimonies of two women are equal to one man". Parda system isolated women from the outer world and confined them to the four walls of their house.

In the holy Quran the women are exhorted to be modest, chaste, lead a life of decorum and decency which was interpreted by the religious leaders in terms of putting the women in Parda, put a veil or burkha on their bodies. This resulted in losing their right to participate in communal activities. Thus Islam differentiated between the man's world and the woman's world.

In early Islam, female education was highly restricted. Only in the families in which the father was educated, the girls learnt to recite the verses of Quran. But her learning was totally dependent on the approval of the father.

In the medieval period women education was by and large ignored. The women were excluded from public gatherings or in any intellectual deliberations. The result was that most of the women remained illiterate and unlettered. Some females had access to tutors and libraries but they were not engaged by men-folk in any intellectual discussion. Hence they could learn through their own individual efforts. By and large women remained in status as inferior, unequal, submissive and ignorant beings. Females were denied access to learning. They were also excluded from the mosques where most of the education occurred. They could not attend the Kuttabs and the Madrasa.

Some of the women who were fortunate to receive education usually came from affluent, prestigious families that could afford to hire private tutors and successfully face the criticism of the community for educating their females.

It is worth noticing that despite Islam giving equality to sexes and permitting men and women to acquire success, education and honour and in spite of it giving equal religious and spiritual rights, the Islamic clergy interpreted it in terms of equality in their own natural sphere of being men and women. They propagated that the roles of men and women are different and so they have to be isolated from each other. While man needs education woman has to stay at home and involve herself in house keeping for which the training in the house craft is only needed, which can be provided in the home itself.

Above we have described the role, status and education of Indian women as determined by the religious order to which they belonged. Let us now look into the status, etc., of the Indian women in historical perspective.

We have already emphasized that from the very beginning of the history of civilization society has been male dominated and the status and the position of the woman depended on how man conceived her in his relationship with her. In India the Rig Vedic society was founded on the home and family and so assigned a place of importance to her. The Rig Vedic sages focus the domestic life on the sentiments centred round the women. The women of the Vedic and Brahmanic literature. The learned lady was held in high esteem.

In the Epic age the woman was considered to be a true friend of man. She was regarded as man's half, his religious partner, giver of joy and sons. Through her man was able to attain immortality. Sita, Savitri, Damyanti, Draupadi born in royal families and in luxury followed their husbands to the wilderness of the forests and endured a life of much hardships along with them. They embodied in themselves extreme love, devotion and selfless service to their spouses. They served without expectations of any return from them. Women of this period were also ideal mothers and true teachers of their offspring.

There is evidence that the Muslim invasion brought about the deterioration of women's position. Restrictions on her rights and freedom were imposed. Muslims adherence to Polygamy and Parda also influenced the Hindus. Restrictions of the rights and privileges of the women were imposed. The women were considered inferior to men and so began to be ill-treated. The women, both among Hindus and Muslims were confined to their homes and their duties, rights or obligations all were interpreted in terms of devoted wife and sacrificing mother.

The position of the medieval Muslim women, according to Muslim law was somewhat better than that of contemporary Hindu women. But in practice it was similar or in many instances inferior than Hindu women because of the rigidity of the Parda system and the denial of education to Muslim women.

There is no authentic account of the prevalence of education among Muslim women of various classes and masses. However, it seems that the majority of Muslim women were illiterate and those few who were educated learnt through oral and non-formal instructions. There were ladies of the noble families who had the privilege of learning the religious texts and various arts and crafts but those they learnt by their own persistence and in their own homes. History reveals that there were highly learned and accomplished Muslim ladies like Razia Sultan, Chand Bibi, Nur Jahan, Jahanara, etc. These ladies could learn and attain dominance by sheer strength of their personality. Thus, we may conclude that during Muslim period while the women from royal families enjoyed much respect and freedom and were interested in learning, the women of lower and middle strata of society were largely ignorant and illiterate.

New Age

At the advent of the British Empire the status and the position of the Indian women were very low. From the ideological point of view women were considered a complete or inferior species. They were inferior to males having no personality, no significance. From the social point of view they were kept in a state of utter subjection, denied any right, suppressed and oppressed.

The customs of polygamy, the parda, the denial of woman's rights over property, child marriage, Sati Pratha and denial of remarriage to widows - all these practices in this period resulted in the development of a very weak personality of the woman. She was not only considered an inferior by the male members of the society but she in herself became rooted to the idea that she was weak, helpless, subordinate and inferior - a non entity, a slave. Hence women themselves became great perpetuators of tyranny on the women over whom they could exercise their sadism. So dowry demands, forcing of the widows to burn or to lead a life of misery and toil, a dominant mother-in-law and subservient daughter-in-law, all such acts were initiated, perpetuated and committed by the women or in connivance with the women.

The British influence was in the positive direction. The close contacts with western cultural tradition, literature and education affected very deeply the minds of the Indian leaders. The result of it was the social movements for reforms in those evils which were prevalent in the society. The reformist movements started in the 19th century. The leaders and the social reformers who were in the forefront of the struggle for women emancipation were Raja Ram Mohun Roy, Ishwar Chandra Vidhyasagar, Swami Dayanand Saraswati, Swami Vivekanand, Mahatma Gandhi, Jawaharlal Nehru and many others.

To Raja Ram Mohun Roy goes the credit of laying the foundations of all the principle reformist movements which subsequently became instruments for modernization of the country. He devoted whole of his life for raising the status and position of the women in India. He propagated his own democratic, rational and human conception of womanhood.

It is said that while Raja Ram Mohun Roy saved the widow from self-immolation or becoming Sati on the funeral pyre of her husband, Ishwar Chandra Vidyasagar released her from a living death, by helping to legalize the Widow Remarriage. He wrote a book on widow remarriage which was published in 1853. It was through his efforts that the widow remarriage Act of 1856 was passed which permitted the legitimacy of the issues born of such marriages. He also gave much importance to the education of the girls which was considered essential for the development of their personality. Swami Dayanand Saraswati felt that the woman's status must be raised. He sought to create equal status for the women in the field of Sacred Thread Ceremony. He considered that education must aim at making women capable of performing her duties in home as well as outside the home. He founded Arya Samaj in 1875 at Bombay. It started Gurukuls for widows, rescue homes for destitutes, etc.

Another social reformer was Swami Vivekanand. He was greatly pained at the miserable condition of women in India. He, therefore, recommended that women should be supported and educated as men. He said, "It is only in the hands of educated and pious mothers the great men are born. The ideal woman in India is that mother, the mother first and the mother last." He suggested that the women should be made ambitious through a sound system of education. For him the ideal of womanhood was not only Sita or Savitri but that of an ideal mother. He said, "Motherhood is the beginning. Motherhood is the end of Indian womanhood."

Mahatma Gandhi considered that if a husband is a God, the wife is a Goddess. Wife is not a slave but a friend and companion with equal rights. Gandhi held the view that women have a right to education. But he was of this view that men and women are not identical but complementary to one another. Education for them should be such that it makes of them capable of performing their duties. Gandhiji's efforts led to the elevation of the woman's status an involved her in the struggle for social progress and political independence. The women were able to develop their latent powers. Women like Sarojini Naidu, Kasturba Gandhi, Kamla Nehru, Aruna Asaf Ali participated in the political arena with all their might and potentials. Indeed India witnessed the rise of many great women.

India gained freedom in 1947. Her Constitution was adopted on 26th January, 1950. The Constitution gave full and equal rights to women as compared to men. Thereafter we arc witnessing a strong, persistent and unrelenting struggle for the emancipation, empowerment and dignity led by women activists, enlightened political leaders, educationists and social reformers.

The western countries being mostly Christianity dominated gave the status and the position to the women as indicated by their religion. Hence in most of them till quite recently women were given a very low status in comparison to men. The Christians considered the women as temptations of the world of flesh and of the devil. The fathers of the church believed in the myth that Eve led Adam into sin.

Earlier, before the advent of Christianity, the women of Greece enjoyed much better status and position than later Christian women. Plato, the Greek philosopher made no distinction of the sexes in his ideal 'Republic'. He, no doubt, admits that women are generally inferior to men but in his view they have similar, if lower, capacities and power. He emphasized that there is no occupation or art for which they may not be fitted by nature and education. He, therefore, wants them to share in government and war as well as in the various mechanical trades. Still the Greek opinion was that women are best suited for household chores. Aristotle had unshakable faith in the value of household and the family and considered man as its natural ruler.

The Romans held women in greatest honour as the words of Cato the Censor show: "All men, rule over women, we Romans rule over all men, and our wives rule over us."

In law, however, the women had an inferior status in that they did not have freedom. They were always put under the control of some male member of the family. Before marriage she was entirely under the control of father, on her marriage she passed into a similar position towards her husband, and if she remained unmarried, she was under the control of her nearest male relative. In spite of this legal position, the position of the women in their family was an honoured one. Roman girls did not, as a rule, go to school. They were taught all that they were to know of book learning at home by their mothers.

When Christianity came a new set of virtues began to be

propagated in place of the vices which had engulfed the later Roman social order. It is to be noted that the Roman society, in the beginning of the Christian era, had become a completely debunked society in which ethical and moral values were completely eroded. Christianity combined and harmonized an ideal of personal morality, sincerity, honesty, chastity, love, loyalty, kindness and unselfishness. Womanhood was elevated and given a new dignity. Before the establishment of Christianity, divorce became frequent, infanticide, child exposure, cruel and bloody gladiatorial shows licentiousness in private life were the evils which had deformed the society. Christianity fought against these evils and created a better and just order. Women, even though remained under the subjection of male members, yet were given an honoured place in home.

In the early middle ages, from the sixth to the tenth centuries, the creeds and dogmas established by the church were accepted without any doubts or questions. But after tenth century, particularly, during the eleventh and twelfth centuries, Christian scholars started questioning the dogmas spread by the church.

They adopted logical methods of discussion and analysed the various beliefs and faiths on the anvil of rationality. This period is, therefore, known as the period of Scholasticism. "The aim of Scholasticism was to support the doctrines of the Church by rational argument, to show essential harmony between reason and faith." The thirteenth century was the Golden Age of Scholasticism. In this age, Scholasticism projected two high peaks. One was that of the doctrine of St. Thomas, who along with Albert built Aristotelianism into a Christian system of thought. The other was that of St. Bonaventure. At this peak, the Augustinian thought of the middle ages reached its highest development , St. Thomas and St. Bonaventure were two sages who led to the construction of Scholastic synthesis middle ages.

We find in general in the doctrines of the church of the

middle ages that woman was represented as the source of all evils in the world. St. Franciscan Bonaventure wrote.

> "Woman is an embarrassment to man, a beast in his quarters, a continual worry, a never ending trouble, a daily annoyance, the destruction of the household, a hinderance to solitude, the undoing of a virtuous man, an oppressive burden, an insatiable bee, man's property and possession ."

The view of St. Thomas Aquinas (1225-1274) about women were almost similar in that he also considered women inferior to men. He might be greatly influenced by the opinion of the age. In his opinion man represents in himself perfection, while woman stands for the imperfect. He also depreciates the functions of the woman. Woman is dependent on man for procreation and for guidance throughout her life whereas man needs woman only for procreation. Man is thus master and woman a mere helper. The woman has weaker body, the smaller growth and weaker intellect and lesser will-power.

During Scholastic period it was not compulsory for girls to go to the school. To them domestic education was given in their homes. The University rules did not allow the admission of women in the Universities.

Martin Luther (1483-1546) criticised and protested against certain practices of the established church of his times. He tried to combine the best ideals of the past with religious morality and a new idealistic approach to Christian religion developed in Protestantism. The Protestants advocated an honourable and equal status for women like men. According to them the man is the embodiment of the strength, power and greatness while woman is the embodiment of the smooth, gentle, softness and beauty. Man and woman are complements of each other. Their relationship is not that of a master and a slave. The Protestant reformers also advocated universal compulsory and free education for all classes and for both men and women.

The Protestant revolt was accompanied and followed by the humanists who initiated the period known as Renaissance. These humanists rejoiced the theological dialectic of Scholasticism. In this period the emphasis was laid on the popular and universal education for both men and women. The woman was now not given an inferior status but was recognized as an active partner of man in bringing progress and Prosperity to the society. Comenius demanded education for all children rich and poor, boys and girls, in all cities and towns, villages and hamlets. John Locke and Hobbes recognized that familial authority belonged to the mother as well as to the father.

The Protestant revolt did not put equal influence in all the countries of Europe. However, in France, the State, church and the government achieved a considerable degree of independence from Rome. At this time Jean Jacques Rousseau introduced the philosophy of Naturalism in education. However, his philosophy of education did not follow the principle of equality in the education of men and women. For him the procreative role of the woman makes her unlike man. Functionally the women are determined by their reproductive role. He also implied in his attitude towards women education that they are the source of evil. Modesty is the only virtue of a woman and man has the absolute right over his wife.

He gave a long list of women characteristics like shame, stupidity, weakness and ignorance. He was of the view that intellectual pursuits are not for the women. Nature intended women for domestic functions mainly. For him the woman was only required to please man. So woman has to learn singing, dancing, embroidery and designing. She may receive an early education in morals and religion so that she can provide a good home for her family.

The psychological developmentalists like Pestalozzi and Herbert and Froebal were however of a different view that the woman is neither physically weak nor morally inferior to man. She is the active sharer of sorrows and sufferings of life with man. Pestalozzi believed that it was possible to improve the status and position of woman only through education. Herbert emphasized that the aim of the education of the woman should be to analyse her interests, to discover which are best for her and for society and apply these interests in the various situations in life. His emphasis was that education of woman should develop the will to be good and the desire to make good moral choices resulting in a high degree of personal character and social morality.

According to Froebel, "Education must be controlled development by which both man and woman come into realization of the life of the all encompassing, unity of which both of them are a part a development by which their lives broaden until it has related itself to nature until it enters sympathetically into all the activities of the society, until it enters into the achievements of the race and the aspirations of humanity". Thus it may be concluded that the developmentalists consider woman having equal position like that of man. They are the active members of the society who help to make a better home and society.

Jeremy Bentham was a covert feminist. He wanted to put untapped brains and energies of women to use. He believed that the sensibility of women is greater than men. The woman is more fit for a family life and man for outside life. But Bentham did not want to exclude women altogether from public life.

James Stuart Mill emphasized that the emancipation of women has a two way effect: "they themselves be happy, they will add to the happiness of society". Hence he laid stress on the women education as the surest way to cultivate them and to free them from the bonds of domesticity by opening up careers for them. Mill criticized the theory of inner inferiority of women as supported by Aristotle and Rouseau. But Mill did not question the traditional family system and its demands on women.

Among the socialists Marx and Engels are predominant. They were the forerunners of the doctrine of communism. According to this doctrine they preached that through the institution of family, the children became private heirs which meant the women's reproductive labour like their productive work underwent a transformation from social to private. And this led to the subordination of women in terms of the emergence of the private property.

The description given above about the status, position and education of the women both in India and western countries indicate that women, by and large, were given much inferior status and position in most of the periods of history and by most of the thinkers with a few exceptions. The great philosophers like Plato, Aristotle, St. Thomas Aquinas, Rousseau and others talked much of equality and goodness of mankind but did not acknowledge the same goodness and equality to women. John Stuart Mill may be taken as an exception. The social theorists considered that institution of private property was the root cause of relegating women to a secondary position.

The situation so far presented started to change in the later part of the nineteenth century and the beginning of twentieth century. The women education began to spread. The Industrial Revolution, American Independence and the world wars awakened the western women. Further the political upheavals and revolutions in USSR, France, India and China made the women aware of their enslavement by the male members of the society. The women began to demand equal rights with men.

The Industrial Revolution in Europe ushered a new era in the emergence of women from their homes to engage various other vocations. It inspired the women's movement for bringing change in their status and position. The First World War brought dramatic alteration in the image of woman. At the end of it the opportunities of women's employment increased many-fold. The women also asserted in their freedom of dress and in smoking and drinking in public.

The Second World War brought almost four million new women workers. There was an upsurge in the demand of women's equal rights with men. The women education spread rapidly. The women now entered in all types of professions along with the right to speak in public, to vote for and hold office. There was a revolt against the double standards of morality and against puritanism. As twentieth century advanced the women adopted swim suits, short skirts, started taking part in sports, driving cars, etc. The women got greater leisure by the introduction of mechanized kitchens. By the middle of the twentieth century women's liberation movements became more vigorous and involved more and more women's organizations, in Europe, in general and in America, in particular.

The women now presented the cult of new feminism. It demanded full social equality for women. The women fought for more independence and discarded the traditional triangular roles for themselves that of children, kitchen and the church. The women's organizations rejected the 'Barbi-doll' stereotypical model of woman. The middle class educated women were in the forefront of the struggle for women's rights and for presenting a new image of feminism. They protest against a passive, conforming, dependent female stereotyped roles and a future which ties them down to the home and family.

The women's movements have achieved much. Still, even in the west the women have not yet attained that position and status which they consider is equivalent to men. They are still fighting for equal pay, status, position and security like that of men. They have become intolerant to any discrimination in their service conditions because of their sex. The battle is going on.

Renaissance

We have traced very briefly the history of women movements for empowerment, equality and recognition and worthy members of the society in the west. Let us now peep into the situation as it exists with respect to Indian women.

The Indian women have fallen from the high position and status held by them in Vedic times to a very degrading position in the medieval period and in the earlier decades of the modern period. It was for the enlightened Indians educated in the western tradition and culture that brought a change in the outlook of the Indian males and females regarding their mutual relationship. In Indian situation the movement for female emancipation was led in the beginning by the male members of the society.

These Indian males who fought for a higher status and the position of women were those who were impressed by the regards and considerations which western women enjoyed but they made the case of women emancipation on the basis of the reinterpretation of Indian religious texts and exposing the gimmicks of the half literate clergy which advocated sati system and approved the ill treatment of widows, parda, system, confining of the women to homes, child marriages and calling any women as Kulta or corrupt if she deviated slightly from the norms of conduct laid by them for women. For the ill-treatment of women they were drawing support from a perverted interpretation of the religious texts and religious precepts. The enlightened Indians exposed their misinterpretation and based their argument for women liberation on their own very well studied and expressed interpretation.

The movement for women emancipation was also undertaken by enlightened women like Pandita Rama Bai and others. They set the trend which was followed by hundreds of women. The freedom movement launched by Gandhiji drew women into the central field of struggle. Women fought for the freedom of the country as well, as for their own emancipation. According to *Manusmriti* Hindu women were given a right to Stridhan properties but not to the joint family property on which she had only the right to maintenance. She was given an inferior position in the law of adoption. The status of the woman was determined according to the nature of relationship she had with a man. She was a "Sarvainini" as a wanton woman, "Veshya" as a prostitute, "Kishkashirii" as a woman discarded by her paramour or a "base" as a woman kept exclusively by the man.

According to Justice Bhandare "It was only later that during the time of Vijanesvera that the archaic Smriti law was freed from religious fetters and changed for the benefit of women". But it took a long time and centuries of oppression that women got some legal rights over their property. It was only in 1937 that the concept of widow's estate was developed in respect of property inherited by her from her husband.

The freedom struggle created an urge in the Indian male and female to ameliorate the conditions of the downtrodden and neglected sections of the society. The women, Scheduled Castes and Scheduled Tribes were some such sections. Hence when the constitution for an independent India was drawn, the emphasis was put on the development of an egalitarian society. For the elimination of discriminatory and derogatory practices against women Articles 14, 150, 16, 39(e) and 51 were introduced. These guarantee equality and special protection for women.

The Article 14 provided for equality of all before the law. Article 15 emphasized that the "State shall not discriminate against any citizen on grounds only of religion, race, caste, sex, place of birth or any of them." Article 15(3) stated that "Nothing in this article shall prevent the state from making any special provision for women and children." Article 16 mentioned that (1) there shall be equality of opportunity for all citizens in matters relating to employment or appointment to any office under State. (2) No citizen shall, on grounds only of religion, race, caste, sex, descent, place of birth, residence or any of them be ineligible for, or discriminated against in respect of any employment or office under the State.

Article 39 States: The State shall, in particular, direct its policy towards securing:

(1) that the citizens, men and women equally, have the right to an adequate means of livelihood

(2) that there is equal pay for equal work for both men and women

(3) that the health and strength of workers, men and women and the tender age of children are not abused and that the citizens are not forced by economic necessity to enter avocations unsuited to their age or strength."

Article 51 A States: "It shall be the duty of every citizen of India to promote harmony and the spirit of common brotherhood amongst all the people of India transcending linguistic, logistic and regional or sectional diversities, to renounce practices derogatory to the dignity of women."

When the Universal Declaration of Human Rights was adopted on 10th December. 1948 its Article I provided that "all human beings are born free and equal in dignity and rights". Article 2 provided for equality of sexes. It states that "everyone is entitled to all the rights and freedoms without distinction of sex."

The International covenant on Civil and Political Rights, 1966 urges every covenant State to respect and ensure to all individuals within its territory the rights recognized by that covenant without distinction of sex. Article 3 of this document emphasize that covenant States should undertake to ensure equal rights of men and women in 1979 the convention on the Elimination of All Forms of Discrimination Against Women reiterated "that discrimination against women violates the principles of equality of rights and respect for women's dignity and is an obstacle to the participation of women on equal terms with men in the political, social, economic and cultural life of their countries, hampers the growth of prosperity of society and the family and makes more difficult the full development of the potentialities of women in the service of their countries and of humanity and urges that change in the traditional role of women as well as role of women in society and in the family is needed to achieve full equality between men and women".

Justice Bhandare writes "In spite of the enshrinement of these provisions, equality between men and women continue to be an elusive goal, not only in our country but all over the world. A wide gap exists between the ideal and the practical in our country, partly due to historical reasons. However, the main reason why such discrimination continues in our country is the attitude, of inferiority and bondage-towards women and an atmosphere in which women are deprived of all basic freedoms, starting with that of education, and are thereby exposed to easy exploitation".

This book concentrates on women's education and its impact on male-female discrimination and on the female psyche. In almost all the chapters, the book highlights the importance of education to the girl child as well as to the grown up woman.

Justice Bhandare raises some questions regarding disparity between man and woman and says that several of those questions do not have an adequate and satisfactory answer.

An attempt is made to seek answers to these and similar questions by focussing our attention on the triad of sociological, psychological and educational aspects of female development in our country. The questions raised by Justice Bhandare are:

(a) How is it that in public life-professions, business and services-women are not adequately represented?

(b) How is it that women put in longer hours of work compared to men and yet do not enjoy equal status or opportunities?

(c) Why is it that property owned by women constitutes a very small fraction of the property owned by men?

(d) Why is it that maternity is not recognized as an essential social function?

(e) Why is the rate of suicide so high among women?

(f) Why is it that fairness vanishes when it comes to giving a fair deal to the 'fair' sex.

The struggle for the emancipation of western women had its impact on the emancipation movements in India. But in India the feminist movement did not take the aggressive and militant form which it took in some European countries. In India the feminist movements were not vehemently or violently opposed by the male members, or clergy or politicians. Rather they were supported by enlightened political and religious thinkers. The agitations for female liberation in India began in the later part of the nineteenth century and were carried on with zeal till the Constitution of India in 1950 gave them equality in terms of their lawful existence.

Those agitations were largely spearheaded by women reformists and male thinkers who had the best of western education. These movements emphasized on the need of the small middle class educated and privileged women. The real breakthrough in the recognition of male-female equalities was made only when the Constitution of the Indian Republic was adapted in 1950.

Before that in 1949 the University Education Commission which was set up under the Chairmanship of Dr. S. Radhakrishnan has observed:

> 'There cannot be educated people without educated women. If general education had to be limited to men or to women, the opportunity should be given to women, for then it would more surely be passed on to the next generation".

The secondary education commission (1952-53) emphasized that:

> "Every type of education open to men should also be open to women". Thus this commission did not make any distinction between the education of men and women and so the era of equality of educational opportunities to women began.

The Report of the National Committee on Women's Education (1958-59) made a strong case for the education .of women. Its important recommendation was:

> "The education of women should be regarded as a major and a special problem in education for a good many years to come and a bold and determined effort should be made to face its difficulties and magnitude and to close the existing gap between the education of men and women in as short a time as possible".

As has been specified earlier the movements for women emancipation in India were largely initiated by the Government on the insistence of the educated and reform-oriented women leaders. These leaders by and large did not lead independent movements but were more dependent on the government help, funding and the initiatives in framing laws and rules for women's upliftment. The National Council for Women's Education played an important role in spearheading the movements for women education and their upliftment. The Council set up a committee to examine comprehensively the problem of curricula for girls at all stages of education. This committee was set up on November 1, 1961 under the chairmanship of Smt. Hansa Mehta.

The committee after carefully examining all the evidences produced before it came to the following conclusions:

> "Our enquiry has not imbued with any conviction that there are clear and ascertained differences between the two sexes on which an educational policy may readily be based. We have encountered a number of facile generalizations about the mental differences between boys and girls; we have found few, if any, which we are able to accept. Men and women have existed for centuries; but either sex is still a problem to the other and indeed to itself, nor is there any third sex to discriminate dispassionately between the two. In the mean time it is the part of wisdom neither to assume difference nor to postulate identity, but to leave the field free to both to show themselves".

The above mentioned conclusions show the confusion in the thinking of the women leaders who failed to arrive at definite conclusions regarding the differences between two sexes. We have endeavoured to point out, that, such conclusions have left the field wide open for discrimination particularly in education. The last words 'but to leave the field free to both to show themselves', sound quite traditional which emphasizes that woman's field is home and the man's work. The committee's observation may lead to the conclusion that both males and females should work freely in their own fields. However, the committee tries to refute traditional view by emphasizing that "the traditional view assumes that there are two different personalities-masculine and feminine, with widely different and complementary traits and that they owe their origin to sex. This view also has however been proved to be incorrect. Recent scientific studies have shown that the differences in the psychological traits of men and women are due, not to innate sex differences but to social conditioning".

The committee on the basis of such observations as above, recommend', for the education of girls and women that "Education is a great levelling force and one sure way to raising the status of women to real equality with men is to eliminate, or to reduce to a minimum, the existing wide gap in the education of girls and women."

The Education Commission (1964-66) endorsed the views of the National Committee on Women's Education and emphasized:

> "The education of women should be regarded as a major programme in education for some years to come and a bold and determined effort should be made to face difficulties involved and to close the existing gap between the education of men and women in as short a time as possible".

Thus we see that year after year various committees and commissions emphasized the education of the women for raising their social status. But besides some progress in the quantitative expansion of women education no significant developments took place in raising the status of rural, downtrodden, Schedule Castes and Schedule Tribes women. Hence the committee on the Status of Women (1971-74) concentrated on this anomaly.

It observes:

> "The deep foundations of the inequality of the sexes are built in the minds of men and women through a socialization process which continues to be extremely powerful. Right from their earliest

> years boys and girls are brought up to know that they are different from each other and this differentiation is strengthened in every way possible-through language forms, modes of behaviour of labour etc. They begin to learn very early what is proper or not proper for boys and girls and all attempts at deviation are noticed, discouraged and sometimes punished. The sissy and the tom boy are equal objects of derision. There is nothing wrong in this if it were merely a question of distinction. But it soon gets inextricably tied up with the traditional concepts of the roles of men and women and their mutual relationships which are based on inequality. The process of indoctrination affects the development of individual personalities.

The only institution which can counteract the effect of the process is the educational system. If education is to promote equality for women, it must make a deliberate, planned and sustained effort so that the new value of equality of the sexes can replace the traditional value system of inequality".

The committee comes to the conclusion that the reasons for the variation of social attitudes and the consequent slow progress of women's education are both social and economic.

It found that a substantial number of girls are engaged in contributing to the family income by their own labour. The prevalence of child labour has been admitted as the greatest deterrent to the spread of education among children of the poor. The committee was appalled by the extent and degree of use of young girls of five to fourteen years in work for twelve hours a day.

The committee also found that large majority of girls by the time they reach the age of eight, are required at home to do various domestic chores, e.g., collecting fire wood, coal waste, cow dung, fetching water, at times from long distances, washing, cleaning, cooling, taking food and water to parents in their places of work, etc.

About the girls education in the rural areas it observed that:

> "education in the rural areas often results in alienation of the girls from their habitat. While this criticism was voiced in many places, the most vocal opinion was expressed by women in the villages of Himachal Pradesh. Since the development of the state and the standard of living of its people depended on the continued efforts of women in agriculture, education in their opinion was becoming an adversary of progress. Girls who completed their formal education in the villages, did not want to continue living in villages or take part in agricultural activities. The problem became more acute when, owing to absence of secondary schools in the villages, they had to study outside, in urban or semi-urban areas. Many of them found village life with its hardships intolerable afterwards. Most girls who complete secondary school develop a desire for white collared jobs, or urban life in some forms".

The National Policy on Education (1986) considered that "Education will be used as an agent of basic change in the status of women." It suggested that "the National Education System will play a possible, interventionist role in the empowerment of women.

It will foster the development of new values through redesigned curriculum, text books, the training and orientation of teachers, decision-makers and administrators, and the active involvement of educational institutions. This will be an act of faith and social engineering".

National Commission on Self-Employed Women and Women in the Informal Sector (1987-88) has emphasized:

> "Education is both an important instrument for increasing and bettering the chances of women's employability and for empowering women as they learn to think for themselves, become confident and also develop the capability of recognising more acutely the areas of exploitation."

The National Commission for Women, a statutory body was set up under the National Commission Act, 1990 to safeguard the rights and interests of women. This commission reviews legislations, intervenes in specific individual complaints of atrocities and takes remedial action to safeguard the interests of women where appropriate and feasible.

In Indian situation the women's movement has not been in terms of radicalism or the violent assertion of the female rights. The reason for it seems to be the sensivity of both the males and female towards the necessity of the upliftment of the women from their miserable existence. The Government and NGOs all laid great emphasis on the empowerment of women for which they all recommended crash programmes for women education.

The feminist movement in India can be characterized by its sensible approach. In this movement almost all political parties except those who have leanings towards fundamentalism and orthodoxy in their outlook lend their support. By and large it is non-commercial and non-sectarian; But this movement has failed to break away, from the traditional approach of motherhood, housewife and kitchen queen. The movement has not yet reached a large section of rural and slum area women. It is the movement essentially spearheaded by urban, educated middle class. This class is in a typical paradoxical situation. It wants the best of both worlds. It wants to secure independence from male domination but is not willing to think in terms of a life pattern in which the male does not figure as a key person in the role of a father, brother or husband or in any other form.

In spite of the feminist movements, political support and increasing awareness of evil influences on national progress of the neglect of women, we find that Indian women's status and position has not undergone any revolutionary change. No doubt the urban middle class women have become more assertive, better educated and economically independent by involving themselves in all types of jobs, some of which were so far under the special male prerogatives like those in the army, police or as airline pilots. But the majority of the women of rural and poor classes are suffering from various types of disabilities. The main reason for such a situation seems to be the woefully low percentage of female literacy. According to Prof Moegiadi, UNESCO's representative in India "four South Asian countries — Bangladesh, India, Pakistan and Nepal account for the largest number of out of school girls and Illiterate women."

Addressing a national workshop on State Policies on Incentive Schemes in Primary Schools and their Contribution to Girls Participation, jointly organised by NCERT and UNESCO, he said:

> "Though progress has been made, we are all aware that according to, the 1991 census of India we have 50.2 per cent literacy, and now according to the latest information we have 64 per cent literacy rate. It is estimated that in near future it can be 70-80 per cent" .

The number of females in the work force is also very limited. The 1991 census figures tell us that the working population was 317 million out of the total population of the country as being 846.3 (males 439.3 and females 407.0) million. The males were 226.4 (71.4 per cent) and females 90.6

(28.6 per cent) million who were working. The males in the organized sector were 23.0 million while women were, only 3.8 million. The respective percentages were 85.8 and 14.2. In the unorganized sector there were 290.2 million persons out of which 203.4 were males and 86.8 million women. The respective percentages were 70.0 and 30.0. Hence the women working in organised sector were very few as compared to men.

The National Commission on Self Employed Women and Women Engaged in Informal Sector observed that the women could be found to be largely confined to strenuous and monotonous work that might be irregular and seasonal and women workers could be rarely benefited from the introduction of mechanization and new technology. About eighty per cent of the total female work-force continues to work as agricultural labour. It may be said that one of the basic hurdles to the development of employment opportunities for the women has been lack of adequate training to women workers.

The percentage of Agricultural labourers according to 1991 census was 21.01 per cent for males and 44.83 per cent for females.

Indian women are also being increasingly victimized. Crimes against women are increasing. Crimes such as rape, bride burning, wife battering and ragging of girls are also on the increase. Emotional violence against females at work is a new phenomenon. The rape cases increased from 3,945 in 1982 to 9,752 in 1989. These figures are on the basis of the National Crime Records Bureau, Ministry of Home Affairs, Government of India. But the Marie Stopes Institute, Delhi thinks that these official figures are not correct. According to it on an average, two million women and girls are raped in India every year.

Thus we find that even now there is much discrimination against women and they are a neglected lot. Rajbala says that "A basic statistics paints a grim picture. Over 400 million women with 75 per cent illiteracy work 10-14 hours daily, undergo 4-6 pregnancies and run low income households".

In India, women have been surrounded in a web of myth and reality. She has been considered as a goddess as well as an evil incarnate. At one stage if she was put on a very high pedestal and at another stage she was thrown into the pits of filth and guilt. The casualty has been the reality of her existence. It is only recently that the emphasis has been put on the understanding of the women as she is, as also on the understanding of her relations with man in the light of the recognition of the fact that both are the equal parts of humanity. In this context her education is now considered as important and worthwhile as that of man.

Historically, in the Indian situation the rearing of the girl child and her education has always been taken with indifference. The only exception may be the Vedic period. The birth of a male child is celebrated with joy and happiness while the birth of a girl child is a matter of sorrow and gloom for whole of the family. This trend is changing in the enlightened households but by and large in majority of the families the situation has hardly changed.

The ambivalence with which the Indian women were viewed, has created a typical situation in the relationship between men and women. It was believed that since energy resided in women, they were objects of worship. The Devi cult assigned all the creative and protective powers to women. But at the same time the women were considered as the promoters of evil, seductress who destroyed men if given freedom and the power to exercise their free will. Thus the women's will power had to be controlled. The husbands were given their absolute rights over her body, soul and mind. The women accepted their subordinate status for centuries. It is only in the later half of the twentieth century that the Indian women started revolting against the stipulations that the women are inferior to men. The empowerment of the Indian women is the battle cry of the feminists of today. The enlightened men are offering their help in the emancipation of the women.

At the advent of the new millennium we find that the Indian women are joining the world of work in increasing numbers. In many cases it is creating stresses in the family life particularly in those homes in which the womens' role is confined to being housewives. The pressing economic demands make it obligatory for women to seek employment in various fields but the old conservative notions that the women's rightful place is in homes, create situations of stress, and conflict. Under the shadows of conflict and stress the education of the women is being planned, propagated and provided. This book highlights the conflicts and the stresses of the working as well as non-working women and also the influence of socio-psychological factors on women education.

In India, there is growing realization that the women education is of great importance to the healthy development of the social and national life. Efforts are being made to provide schools, for all the girls of school-going age and to give incentives to them to learn. Still the situation is far from satisfactory. The literacy percentage among Indian women is lawfully low. This may be due to the lower social status and the psychological make up of the women, particularly of the lower classes and castes.

The Dalit women and the women of the minority communities have by and large miserable existence. The Dalit women are exploited not only by the higher caste people but also by their own male relatives. Similar is the case with the women of the minority communities, especially in the case of lower class Muslim women. The reasons for their exploitation seem to lie in their ignorance. Most of them are Illiterate and so have neither the means nor the will to fight against their exploitation. Hence their education is a matter which has to be given top priority.

What will be the futuristic trends of women education? Whether women education should be of the same pattern as the education of men? If not then why and what type of education is required for them? Should women be trained for joining the world of work or only for the household work as the housewives? These are some of the questions which are being raised about women education. In the present book an attempt is being made to discuss these and some other vital issues concerning women education so that some appropriate measures may be taken for organizing it thus ushering in an era of equality, dignity, esteem, self-respect and self-confidence for the Indian women.

It may be emphasized that the issues in women education are not only confined to quantitative development. Equally important are qualitative aspects. In an article "The Burning of Roop Kanwar - Madhu Kishwar, who visited Deorala where bride burning of Roop Kanwar took place, reported that "the fascination with the sati cult has been attributed to the superstitious ignorance of illiterate village women, but it is noteworthy that the entire cult being created at Deorala is in the hands of educated men". When we think of women education we are concerned with the development of progressive outlook in them. We will not like to provide that type of education to our women which the menfolk of Deorala got, which led them to close their minds rather than broadening their vision. The leaders of the pro-sati campaign were urban, educated men in their twenties and thirties.

The main premise on which the argument throughout is based is that Indian women are by nature not docile, nor are they devoid of a mind of their own. It is due to four fold major factors that we find them in the state in which they are. These factors are: 1.Religious precepts from some eminent sages motivated by the desire to subordinate the assertive women. 2.The physical weakness perpetuated by multiple pregnancies and childhood marriages. 3.Women's own desire for showering motherly affection on their own men and for maintaining domestic peace at their own cost. 4.Lastly their complete economic dependence on malefolk.

Fight for Independence

Around the globe, the Women have been known to participate in national liberation movements. Although they have not been found to be politically very conscious or involved in day-to-day political issues, women have mobilised themselves during crisis situations. In India, women have participated in the national freedom struggle. However, a clear picture has not emerged. There have been debates and counter debates about the magnitude of women's participation in national struggle as to:

(a) Which section of women did participate?

(b) Did it help in the emergence of female political leadership?

(c) Were women able to create some niche for themselves in the political sphere?

(d) Was their participation in some way a reinforcement of patriarchy or it created and acknowledged the separate identity of women as individuals?

In attempting to analyse the role of women in Indian Freedom Struggle, one is beset by a series of problems at the very outset. For, one, the political role of women as a subject of research is of recent origin in India. There are very few comprehensive studies on women's participation in the Freedom Struggle. Studies published between 1968-88 do touch upon various aspects and dimensions of women's participation. Some date has also been generated, some factual accounts made such as most standard histories of The National Movement mention women's participation and role in the Civil Disobedience Movement. Women in revolutionary terrorism have also been described. Some accounts of contemporaries who participated in the movement refer to the strength and broad base acquired by it as a whole through women's participation.

However information on women in the writings prior to 1975 have been mainly on women of elite sections of society. Large majority of women have not figured in these accounts, and their role has remained Unexplored and marginlined. Except some accounts by some elite women participants not much is known about the lives or the social background of the mass of women, who entered the movement in different regions of the country. But recently some work has been done in this area.

Further most of the accounts of women's participation have been mainly descriptive and not analytical. They do not examine either the reason or the implications of this spontaneous upsurge of political activity by women of all classes. The elite perspective is dominant, which relates women's participation to reform movement and education but ignores the role of peasant women.

Women from different sections including even prostitutes or thousands of housewives, who directly or indirectly supported the freedom fighters by shouldering family responsibilities have not been discussed. The impact of colonialism on women's lives and beliefs, created a source for radicalism among Bengali youth. Strangely, it was recorded by an English as early as 1907, and repeatedly mentioned by Mahatma Gandhi.

Some have described existing research on women's participation in national struggle as non-comprehensive, cursory in nature and generally a history from above. Thus, one has to start with caution and carefulness in recording and analysing women's participation in national liberation movement.

Active Conduct

Generally, one starts with the presumption that the social reform movement from the mid 19th century prepared the base for women's awakening and their entry in the movement later on. The elite class-led social movement of the 19th century, was a movement run by men on women's issues. Pandita Ramabai stands solitary in the galaxy of names like Raja Ram Mohan Roy, Agarkar, Ishwar Chandra Vidyasagar and Veerasalengam.

Their efforts rallied round issues affecting women's life adversely such as the practice of sati, female infanticide, plight of the widow, child marriage, polygamy, etc. Raja Ram Mohun Roy championed the ban of the practice of sati. His campaigns resulted in the governmental resolution of 1829, banning the practice of sati. Raja Ram Mohun Roy was trained in western liberal education. He founded the Brahmo, Samaj in 1929, which by the second half of the century practiced a Christianised version of Hinduism.

The Brahmo Samaj split in 1886 into Adi Brahmo Samaj led by Devendra Nath Tagore, and Brahmo Samaj of India led by Keshav Chandra Sen. This faction opened schools for girls, started a women's magazine in 1863 and founded the Brahmitra Samaj in 1867. This Samaj taught Brahmo religion, handicrafts and social skills to the female relatives of the Brahmo Samaj members. Keshav Chandra Sen exhibited a mixture of reformist, revivalist and traditional ideas about women. On the one hand, he pressed for a law to legalise cross-caste marriage within the Brahmo community, and to raise the minimum age for marriage of girls to 14, on the other hand, got his daughter married at the age of 13.

The Brahmo Samaj was further split in 1878 into liberal and conservative factions. The liberal Sadharan Samaj sponsored women's education, but the Nava Vedhan Brahmo Samaj did not favour higher education for women. Vidyasagar took up the cause of widows, and started a movement in support for widow remarriage in the 1850s. It resulted in Hindu Widows Marriage Act of 1865, but in actuality not much was achieved. It met with strong opposition from the Bengali orthodoxy. There were signature campaigns but most effective was the social pressure from the reform leaders, ranging from social out-casting to threats of violence.

The real explosion came with the campaign against child marriage and the debate over age of consent bill, initiated by Behramji Malabari in 1884, who started a nationwide debate. It met with strong opposition from the orthodox. The attack was spearheaded by Lokmanya Tilak, who defined the legislation as an attack on religion. The orthodox were not wrong in connecting the issues of reform and religion. Throughout the 19th century, the conservative Brahman elite class was making a very successful attempt.

It remains the major factor in Indian politics even today to define Indian culture and Indian nationality in terms of reconstituted Hinduism. There was no way the reformers could avoid the issue. This 'Hindu identity' had to be challenged to make active even a consistent democratic liberalism or liberal feminism because it had remained caste ridden and patriarchal. Numerous low-caste radicals were willing to meet this challenge, but only few of the elites were eager.

As a result, the movement was almost totally overwhelmed by Hindu revivalism by the end of the 19th century. The new revivalism was embodied in powerful organisations such as Dayanand Saraswati's Arya Samaj (1875), Vivekananda's Ramkrishna Mission (1897) and Annie Besant's Madras Hindu Association (1904). These new organisations attacked the reformers, but supported some reforms of the Hindu society. They did incorporate a good deal of the programme of reformers such as educating women, raising the age of marriage, remarriage of child widows etc, but all this was to be done within the framework of Hinduism. The ideal of Sita, the subordinate and oppressed 'Pativrate', defined the limits of Indian women's advance.

Barring a few exceptions, the modernists and the revivalists were not really concerned with gender equality, women's own desires or their perspectives on dignity and justice. Nor were they aware of the inter-relationship between patriarchal control over women's freedom, roles and behaviour and the carefully preserved pluralist hierarchical Organisation of the Indian society.

Some regard the reform movement as a failure, but Gail Omvedt maintains that it helped to lay some of the foundations for the women's movement that emerged in the 1920s. Though men kept control within the family and within public life, the slow movement of women out of the home and the women's groups sponsored by male reformers and later the nationalists helped to 'extend the female space' for action.

One generation later Jyotiba Phule spearheaded the middle class and low caste movement for their rights all over India in the mid 19th century. He pushed the analysis of the inter-relationship between women's sub-ordination and maintenance of caste hierarchy far beyond the point that Vidyasagar had managed to articulate. Phule identified women's subordination as an instrument to perpetuate existing models of hierarchy. Periyar called for rejection of the mangalputra and wrote, "our ladies must come forward to compete with males in all spheres." The main social organisations founded by men centred round ceremonies. 'Satyashodhak marriages' dramatised the defiance of caste ideology by refusing the use of Brahmin priests or traditional rituals and by institutionalising women's equality. The ceremony concludes with the mangalashataka and garlanding. Periyar also emphasised garlanding and equality. In this respect, both were ahead of even the best laws of today the reformed Hindu 'Civil Code' includes the patriarchal saptapadi ritual and even registered marriages make not even a rhetoric mention of women's equality.

The ideology of Phule and Periyar had a strong feminist element in it. They definitely connected women's oppression and exploitation with other forms of social inequality and called rigorously for a fully liberated society.

However, in the long run, the reform movements strengthened women's "socialisation for inequality" within the middle class as a whole and heightened the growth of institutions like dowry and the supremacy of the patriarchal family in women's lives. Instead of its expected liberating influence, education became a powerful force in strengthening the sanskritisation process, which manifests the integral links and mutually supportive relationship between patriarchy and heirarchy.

Women's participation in the Freedom Struggle dates back to 1905. The Swadeshi movement, which was triggered by the British decision to partition Bengal in 1905, saw women's entry into the movement, and the skilful tactics of several women leaders contributed to increase the participation of women in public life. Attempts at mass mobilisation also facilitated this participation. Pamphlets were written in Bengali and widely distributed. One of those was a pamphlet by Ramendrasundari Trivedi entitled 'a vow for Bengali Women', which tried to explain the Swadeshi movement in simple language for a village woman to understand.

The pamphlet called upon women to participate in the ritual of Rakhi bandhan and arandhan (not lighting cooking fires), and to boycott foreign goods. Nirod Choudhary reported that the Swadeshi movement aroused a strong sense of patriotism in his mother who smashed the family's foreign made cooking pots. The traditions of Hindu mela were revived and exhibitions became a regular part of Congress meetings. Meetings were regularly held by women, although there was strong opposition, especially against the young unmarried girls in the leadership. Sarla Devi, daughter of Swarna Kumari Devi, started physical culture clubs, began a Swadeshi store for Women's work and organised festivals which celebrated Bengali traditions. She played an important role in the Swadeshi movement until she moved to Lahore in 1905 after marrying Arya Samaj leader Ram Bhoj Dutt Choudhary. Some British women who made Indian nationalism their own cause, played important roles as helpers as well as 'catalysts', such as Annie Besant, Dorethy Jinaragadasa, Margaret Cousins, an Irish feminist and Sister Nivedita.

The Swadeshi movement also marked the formation of several women's organisations. Mahila Shilpa Samiti (1906-1908) was clearly inspired by the Swadeshi movement. Earlier, in 1901, Sarla Devi Choudhrani had formed the Bharat Stri Mahamandal after serious differences with the male leadership of the National Social Conference (NSC). In fact, women's associations had started coming up in the latter half of the previous century.

In the Presidency of Bombay a women's magazine 'Stress Bodh' was started in 1857 by the Parsies. The 'Prasthana Samaj' which had organised Arya Mahila. Samaj in 1882 under the leadership of Pandita Ramabai Ranade associated with the modern faction sought government funds for a girls' high school and legal authority to discourage child marriage. She formed NSC to provide an all-India forum for discussion of social reform after the leaders of the National Congress had decided to eliminate this subject from their agenda in order to present a united front to the British. Tilak was bitterly opposed to Ranade's action. In 1895, Tilak's opposition to NSC forced the holding of separate sessions by the Congress and NSC.

Female relatives of the reform oriented leaders began forming local women's organisations, justified by revivalist ideals, and there were no campaigns for social legislation. The

Hindu ladies social and literacy 'cell' was started in 1902, Gujarati Street Mandal in 1903 and Women's Zoroastrian Association in 1903. In 1908, Seva Sadan was started by the reform oriented leaders of the different communities. In 1904, the leaders of Maharashtra Social Conference (MSC) organised a women's section which held an annual conference during MSC sessions. This conference, the Bharat Mahila Parishad (BMP) organised educational and inspirational programmes in which women of distinction - Ramabai, Annie Besant, Sarojini Naidu and several others - gave speeches before women.

In the Madras Presidency, a women's magazine was started by Kamala, wife of Indian Christians' social reformer Satlinadhan. A Brahmin widows' home was founded in 1913 by Subhalakshmi Annal, and a Mahila Seva Samaj in Mysore in 1913.

Local Muslim women's associations were found in the early 20th century by upper class Muslim women in several cities. In 1916, the Begum of Bhopal formed the All India Muslim Women's Conference, at which papers on social reform and education were read and resolutions passed. In 1917, Abu Begum proposed a resolution against polygamy that provoked opposition from Muslims. However, Gail Minault points out that in other cases Muslim women skilfully utilised religious themes and anti-British feelings to justify their activities during the Khilafat and Non-cooperation Movement.

After 1910, women experienced in organising and working in local women's associations, and convinced that women should take the leadership into their own hands, started provincial and national women's organisations. There associations were inevitably elite, bourgeois and urban, consisting of women from the upper class with the advantage of social status, education and privilege, but redeemed by their desire to serve all women. The Young Women's Christian Association of India (YMCA) had become national in 1896. The

Women's India Association (WIA) was formed in 1917 in Madras (now called Chennai). In the same year, Sarojini Naidu led a delegation of women formed by Margaret Cousins to the Constitutional Reforms Committee, demanding universal adult franchise women.

The National Council of Women in India (NCWI) was formed in 1925, All India Women's Conference (AIWC) in 1927. By mid-1935, WIA and AIWC claimed membership of over 10,000 women. NCWI developed eight provincial councils by 1934 and had 180 affiliated societies with a membership of over 8000. WIA did not limit itself to fund raising, social service and women's education, but also sought to influence government policy on equal rights for women in some areas, and was involved with the issue of suffrage, education and social reform. WIA founders included women like Margaret Cousins and Annie Besant who were not only suffragists, but political radicals and critics of imperialism in their own country.

AIWC, which had originally convened only to discuss women's education, became a permanent body which succeeded in developing branches all over India. It called itself a political, even had a clause in its constitution prohibiting its engagement in party politics. But by 1932, however, AIMC had involved itself with political rights of women. Although its major focus and priority remained women's question and elimination of women's backwardness, the future of India gradually became and important concern.

From the beginning, WIA had an interest in home rule and women's suffrage, which was clearly patriotic. Yet, even in troubled time of 1928-29, the WIA insisted that their policy was to work for reform through the Legislative Council. They were not prepared to accept Civil Disobedience, for this would jeopardise the relation they had so carefully worked out with the government to secure for women, positions of magistrates on various councils and committees and to urge the legislation for the improvement of women's status. However, when the Civil Disobedience Movement started in 1930, WIA was faced with a dilemma. Dr Muthulakshmi Reddi, a founder member of WIA and later as Vice-President signed a protest in 1928 against the all British Composition of the Simon Commission. The choice was between aligning with the national movement or adopting an apolitical stance. Situations caused leaders of these organisations to redefine their aims, amend bylaws, argue with each other, and finally end up with organisations which were somewhere between autonomous women's associations and women's auxiliary of the Indian National Congress.

Kamala Devi Chattopadhyay observed, though the Women's Conference had originally stated it would not participate in politics, it realised that it would have to concern itself with public in its wide term, without alignment to any particular political party. It also accepted women as members from any party. It took a strong nationalist stand, and demanded equal rights for women to enable them to play their full and legitimate role in the national affairs. Otherwise, all other rights might become illusory.

Many members of WTA were also members of AIWC, and many such members were members of the Indian National Congress, and leaders in the National movement as well. This factor led to close relations between women and the national movement.

Although women's associations could never decide their stand on the involvement of women in politics, the women in general were ultimately drawn into the vortex of the Freedom Struggle by Mahatma Gandhi. In South Africa, his stayagrah 'army' had women in it. With his experience of South Africa behind him, Gandhi was aware of the potentialities of women as passive resistance. As he experimented with his weapon of satyagrah in India, he realised that women could participate in it together with men.

With the belief that for the Freedom Movement to be successful it had to be a movement of masses, Gandhi felt that swaraj would be meaningless without reform of social structures and upliftment of the weaker sections, namely the women and the lower social strata, to a position of equality with others. While lending support to the cause of improving women's condition through education and reform of marriage laws, he declared himself to be uncompromising in the matter of women's right.

He remarked, "woman has been suppressed under custom and law for which man was responsible and in the shaping of which she had no hand .... Woman has as much right to shape her own destiny as man has to shape his .... It is upto men to see that they enable them to realise their full status and play their part as equal of men." He differed from the early reformers by his revolutionary approach to women's role in society and their right to personal dignity as individuals. Without belittling their roles as mothers and wives, he insisted that they must play an equal role with men in the achievement of freedom and social justice. In his opinion, women had natural abilities to lead in a non-violent struggle for human liberation. The most significant aspect of Gandhi's ideas lies in the remarkable similarity between them and the demands now voiced by the women's liberation movement all over the world equality in the family and society, the right to one's own body; the opening of wider opportunities for self development; and, a refusal to be treated as sex symbol.

Equality of Stature

As president of the Indian National Congress in 1931, Pandit Nehru accepted equal political and legal rights of women, and introduced the concept of equal obligations along with equal rights in the Fundamental Rights resolution passed by the Congress that year. Along with adult suffrage, the resolution emphasised the need for protecting women workers, particularly granting them maternity leave. He asserted that "women must be trained to participate in every department of human activity and play an active part in all professions and sphere. For this purpose, they must fight social institutions like pudah, untouchability, caste system and marriage laws. But above all, they must participate in the struggle against the root cause of political subjugation and the economic system. The women's movement would suffer set back if it remained isolated from the general political and economic struggle for liberation in the country."

Some historians of the social reform movement have held that this merger of the women's movement in the political struggle diluted its strength, though perhaps it gained in legitimacy by the championship of national leaders. Some others, however, claim that the India perspective gave the women's movement in India an identity distinct from similar movement in other countries.

Thus, women and their associations were drawn inside the vortex of national struggle for freedom under the inspiration and guidance of national leaders like Gandhi and Nehru. During the Non-cooperation Movement, women in different parts of India joined processions, propagated the use of khadi and charkha; some of them left government schools and colleges. Renuka Ray in Calcutta gave up her studies along with her friends and joined the movement. So did Vijayalaxmi Pandit.

Basanti Devi, wife of C R Das, accompanied her husband in his tour of Bengal and asked women to boycott foreign goods. She was arrested on December 7, 1911, on the charge of obstracting the gentlemen of Calcutta, by selling khadi She presided over the Bengal provincial conference of Chittagong in April 1922, and Kasturba Gandhi presided over the Gujarat provincial conference appealing to women to take to spinning and weaving khadi. In Allahabad, Rameshwari Mehra formed a kumari sabha to encourage girls to take part in public discussions. There were women like Hemprablia Majumdar, who received lathi blows. Bee Amman, mother of the Ali Brothers, discarded her veil and addressed meetings all over India, advocating the use of khadi supporting Hindu Muslim unity.

In Borsad satyagrah of 1923-24, women turned out in large numbers. It is on record that women displayed greater courage than men, when police confiscated their house, buffaloes and other property.

In the Bardoli satyagrah of 1928, the women gradually outnumbered men in political gatherings. Sardar Patel commented that in stead-fastness of purpose, simplicity and purity, they were better than their men. Maniben Patel and Bhakti Desai fixed their tents and huts on the land declared to be sold by the government.

The salt satyagraha launched by Gandhiji in March 1930, was extended to a mass campaign at the beginning of April 1930. Gandhiji had initially exclude women from participating in 'salt satyagraha'. This was not taken lightly by women. Margaret Cousins sent a spirited reply on behalf of WIA, protesting against the division of work by sex, as women had been left in charge of the ashram of Sabarmati while men were to accompany Gandhi in the march to Dandi. Kamla Devi Chattopadhyay met Gandhi and expressed her desire to be involved in the satyagraha. Durgabai Desmukh met the local leaders of Madras and suggested that they be included in the movement.

On April 6, 1930, the salt laws were ceremoniously broken by Gandhi. Sarojini Naidu and Muthuben Patel were with him. Many women had walked to Dandi and the awakening in the villages was astonishing. Gandhi was arrested and in a statement to the press on 7 April, 1930, Gandhi said that he was becoming increasingly certain that in the struggle for swaraj, the women of this country could contribute a greater share than men.

Gandhi had nominated Sarojini Naidu to lead the raid on Dhasana salt fields. She declared that the "time has come when women can no longer seek immunity behind the shelter of their sex, but must face equally with their male comerades all the pains and sacrifices for the liberation of this country." Lilavati Mushi and Sarojini Naidu organised women and led them in different parts of Bombay (now called Mumbai) to make salt. Kamala Devi Chattopadhyay stood outside the law courts and sold salt at high prices.

Women's role in salt satyagrah was significant in two ways. First, among Congress women, this represented a shift from role of supportive auxiliaries to direct participation in the struggle, even when it involved defiance of the leadership. Secondly, the impact of the women's role resulted in the conversion of a section of the leadership, especially Gandhi and Nehru. Kamala Devi Chattopadhyay commented, "ancient prejudices melted, walls of tradition cracked and rays of new hope is creeping in." Nehru remarked, "our women came to the forefront and took charge of the struggle. Women had always been there of course, but now there was an avalanche of them which took not only the British government, but their own men folk by surprise. There were these women, of the upper or middle classes leading sheltered lives in their homes, peasant women, working class women, rich women coming out into tens of thousands in defiance of government orders and police lathis. It was not only the displays of courage and daring, but what was even more surprising was the organisational power they showed." Thus, the women had turned this struggle into a beautiful epic.

In July 1930, when Lord Irwin was to address the Central Assembly, it was decided that there should be picketing by a group of women volunteers on the first day, and 27 women from Lahore, Ambala and Simla were chosen for this purpose. Women went in groups of twos and threes and stood outside the Central Legislative assembly Hall. They had black flags hidden under the fold of their sarees. As soon as the viceroy came and got down from his car, they took out their flags and shouted "Irwin, go back." In Lahore, Manmohine Sehgal organised picketing in front of college gates and also student's strikes. Arrested women in Lahore jail were Zutshi, Kamala Nehru's mother Raspati Kaul, Parvati Devi, Asaf Ali and Satyavati from Delhi.

Same happened in Bihar, where a number of women were arrested. Hasan Imam addressed several meetings of students in Patna and Barh together with her daughter Sami, Suit. CC Das and some other women she organised a procession of women in Patna on July 15 to inaugurate an intensive campaign of boycott of British goods. During the week ending July 25 Patna witnessed two demonstrations, in which nearly 3000 women took part. Hasan Imam, Sami, Smt. C C Das, Gauri Das and Vindhyavasirii Devi were summoned to court. Imam formed a committee of women in Muzaffarpur to propagate spinning. Women leaders were also advocating non-payment of chowkidari tax.

In Karnataka women who took part in the struggle were Kamala Devi Chattopadhyay, Umabai Kundapur Krishnabai, Panjikar and Ballasi Seddama. Gowramma and her coworkers offered satyagarh in front of the house of the Patel of Akoriji in north Kanara. The police dragged women, beat them with canes and harassed them. Women gave food and shelter to Congressmen, often acted as messengers carrying secret information from one camp to another, and when the call for satyagrah came they had to be proved fervent satyagrahas.

Women in princely states did not keep aloof. In Viramgam satyagrah in May 1930, 700 women were lathicharged. In the Rajkot satyagrah of 1938-39 and the movement in Linodi, women were active. In Rajkot, Kasturba was jailed along with Manibelm Patel and Mridula Sarabhai. Kamala Devi organised agitation in Ram Durg state in Karnataka in 1930.

The Move

In the Civil Disobedience Movement inaugurated by Gandhi in October 1940, women courted arrest in large numbers. One of the first to do so was Sucheta Kripalani, who had been in charge of the women's department of the All India Congress Committee since 1939.

In the 1942 'Quit India Movement' almost all the top leaders were immediately arrested, and the movement was practically leaderless. However, women joined in taking out processions, holding meetings and demonstrations and organising strikes. In Assam, a young girl, Kanaklata Barua, led a procession of 500 and was killed in the police firings. In Midnapur, Bengal, women played a notable role and were victims of police atrocities. In Bombay, Usha Mehta operated an underground radio station. The Congress Radio, broadcasted news at 7.30 P.M. from August to November 13th, 1942, till Usha Mehta along with her colleagues were arrested. She as sentenced to few years rigorous imprisonment and was sent to Yeraveda jail, where she found herself among 250 women political prisoners.

Aruna Asaf Ali was one of the most important figures of 1942. For four years she remained underground, avoiding arrest. She published bulletins and edited along with Ram Manohar Lohia 'The Inquilab'. A price of Rs 5,000 was announced as a reward for her capture.

Besides the women who joined the Freedom Movement on the call of Gandhi, there were a few who could not believe his creed of non-violence. They were revolutionary and in the 1930s such organisations sprang up rapidly. They were active in Bengal, Dakha, Commilla and Chittagong where the storm centres. Young college girls joined these secret societies. Kalpana Joshi, Preeti Waddadar were associated with Chittagong armoury raid. Preeti led a raid on the Pahartali railway officers' club. She later committed suicide. Shanti and Soniti shot dead

Stevens, the district magistrate of Commilla in December 1931, and were given life sentences. The Chchatri Sangh started in Calcutta in 1928 was an important training and recruiting ground for future revolutionaries. In Delhi, Rocpvati Jain, at the age of 17, was in charge of a bomb factory under Chandrashekhar Ajad. Sushila Devi cut her finger and put tilak on the forehead of Bhagat Singh and Batukeshwar Dutta on April 9, 1920. She was arrested and imprisoned. Durga Devi played the role of Bhagat Singh's wife. She shot a police sergeant at Hamilton Road, Bombay. She was elected president of the Delhi provincial Congress Cominittee in 1938.

In January 1942, the Indian Independence League was formed in Kualalampur and Indian women in Southeast Asia worked for the cause of India's freedom. In March 1943, a women section of the league was started and Indian women in Malaya, Thailand and Burma, enlisted as volunteers on the call of Subhash Chandra Bose. In July 1933, a women's regiment-the Rani of Jhansi Regiment was formed with Lakshmi Saligal as the captain.

The general idea or myth circulated for quite a long period has been that women's role in the national movement(s) against imperialism was male-dictated or male manipulated. Uma Rao and Ishani Mukherjee in their writings offer enough evidence against it. Various writings in recent years indicate that once mobilised, women moved on their own, acquiring new confidence and articulating new priorities. The number of women directly involved in revolutionary movements in Bengal, Maharashtra, Punjab, in Uttar Pradesh and the erstwhile Madras Presidency in the turn of the century may have been small, but the inspirational support base of the revolutionaries included more women whose names will never feature in dictionaries of freedom fighters. The women who provided shelter and food, carried messages or arms, or instilled a passion to 'serve their country' among their children, telling them about the 'heroes' and 'martyrs' who sacrificed their lives for the country's freedom, did not belong to the elite class only. Many were uneducated and poor. They played such roles without waiting for any social sanction. They provided a communication channel for the message of nationalism when nationalist literature was under severe control. The stories continued to spread and the songs and poems were eagerly observed by young people, often from women in their homes. Women's invisible role, which provided greater force, has received little formal acknowledgement.

Similarly, women's active and even militant roles as participants and leaders in quasi-national peasants' and workers' struggles remained strongly invisible till recently. Recent attempts to reconstruct life stories of women activists and to obtain oral history from surviving women freedom fighters provide little substance to the theory of male direction, guidance or manipulation.

Some find it difficult to believe that leaders of the national movement were not aware of the growing base of women's support and feelings of national cause, and were 'surprised' at the intensity and the degree of their response to the Civil Disobedience Movement. The history of national movement records various instances when women defied the national leadership. It was evident during the salt satyagrah of 1930. Sarojini Naidu was defiant, Margaret Cousins wrote a spirited letter to Gandhiji, protesting against the division of work by sex, as women had been left in charge of the 'ashram' and Sabarmati, while men accompanied Gandhi in his famous Dandi March. Despite the reluctance on the part of Gandhi, women participated in a big way in the satyagraha.

By and large, the leaders of the national movement envisaged a supportive role for women. They did not want women to involve in direct action. Gandhi himself described the difference between men and women as follows. "She is passive, he is active. She is essentially the mistress of the house.

He is the breadearner." This sexual division of labour was perpetuated even during the National freedom Struggle. In fact, Gandhi inducted women in the Freedom Struggle because they were considered to be self-sacrificing, able to endure pain, and were essentially non-violent in nature. Gandhi did not visualise any fundamental change in the sexual division of labour, or any departure of women from their normal social roles as wife and mother. Madhu Kishwar remarks:

"The symbols put forward to draw them into public life are those of ideal wives whose chief qualification was that they spent their lives in self-less service and unending devotion of husbands, following them to the end of the World. There was some inherent dichotomy in Gandhiji's thinking on women. On the one hand, he asserted that women had the same rights of freedom and liberty as men. On the other hand, he kept reforming to the mythical figures of Sita and Damayanti and their devotion to duty despite sufferings.

The deduction- "participation in politics would be simply an extension of this duty." This approach has been criticised by Gail Omvedt and Maria Mies. Mies claims that Gandhi created a new myth of Indian womanhood, Sita-like in her devotion to service and self-sacrifice, weather to her family or her nation. As a consequence, Gandhi attracted women from well-to-do classes with "good education, well placed husbands and servants". For these women, family came first and concern with sociopolitical issues afterwards. May be Gandhi was not prepared for radical changes at the structural and institutional level. The status of women had to be improved, but institutions which impinged on and curtailed their freedom were to be retained.

However, in all fireness to Gandhiji, it has to be accepted that he has a broader vision in comparison to other leaders of the movement. Unlike social reformers, Gandhi had realised some of the negative consequences of colonial role on women's economic status. He decided to launch the khadi movement which would offer to the masses of women an immediate open channel for their participation in the national struggle. Even more, Gandhi used women's role in the khadi movement to convince men that women's participation as equals was essential if the swadeshi or boycott movement was to succeed- an argument that he extended later to the winning of full freedom for India and nation building. For women to provide leadership in the movement was not enough. They had to understand the dignity that came from being productive and independent. Such an understanding would help them to identify with poor women, emancipate themselves and achieve the new identity necessary for nation building.

Nehru's understanding of women's subordination was both limited and static. Though fully aware of the problems of building a democratic and eqalitarian society on the foundations of a social and cultural structure divided by multiple allegiance (or identities) - religious, linguistic, caste and tribal and hierarchical beliefs that prevented a "sense of equality", he did not understand the "critical connections between the control over women and the maintenance of that differentiated and hierarchical social structures. While he certainly accepted the emancipation of women as a value in itself, and claimed improvement in Indian women's status as his greatest achievement, some argue that his approach to women reflected the elitist vision of social reformers, relieved to some extent by his fascination for socialism, with little or no understanding of the deeper causes of women's subordination in India. While he introduced the emphasis on women's rights in the constitution, he did little to reduce the controls of the collectives that determined the boundaries of women's lives and behaviour- the family, community, caste, class, and religion.

Some argue that the issue of gender equality was given a back seat, and women's issue lost its appeal and fervour by being subsumed within nationalism. The new politics of nationalism glorified India's past and tended to defend everything traditional. Nationalism in this phase fostered conservatism in social beliefs and practices. Partha Chatterjee maintains, "the new patriarchy of nationalism gave women 'a new social responsibility' not to alienate men, but "to maintain the cohesiveness of family life and solidarity with the kin group. In addition, by associating the task of 'female emancipation' with 'sovereign nationhood', nationalism "bound them to a yet entirely legitimate subordination." Partha Chatterjee also explains the "disappearance of the women's question from the political domain by the end of the 19th century as the result of nationalism's "refusal to make the women's question an issue of political negotiation with the colonial state."

Some feel that this analysis suffers from the basic problem arising out of a tendency to find a linear connection between the reform movement, growth of nationalism and the roles prescribed for, or played by women in the Freedom Struggle. It neglects the fact that of women's own response to the challenges of colonial rule. Gail Minault and Geraldin Forber argue that women adapted the institution of purdah or seclusion, to form their own institutions, purdah, otherwise a hindrance to women's advancement, helped them through women's forums in which they could voice their concerns. Despite the restriction of purdah and without challenging patriarchal structures, it was possible for this rudimentary women's movement to acquire a unique strength.

Some opine that women's involvement in the national movement or the merger of women's movement with the Freedom Struggle diluted its strength, though perhaps it gained in legitimacy by the championship of national leaders. It has to be accepted that gender equality was not the main thrust, either of the social reform movement nor the National Freedom Movement. The social reform did help to improve the status of Indian women and placed great on education as the emancipator of women. However education never became the sole agent for gender equality, it suffered from the basic contradiction between upliftment of women and limited vision of that upliftment. Everything had to be done within the framework of patriarchal family. Women were not seen as individuals. Similarly, the national movement leaders envisaged an auxiliary role for women in the movement. It was by sheer hardwork and readiness for come what may, that women were able to prove their worth during the Civil Disobedience, salt satyagrah and the Quit India movements.

The so-called extremist movement of Bengal witnessed a galaxy of brave young girls, who readily sacrificed their lives for the freedom movement. Innumerable number of women provided support to freedom fighters, looked after their families in the absence of their fathers, husbands and sons. Participation in the national movement was not limited to elite class women only. They did provide organisation base and ideas and vision to the masses of women. But once aroused, the common women surged forward and became the most solid base of the National movement, we salute those masses of invisible and unnamed women who added strength to the movement, which by many is termed as the 'elite agitational politics'. Recording the participation of such women is a mammoth task. Efforts in this direction are commendable. It is hoped, someday a new history will be written about the national struggle.

2

INDIA AFTER INDEPENDENCE

After the independence, the political scenario in India has been characterised by a rather curious feature with most of the political parties and combination of parties accusing one another of striving to subvert democratic institutions. The Narora document has done the right thing to focus on the central fact that politics in India today faces grave threats. It is also correct in underlining the fact that most of the political issues the country is agitating on, are directly or indirectly related to this central fact.

For a proper understanding, however, of the current turmoils and conflicts in this vast country of nearly 900 million population, into which gigantic social forces are being inexorably drawn, it is necessary to start with an analysis of the real nature of politics in India, and its active role in the course of sociopolitical development. Only an examination of the nature and role of the existing political institutions can lead to an understanding of the nature of subversive attacks on them and, consequently, of the imperatives for overcoming them. The debate on women's entry into politics in India is closely related to this analysis, In order to start this debate, one has to look at the nature and working of politics in India.

Conclusive Activation

The basic nature of a political system is judged not by the speed of its ways, nor even by the proclamations it may have chosen to make, it has to be judged by its actual working-by the resultant of the social processes it seeks to encourage, control and repress. Earlier, even before the transfer of power, on January 22, 1947, a resolution moved by Jawaharlal Nehru in the Constituent Assembly of India, which set the objective of framing a Constitution — "wherein shall be guaranteed and secured to all the people of Indian justice, social, economic and political; equality of status, of opportunity, and before the law; freedom of thought, expression, belief, faith, worship, vocation, association and action, subject to law and morality". The Preamble of the Constitution proclaims the resolution on the same lines. Devices like confided Fundamental rights, Directive Principles of State Policy, special safeguards for minorities, Scheduled Castes and Tribes and so on, have added to the attractive look of the Constitution.

The democratic and egalitarian appearance of the political power in India has been further reinforced by the adoption of the socialistic pattern of society as the goal, still later by the full-threaded declaration of war against mass poverty----'garibi hatao' and, finally, by the 42nd amendment of the Constitution to declare the Indian Republic as a socialist and secular state. However, observers within the country and from abroad have refused to take these proclamations at their face value. They have clearly and categorically characterised the existing political power structure in India as exclusive and elitist.

For instance, Professor V K Rao, a former Union minister, identifies the locus of political power in India in "a political alliance of the intermediate classes with the upper classes, resorting to socialist ideology only to win mass support but using all levers of power to facilitate a type of capitalist development in the interest of a narrow section of Indian society". Another Indian analyst says, "whether in agriculture or industry or infrastructure or even scientific research, the advantage has invariably gone to that segment of power elite, which holds the political levers of parliamentary democracy. The present power structure constitutes the greatest stumbling block to any successful effort to relieve the poverty of the poor. According to Gunnar Myrdal, "India is ruled by a select group of upper class citizens who use their power to secure their privileged positions". He defines the elite groups as the product of a linking up of the vested interests of business, permanent officials and political leaders.

Barrier of Caste System

The process of politics is one of identifying and manipulating existing structures in order to mobilise support and consolidate positions. When the caste structure provides one of the most important organisational clusters in which the population is found to live, politics must strive to organise through such a structure. The alleged casteism in politics is thus no more and no less than the politicisation of caste. Caste in contemporary Indian politics plays a very important role behind the facade of parliamentary democracy. The political behaviour of people is influenced by caste considerations as is quite evident at the time of distribution of tickets by political parties for elections and composition of ministries. As far as possible and practicable, the people prefer a candidate of their own caste, irrespective of his merits and demerits. Similar regard is paid when the list of party's office-bearers is prepared. When a single party is not in a position to have its own candidates, alliances are formed on the basis of caste to recommend the name of a person after arrangements of 'give and take' are made to the satisfaction of the constituents. The central discovery is that politics is more important to caste and castes are more important to politics than before.

There is a widespread impression among educated Indians that caste is on its last legs and that, educated, urbanised and westernised members of the upper classes have already escaped its bond. Both these impressions are wrong. These people may observe very few dietetic restrictions, marry outside caste and even religion, but this does not mean that they have escaped the bonds of castes entirely. They show caste attitude in surprising context. That is the reason no political analysis of Indian politics that neglects caste is worthwhile. In fact, caste has become a factor to be reckoned with and none of the political parties, including Congress, Bharatiya Janata Party (EUP) and Communist, can ignore it.

Some of the political parties are organised purely on caste basis. For example Dravida Munnetra Kazhagarn (DMK) and All-India Anna Dravida Munnetra Kazhagarn (ALADMK) are anti-Brahmin parties, National Democratic Party of Nair community, Socialist Republican Party of Ezhava community, Kerala Congress of Catholic community and Bahujan Samaj Party (BSP) of lower caste communities are purely casteist parties. In Madhya Pradesh, it is a general observation that whenever there was Thakur Chief Minister, the Yadava, Kurmi and Brahmin legislators felt themselves neglected. Thakur officers were being promoted out of turn, despite the fact that some of them had adverse service records and inquiries were pending against them. Furthermore, few of the senior IAS Brahmin officers have been suspended. More or less, this has been observed all over the country.

To a limited extent, caste system was recognised by the framers of the constitution when they reserved seats for Scheduled Castes and Scheduled Tribes in the House of People and Legislative Assemblies of the states, made a provision for the appointment of a special officer for Scheduled Castes and

Scheduled Tribes to investigate matters relating to the various safeguards provided for them in the Constitution and also by providing for a minister in charge to look after the welfare of Scheduled Castes, Scheduled Tribes and other backward classes in the states of Bihar, Madhya Pradesh and Orissa.

There is also a provision which empowers the President/ Parliament to indulge/exclude certain castes or groups therein in the category of Scheduled Castes. Subsequently, the Constitution was amended in 1951, and a provision was also made for protective discrimination in favour of Scheduled Castes, scheduled tribes and other socially and educationally backward classes of citizens in services. Keeping in view the social hierarchical caste based structure, which exploited the weaker sections of society, there was and is a justification for such a provision in the Constitution, but only to limited extent for a limited period. However, while doing so efficiency of administration should also not be blindly ignored, otherwise, their condition would become more miserable.

It is important to note that the expression 'Scheduled Castes and Scheduled Tribes' as used in Article 338, include "such other backward classes as the President may, on receipt of the report of a commission appointed under clause (1) of Article 340, by order specify and also the Anglo-Indian community". About reservation, it should be remembered that reservation can neither be made on communal considerations nor more than 50 per cent seats be reserved. While caste has been politicised, in the process it has provided the Indian politics with processes and symbols of political articulation. Thus, within the new context of political democracy, caste remains a central element of Indian society even while adapting itself to the values and methods of democratic politics.

Different Classes

In a literal sense, castes and classes have different

implications. But in the politics of our country, they have come to be identified with each other. Even courts have accepted the view that in certain situations, the class as a whole may be taken as a caste and thus, caste may be entitled for the benefits of reservation that are available to a backward class.

We find that most of the tensions and conflicts have their source in social stratification and, for this reason, a possible solution to such political problems should be discovered in the rectification of the balance between different classes. The dialectics of Indian politics demand grappling with complex and contradictory trends in the country which has shown many positive and negative features during the past few years. Simply stated, the term 'class' signifies an aggregate of persons within a society possessing approximately the same status. It is a set of relationship constituted by the granting of deference of individual roles and institutions in the light of their place in the system of power and occupation. What really makes a class is the factor of economic interest.

The factor of economic interest is so deep that, as suggested by Karl Marx, it differentiates between the rules and the ruled, the exploiters and the exploited. Marx, however, makes the meaning of the term 'class' very rigid by applying the criteria of ownership and control over the means of production and distribution of goods. It may also be added that in common parlance, this term is used in greatly varying senses as upper or middle classes, propertied and non-propertied classes, educated and uneducated classes, even productive and unproductive classes. Liberal writers dwell upon the doctrine of three broad stratas of society-upper, lower and middle-living in harmony and peace. Max Weber takes a middle view in this regard and while dealing with the objective and subjective dimension of this important issue, builds the concept of class on three factors-possession of economic means, external standard of living, and cultural and recreational possibilities.

The struggle of the members of different classes, for the sake of protecting and promoting their specific interest, leads to the creation of conflicts and crises that demand their solution, sooner the better, and thereby the relationship between social set up and political system is established. In the context of Indian politics, class cuts into caste and is also cut into sub-caste by it. Low standing in the social hierarchy has been commonly taken as a sufficient indicator of backwardness. The cause of most of the social conflicts and tensions lies in the want of economic justice.

Illiteracy

The socioeconomic analysis of educational advance in the post-independence period is available from a number of village surveys. From these, it is clear that the spread of literacy and education is much in evidence among the more affluent and socially advance sections of society than among the poorer and more backward sections. The traditionally upper castes are almost all literate and have progressed much further in higher education, the middle castes have registered significant educational progress; but the lower and other backward sections of the population are lagging considerably behind. Literacy is crawling at snail's pace, and female education has not even touched these sections of society particularly in rural areas. Thus, backwardness in education is closely related to the economic and social backwardness and bears the same hallmarks of a society divided against itself. The benefits of high agricultural productivity have not trickled down to the lower castes, the majority of whom work as agricultural labourers. The rigidity of social customs and the relatively poor bargaining power have kept the lower castes in their caste-ordained position.

The economic and political power essentially belongs to the propertied classes, mostly from the upper castes, who have continued to monopolise education and culture too. The vast masses at the base of the social pyramid are not only deprived of the real power, but the power mechanism so works as to perpetuate and intensify this deprivation of the masses lower down. Lower caste segments of population who have historically constituted the most oppressed and exploited mass of the Indian people, practically deprived of any share in the economic, political and educational cultural developments in the country, continue to live in almost the same socioeconomic conditions, some symbolic improvements in certain sectors notwithstanding.

Can a nation of 960 million catch up with the rest of the world with nearly 48 per cent of its population totally illiterate? It cannot, if it does not take up bold measures to tackle the chronic problem within a timeframe. Though we have impressive statistics on education: 590,421 primary schools, 171,216 upper primary and 98,134 high schools, 6,596 colleges for general education, 1.354 professional colleges and 226 universities, for the 150.7 million children enrolled in the age group of 6-14 years, there are 2.90 million teachers. But India of 1999 is caught between the paradox of high technocrats. IIT professionals, MBA, graduates and other literate and another India overflowing with an illiterate population of more than 400 million.

Monetary View

Economic power has paved the way for capturing political power and thereby using state apparatus for suppressing the opponents belonging to the poor and backward class. For instance, it is the power of money that purchases the vote bank and thereby manages to have the induction of legislators and administrators, who protect and promote the interests of the rich and upper class. Likewise, in rural areas, the rich peasants have established linkages with the administrative apparatus that work against the rural poor who are immensely vulnerable because they are non-owners and the power-wielders are supported by their ownership of land. Corruption breeds corruption. When it sets in, it grows like weeds in a garden. There is no known antidote for it except exposure and punishment.

Due to expensive elections, degeneration of moral values, and the desire to be rich overnight, political corruption has now become a great threat to our political system. It has diluted moral and ethical standards over the years, has seeped into all walks of life, and hampered the economic development of the country. Since Independence, all the Prime Ministers not only ignored, but actively helped some of the politicians who were very close to them in the matters of financial improprieties. This approach of Prime Ministers of not only shielding but also promoting the corrupt politicians, had its adverse impact on the Indian political system because it encouraged political corruption and hence, corruption started spreading from top to bottom.

It is interesting to note that on the one hand Prime Ministers refused to appoint a commission of inquiry against their ministers or chief ministers, belonging to their party, but were quick in appointing such commission whenever a minister or chief minister belonging to some opposition party was involved. This shows that all the Prime Ministers have dragged their feet in appointing commissions of inquiry when their own kith and kin or lieutenants were involved. With the passage of time, links with the underworld of gamblers, smugglers and FERA violators on the one hand, and further deterioration in moral and political standards on the other, has further increased corruption in political life. When politicians indulge in corruption on a large scale, bureaucracy cannot remain far behind.

The selling, of national secrets by officials occupying sensitive places is a sad commentary on the political and bureaucratic leadership of the country. Public Service

Commissions and other recruiting agencies in some of the states have also become dens of corruption.

One of the most disturbing developments which has encouraged corruption is that politicians have undermined the process of rule of law by withdrawing cases of corruption lying in the courts of law. It follows that when politicians who amass wealth by misusing their powers and position and are still not punished, then how can bureaucrats who are stunningly corrupt and serve their political masters, be punished? In fact, Indira Gandhi had once said that corruption is a worldwide phenomena. She had also admitted that it is not true that the Congress alone gets the money or gives the favours.... We do collect money, but everybody does". According to Viren Shah, the ex-president of the Indian Merchants' Chamber of Commerce, "Can we say that we have not contributed to corruption by bribing those in authority or making clandestine contributions to party funds?"

It is important to note that the history of many Third World countries tells us that when corruption and crime jointly act upon economic and political institutions and state power is employed for partisan political objectives, the result inevitably is both massive violence and authoritariatism and this is exactly the direction in which Indian polity is now heading which is very dangerous and unfortunate.

Illegal Activities

Nani A Palkhivala, the eminent constitutional expert observes, "I do not think India, in its entire history of five thousand years has ever reached a lower level of degradation than it has reached now.... The picture that emerges is that of a great nation in a state of moral decay, of which crime, chaos and corruption are three of the several facets." In order to protect themselves, citizens in some parts of the country have begun to organise private armies. Sooner or later, all developing countries become difficult to govern, and over the past two decades, India has been moving in that direction.

The much talked report of the Vohra panel categorically points out that crime syndicates mafia. Organisations have developed muscle and money power and established linkages with government functionaries, political leaders and others. The CBI has reported that the nexus between the criminal gangs, police, bureaucracy and politicians has come out clearly in various parts of the country. There has been a rapid spread and growth of criminal gangs, armed sertas, drug mafia, smuggling gangs, drug peddlers and economic lobbies in the country, which have, over the years, developed an extensive network of contacts with the bureaucrats/government functionaries at the local levels, politicians, media persons and strategically located individuals in the non-state sector. In certain states like Bihar, Haryana and Uttar Pradesh, these gangs enjoy the patronage of local level politicians, cutting across party lines and protection of government functionaries.

The big smuggling syndicates with international linkages, have spread into and infected the various economic and financial activities including hawala. Transactions economy causing serious damage to the economic fibre of the country. The network of mafia is virtually running a parallel government, pushing the state apparatus into irrelevance. The cost of contesting elections has thrown the politicians into the lap of these elements. Another feature in the political culture of the ruling class is the politicisation of crime and of politics. Politicisation of crime involves competitive use of anti-social forces for the mobilisation of party funds, for managements of elections, for organising meetings and conferences and even for recruiting workers at lower levels from among anti-social elements. It also means the misuse of criminal intelligence as a political tool for black mailing political opponents.

Criminalisation of politics means direct entry of criminals

into political parties and legislatures, including Parliament. Today politics is no longer decent: hooligans and hoodlums are gaining control of public life. The notorious criminals, history-shelters, smugglers and murderers are swarming into politics. Formerly, they were on the periphery of Indian political life, now they have moved considerably towards the centre to manipulate the gears and levers of political machine.

Kuldeep Nayyer wrote that according to the Chief Election Commissioner, 180 out of the 425 members of Uttar Pradesh Legislative Assembly had criminal records and the last general elections in Bihar were contested by as many as 243 candidates against whom charges were pending. According to India Today, "of the 424 members of the Vidhan Sabha, 132 are suspected criminals, 16 of them now actually sit in cabinet meetings. Election Commissioner G V G Krishnamurty, while addressing press persons on August 20, 1997, said as per records, 40 members of Parliament have criminal cases pending against them while nearly 700 members of state assemblies out of 4,072 are named in criminal cases, though It was an international accepted norm that 'law breakers cannot be allowed to be lawmakers", which India must also follow.

In a historic judgement on March 20, 1997, the then Chief Justice of India, A M Ahmadi, warned the nation of the emergence of new crime syndicates with a very strong nexus with politicians, bureaucrats, media, personalities and even members of the Judiciary. It is unfortunate that no counter moving force to check criminalisation of politics is emerging. The historic resolution passed by the Lok Sabha at the special session of Parliament on the occasion of the golden jubilee of Independence, August 26 to September 1 1997 observes:

> "The meaningful electoral reforms be carried out so that our Parliament and other legislative bodies be balanced and effective instruments of democracy and further that political life and processes be free

of the adverse impact, on governance of undesirable extraneous factors including criminalisation."

Women of India are paying a heavy price in terms of a rising tide of violence and assent on their honour just because of distorted social values, a band of politicians, hand in glove with criminals and anti-social elements, caste conflicts, etc. Crimes against women are on rise despite all sacrosanct provisions in the Constitution, criminal law, Parliament, judiciary, police, media coverage, the National Human Rights Commission and the National Commission for Women. Perhaps every segment of India has to own the blame and should dip its head in shame for the continuing assault on womanhood in India.

Power of Women

The women of India have been exposed to greater insecurity, to poverty, illiteracy, casteism, orthodoxy unhealthy living conditions, traditionalism, backwardness, corruption, criminalisation and male dominance in most of the fields. They have been affected by lack of opportunities and facilities owing to the innate discrimination prevalent in the society. In the last 20 years, there has been a global effort with a strong support from the United Nations to understand the discrimination and restore a status to women of the world. The slogan has been equality, development and peace.

The United Nations General Assembly declared the International Year of Women in 1975 followed by the International Women's Decade and organised three world conferences-Mexico in 1975, Copenhagen In 1980 and Nairobi in 1985. The Nairobi conference decided strategies for the advancement of women upto 2000 AD. The world has consciously marched forward with various instruments for eliminating discrimination against women during the 20 years. The fourth world conference on women held in Beijing in 1995, focused on the structural changes that are necessary in the society. It emphasised that no enduring solution to society's most threatening social, economic and political problems can be found without the full participation and full empowerment of the women. India's strategies and action plans are to eliminate all discrimination against women; remove the chasm between legal status and defect status; create an environment of harmony and partnership of men and women.

There are countries like Sweden, Finland and Norway, where women make up almost half of the national legislatures. Stories of smooth succession of power from husband to wife are in plenty. Commenting on how widows and daughters have been thrust into power by dynastic imperatives in Asian countries like Philippines, India and Indonesia. Rounaq Jahan, a Bangladeshi political scientist had observed, "They think that they can manipulate these women. But every time they were surprised that once in power, Women handled the men and mastered old style politics."

But behind most successful women leaders in India, there has been the hidden hand of a man. Just as Jawaharlal Nehru groomed Indira Gandhi, MG Ramchandran did for his screen partner Jayalalitha and Kanshi Ram is doing for his acolyte Mayavrati. Even Laloo Prasad Yadav is not far behind these veterans in propping up his wife Rabri Devi, who confidently faces the camera today instead of taking shelter in her kitchen. There may be a sharp variance in their life style, levels of political sophistication, in their dress sense, but they have one thing in common, that is, their valuable grooming in a political career by their mentors. Grooming Includes training in developing their ethos, political issues and marketing them to their selected audience (voters). Many of them would be raw, without a political or famed godfather to lend support. Like one-third reservation for women at rural and urban local bodies, 33 per cent quota may help women in increasing their numerical strength to 181 in the Lok Sabha, it certainly may not be enough in attaining empowerment in the real sense, which would still remain a far cry. After all the road to empowerment is circuitous. Attaining political power may not mean enjoying or utilising it for the betterment of the country or her constituents, till they are trained to cross the rough and tumble of Indian politics.

Therefore, the present political scenario and demand for women's quota have generated a need for starting grooming courses for women politicians in India. Just as the path of empowerment became easy for the American women by mastering political skills. The Indian women can also attain empowerment if only they are groomed well. For women in the West, there are no reservations on the road to political empowerment. But they have the 'primaries' and other sundry opportunities to make themselves hard enough for the long grind in the political arena. Strangely, the idea has not struck us, where women advancement in the political domain is just a matter of time. A politically ambitious woman in our country is just thrown in the thick of things, to fend for herself.

As more and more women get into the thick of things there is an urgent need to evolve a system that will prepare them for this opportunity. Though there are many examples of women who have come through the system, they are seasoned, and experienced. But they have never been to any finishing school. What they have learnt is through sheer experience. There are no caucuses and no primaries where they can cut their political teeth. In effect, they have to behave, react and act as a politician from the word go. It is not an easy task. There are few women in public offices because few of them run for elections. The reservation in panchayats and municipalities will gradually bring more and more women into the political field. They will gather experience at a level, which will teach them the indispensability of a plural society. Among the women at the local institution level, those who want to adopt politics as a full-time career, will move up to the higher bodies in course of time, and their male colleagues will regard their ascent as a natural and legitimate progression. The training institutions or organisations will teach these political women not only the finer things of decision-making and use their power properly, but also the awareness, understanding of outer world, public dealings and if required, literacy, can also be taught to them. Such a process will not cause any political or social upheaval. The benefits of empowerment would also come in due course without the element of confrontation with other groups.

At present, like other Asian countries, there is very slow rise in the percentage of Indian women in Parliament, central ministry, administration, higher education and technical Institutions.

The Union government obviously thinks this call for affirmative action as is evident from its decision to introduce the Constitution (81st Amendment) Bill in the Lower House. If passed by Parliament, the amendment will have a third of the seats reserved for women in the Lok Sabha and the state assemblies. In this situation, the need for grooming institutions becomes very relevant.

Mohini Girl wrote, "the country is facing, as never before, a torrent of crime due to various socioeconomic reasons not to speak of infiltration of illegal migrants, besides other state sponsored terrorism ... much of these kinds of heinous crimes and atrocities have their roots in the drug mafia, foreign patronage and other country strategies to destabilise civilian population." Criminalisation is a big problem as most Asian cities are unsafe to live in despite the economic growth in the region. Compared to them, the law and order situation in Indian metros is better. The crime rate in Bangalore and Delhi is much lower than that in Seoul or Tokyo.

Apart from this situation, women's status in Asia is clearly in flux. Democracy seems to have helped by creating an environment in which autonomous women's groups could form, network and develop some political influence. Progress in terms of formal political representation of women has been much more gradual in most Asian nations. The practice of reserving parliamentary quotas for women seems to be spreading, although this obviously is a lengthy process. Women in Asia, therefore, face substantial political challenges with significant, but limited resources at their disposal.

Fortunately, in recent times, women have awakened to the fact that in order to break gender-barriers and overcome social bias, women's participation in the political process is essential. Though women constitute nearly half of the total population, politics has all along been men's domain. A February 1997 report on inter-Parliamentary unions says that Indian women hold only 7.2 per cent seats in the Lower House and 7.8 per cent seats in the Upper House. This can be called as token representation.

The percentage of women MLAs in state assemblies is also not very encouraging. Though in comparison to 1952, the percentage in the years from 1993 to 1998, has been certainly increased but still it is insignificant.

The truth is that except for mouthing political platitudes during elections, men are not prepared to give political space to women. One must realise that advancing the status of women is not only a moral imperative, but women's presence at the decision-making level is sine quanon for strengthening democratic traditions and fighting against injustice and oppression.

However, laws alone do not lead to social transformation unless followed by resolute action and socialite awareness of the wrong that have been perpetuated on women from time immemorial. But first of all there should be a revolution of consciousness in the minds of women-in the way they thought about themselves. Women must realise that gender deprivation is inconsistent with the basic human rights of women.

They must realise that they have constitutional rights to equality, health care, economic security, access to education, employment opportunities, pay equity and political *power*. As India has celebrated more than 55 years of its Independence, this is a historic opportunity to invest in India's future for when a woman thrives, her family thrives, when families thrive, communities flourish and the nation reaps the benefits eventually.

3

WOMEN WELFARE

As recognized in the Fifth Five-Year Plan, even with expanded employment opportunities, the poor will not be able, with their level of earnings, to buy for themselves all the essential goods and services which should figure in any reasonable concept of a minimum standard of living. The measures for providing larger employment and incomes to the poorer sections will, therefore, have to be supplemented up to at least certain minimum standard, by social consumption and investment in the form of education, health, nutrition, drinking water, housing, communications and electricity, and social welfare services. Social welfare services are intended to cater for the special needs of persons and groups, who by reason of some handicap-social, economic, physical or mental-are unable to avail of or are traditionally denied the amenities and services provided by the community. Women are handicapped by social customs and social values and therefore social welfare services have and should specially endeavour to rehabilitate them by inducing a change in the attitudes of society towards women, their role and contribution.

Zone of Complication

A statement of a plan of social welfare programmes relating to women, even if, it is within the purview of the overall social welfare programmes, will help in providing the correct emphasis on the problems and development needs of the weaker sections of women and provide voluntary organizations and voluntary effort "a certain" direction. The problems and consequently the developmental action required are, it appears, unlimited and the resources are limited. As such, priorities have necessarily to be assigned.

Among women, the following categories and some of the problems faced by them, call for special attention on a priority basis. The categories are:

(A) Working women. To include
  (i) The low-income women living in tribal and backward rural areas and urban slums.
  (ii) The migrant women.
  (iii) The divorced /separated.

(B) Physically and mentally handicapped women.

(C) Widows with or without children.

(D) Destitute women.

(E) Women who come into conflict with law.

(F) Exploited women and unmarried mothers.

The problems faced by each of the above categories are numerous and some of them are common to other categories. To decide on action plan priorities, the handicaps and/or the factors which impose constraints need to be understood.

Women at Work

According to 1971 Census, women workers constitute nearly 12 per cent of the total women population and well over 90 per cent of the women workers are found employed in rural areas. It should be recognized here that the problems faced by women workers in rural areas are altogether different from those in the urban areas.

Rural areas including tribal and backward areas: Women workers in rural areas are largely landless agricultural labourers; members of households with uneconomic holdings; those engaged in traditional household industries like hand-spinning, hand-weaving, oil pressing, rice pounding, leather, tobacco processing, etc. These household industries-which are predominantly female labour intensive and which have been a major source of employment in villages appear to have declined in importance during the post-independence period. This is also evidenced by the distinctly declining trend in employment of women workers in the rural areas between the decennial Censuses 1961 and 1971. It has not been possible to reverse this trend because:

(i) Almost all the women workers in the rural areas are handicapped by illiteracy and lack of mobility.

(ii) In addition to this, incessant child bearing coupled with hard domestic work does not provide them any time to go through formal education/training to acquire new skills. Facilities for acquiring new skills are still sparse.

Urban Areas: Women workers in the urban areas fall into three distinct categories:

(i) The first category consists largely of migrants from villages and members of families whose economic position has deteriorated to near starvation. The women of this class work mainly as domestic servants and as unskilled labour in various unorganized industries.

This category of women workers, who are largely slum dwellers, are below subsistence level. Their problems are to find a job which is secure or provides them regular income at least to subsist, a place for comfortable living, as most of them are away from their homes located in villages; and rehabilitation facilities for their families, particularly children and preparing them for better livelihood, through better education and training; in that order.

(ii) The second category consists of women, who need employment either to keep their families away from starvation or to ensure better standard of living. Most of such women are found employed in industries, services and professions. Some are even self-employed. In the case of this second category of women workers in urban areas, their existence ranges from subsistence to security. Some of these women, particularly those residing away from their families, are likely to be exposed to the dangers of exploitation from undesirable and anti-social elements. Personal security is therefore a major problem for them.

(iii) The third category consists of women who are highly educated and work in higher ranks of services and professions for personal satisfaction and independence. Belonging as they do at least to the upper middle-class families, they do not as group face any serious problems requiring immediate attention here.

Divorced/separated women are part of each of these categories.

Uneligible Ones

There are several types of physical handicaps like blindness, deafness, orthopaedic handicap, leprosy, mental retardation, etc., which hinder two persons from even entertaining the hopes of equal participation in the overall social activity. These problems are common to both men and women.

Estimates of physically handicapped women are not separately available. To provide a basis for the formulation of Fifth Five-Year Plan, the working group on the Handicapped constituted for the purpose, estimated that "India may have well over 12 million blind, deaf and orthopaedically handicapped persons. In addition, an estimated 2 million suffer from moderate to severe retardation. The number of persons suffering from leprosy is believed to be around 2.5 million".

The basic problem concerning these physically handicapped persons is lack of adequate facilities for differential medical care, education, training and rehabilitation programmes and a lack of knowledge about these facilities by handicapped persons. Further, it is widely known that though the existing facilities are largely used by men, a majority of physically handicapped women are not coming forward to utilize the available facilities.

Widowhood

The 1971 Census distribution of women according to marital status indicates that roughly about 9 per cent of the women are widows. Further, they are almost evenly distributed between the rural and urban areas.

Widowhood is a curse for most of the women in India for various reasons:

(i) It is almost invariably accompanied by economic disaster. This is because a large number of the families in India survive at below subsistence level and hence death of a male earning member pushes down the families concerned to near starvation. Also many of the females are voluntarily out of work force, and illiteracy remains the greatest barrier for the improvement of the economic position of widowed women, particularly in the rural areas.

(ii) Age-old traditions, social prejudices and cultural practices almost exclude widowed women from any socially productive work. Social acceptance of women is reduced with widowhood. In some communities/ regions. There is almost a sort of social boycott of widowed women.

Problems faced by Widows of Different Age Groups: The problems faced by widowed women are not all the same as between different age-groups; and as between rural and urban areas:

(a) For widows in the younger age group - particularly those belonging to 15-44 years of age - the problems are more - related to economic independence and rehabilitation in the society - preferably through remarriage.

(b) For widows in the age group 45 and above, the problem is more of social acceptance and security. Most of such women, if not previously employed, will be unfit for employment. Even in respect of employed women -widowed after 44 years of age - it is difficult to impart -of the needed training/skills for more remunerative jobs within the existing framework of education/ training facilities.

Problems of widowed women in the rural areas are even move severe than those in the urban areas. In addition to economic dependence and the social stigma attached to widowhood, there are no opportunities for their emancipation. Many of them are possibly not even aware of the efforts being made by the government agencies through voluntary organizations to redress their miseries.

These destitute women can be classified into three age-groups as their problems are different:

Below 15 years: Persons in this group can be categorized as children. They are mostly orphans and are, therefore, deprived of the tender parental care. They are also subjected to malnutrition and the consequent diseases. This age group, viz., below 15 years of age constitutes the formative years in a person's life, as the process of development and learning are most rapid during these young years. During these formative years, the effects of environment greatly influence the personality development, mental attitudes, moral character, etc. Often, destitute persons in this age group fall a prey to the environmental disadvantages.

15-44 years: This second group of women are both in the productive and reproductive age group. Their main problems are those pertaining to economic independence, social acceptance and security.

45 years and above: In the case of third group of destitute women, their major problem is social security. They are mostly unfit to be employed. They cannot even be trained to earn their livelihood.

Women and Law

Women who fall under this category are:

(i) juvenile delinquents,

(ii) women in moral and social danger - particularly those who indulge in immoral traffic and

(iii) women prisoners.

Juvenile delinquents: are again a creation of the society and the environment in which they are brought up; the deprivation of proper nutrition and training/education which would enable them to earn a better livelihood, etc.

Prostitutes: Women subjected to severe economic distress and hardships often come into the clutches of persons who have vested interests in immoral traffic. Once they succumb, they do not receive proper health care - curative and preventive treatment for the diseases associated with immoral traffic; many of them are not aware of the existing health care facilities and added to it is the innate fear of being exposed to the general public and the resulting social reactions. The existing health facilities are also not adequate and are not perceived as being sympathetic towards their health problems.

Female Prisoners: Many of the problems faced by female prisoners are in common with male prisoners. However, some of the problems are peculiar to females alone. For example, women prisoners with children - particularly in case children are below five years - have problems in arranging for the care of their children. Also, problems in getting rehabilitated, after they are free, are more severe in the case of women prisoners than men prisoners.

Child before Marriage

(i) Out-of-wedlock pregnancies are on the increase, judging from the number of abortions and live births among single women recorded at various institutions. Estimates of medical termination of pregnancies (MTP) in the case of single women alone range from 10 to 30 per cent of total MTP cases. In respect of live illegitimate births estimates based on hospital records range from 2 to 3 per cent of the total confinements. In reality many more clandestine live illegitimate births may be taking place which are not brought to public notice.

(ii) Premarital pregnancies, are as generally believed, no longer confined to the illiterate and depressed classes. According to some case-studies in this field, nearly 50 per cent of the pre-marital pregnancies were observed in the case of women who are at least matriculates. A few were graduates. Some of them were observed to be belonging to the privileged classes of the society. A more distressing feature, however, is that pre-marital pregnancies are being observed even in the case of school girls.

Among the reasons attributed to premarital pregnancies are:

> Interactions between various social, psychological and economic forces like break down of joint families; overwhelming poverty, rapid urbanization bringing in its wake the social transformation which leads to increasing permissiveness, lack of communication between children and parents; emotional immaturity and craze for excitement among the youth; antipathy towards the introduction of basic sex education among school children, etc., are the most important reasons cited.

Permissiveness and promiscuity increase with rapid urbanization and measures to avoid such premarital pregnancies is a long drawn social education problem and cannot be expected to decline rapidly. However, the problems concomitant to premarital pregnancies can and should at least be tackled effectively.

The action plans should be directed primarily to solving the problems of these six target groups of women.

Action taking Group

There is considerable overlap both in terms of the causes and programmes and agencies concerned with eliminating the problems and building rehabilitation/development plans for these target groups. As such, the action plans are classified under broad groups of actions rather than in terms of categories of women discussed above:

I. Provision of Services/Infrastructure.

II. Education/Training Programmes for the Target Groups.

III. Promoting Voluntary Effort: The Role of Women.

IV. Development of Human Resources.

V. Administrative Set-up and Coordination.

VI. Legislative Measures.

VII. Areas of Research.

The Fifth Five-Year Plan has rightly emphasized the need for a shift in the approach towards social welfare, from a mere provision of curative and rehabilitative services - the kind of approach adopted during the past two decades of planning - to promoting the needed preventive and developmental aspects of social welfare. The action plans should necessarily have such a preventive and development orientation.

Programme for Action

Provision of Services/Infrastructure

(i) Services for the care of girls below 15;

(ii) Facilities for women in the productive age group, i.e. 15-45 years;

(iii) Programmes for the care of aged and infirm women; and

(iv) General welfare programmes.

Services for the Care of Girls below 15: There are three categories of children who need particular attention, viz., children of working women, destitute children particularly female children and juvenile delinquents. The following action plans are suggested:

(1) The child population below 6 years of working mothers in urban and rural areas is estimated to be around 20 lakh and 166 lakh, respectively. With a view to helping the working mother discharge her duties - both as a mother and worker better family aid services like Anganwadis, Balwadis, creches and day care centres might be launched in a big way.

Both in the rural and in the urban areas efforts should be made to cover more than 40 per cent of the children of working mothers.

(2) There are about 11 lakh destitute children in the country. The girls among them need particular attention, because they are likely to be exposed to social and moral dangers when they grow up. Efforts should be made to provide institutional facilities whether through the foster care programmes or otherwise for taking care of a majority of the destitute female children.

(3) It is impossible to discriminate between male and female juvenile delinquents, as the problems are common to both. However, the approach towards juvenile delinquency as such should be to provide the needed atmosphere for a child to develop personality, character and social conscience through setting up of clubs, play centres, juvenile guidance units, workshops, etc.

(4) Holiday homes schemes initiated earlier to provide organized and guided recreational facilities to children and be one of the measures to prevent juvenile delinquency. Such facilities should at least be extended to cover all the children residing in the slums of major cities.

Facilities for Women in the Productive Age Group: In some selected urban areas, hostel facilities are available for working women of the lower income groups earning Rs. 50 to Rs. 800 per month. However, the coverage of the programme in terms of the proportion of working women needs to be stepped up considerably. Similarly, district-wise investigation would be undertaken about the need for working women's hostels and appropriate facilities set up. The matching contribution for grants for construction/ addition/ alterations should be stepped up.

Socio-economic programmes were initiated in 1958 with

the objective of providing full or part-time work to the needy/ destitute women and the physically handicapped either through full wage or a wage sufficient to supplement the meagre income of their families. These programmes should be expanded considerably in both rural and urban areas, as they have the potential to provide the needed economic independence to women belonging to the weaker sections and thus act as a preventive measure to many of the social evils.

For effectively implementing these socio-economic programmes, active collaboration should be sought from agencies like Handicrafts Board, Handloom Board, Khadi and Village Industries Board, Small Industries Service Institutes, Small Industries Development Corporations at the State level and the nationalized banks.

To increase the employment potential for the following types of schemes additional steps should be undertaken within the purview of socio-economic programmes:

(i) Small-Scale industries.

(ii) Units as ancillary to large production of handicrafts.

(iii) Units for the procurement and production of handicrafts.

(iv) Handloom training-cum-production units.

(v) Agro-based industries like dairy, poultry farms, etc.

(vi) Traditional female labour intensive industries like rice pounding, oil-pressing, etc.

Attempts must be made to revitalize and activate the existing sick units falling under the purview of socio-economic programmes.

Ways to improve the working, efficiency and effectiveness of Mahila Mandals must be studied and necessary action taken. They should be reoriented to aim at increasing the earning power of women in the rural areas.

It is suggested that by the end of the Fifth Plan, about 10,000 Mahila Mandals, should be developed throughout the country to provide an effective media for organizing women welfare activities in the rural areas.

Scholarship programmes of the Central and State Governments for the handicapped should be expanded considerably and efforts should be made to encourage women to make use of the scholarships available. Sheltered workshops should be organized.

Schemes for the welfare of destitute women between the ages 18-44 and 45-65 providing for basic amenities of food, shelter, clothing, basic education and training in crafts should be implemented through voluntary organizations who may be given grants to cover 75 per cent of the expenditure. It is suggested that this scheme should be revived and implemented in all the States.

Homes for the rehabilitation of rescued and released women prisoners should be started in all towns with a minimum of 5 lakh of population. Apart from providing shelter, food and clothing, the inmates should also be provided training in crafts like sewing, embroidery, knitting, etc. Efforts should, however, be made in the direction of making inmates self-sufficient and earn independent livelihood.

In some such protective homes, insane women are housed along with other women which is an unhealthy and undesirable practice and should be discontinued.

Programmes for the Care of Aged and Infirm Women: Women in the age group 65 years and over constitute roughly 85 lakh according to the 1971 Census. Many of the women lack absolutely any security They are mostly dependent on their children who often desert them. Thus, even women belonging to upper middle classes are sometimes reduced to the status of destitute. Efforts should therefore be made at least in a modest way to initiate social security measures through old age pension with the objective of providing economic independence to at least 25 per cent of women in the age group particularly in the rural areas.

For the women retired from active service and for those who are in need of some residential facilities, hostels should be started in all the major cities. If necessary, subsidies may also be extended under the grants-in-aid programmes.

General Welfare Programmes: Slum clearance programmes should be initiated in all the major cities and towns with a minimum of 5 lakh of population. People displaced should be provided alternative sites, with proper environmental sanitation, for building their homes.

Zila Parishads and youth in the districts should be entrusted with drinking water supply projects.

A vigorous campaign of education and action should be launched in favour of community sanitation and hygiene. Public utility services should be expanded. The practice of carrying night soil as headloads must be eradicated.

Education/Training Programmes for the Target Groups: Analysis of the problems faced by the target group of women indicated that illiteracy, inadequate education/training, lack of facilities for training in alternative skills and lack of knowledge about the existing facilities are some of the major problems that have hindered the progress of women in India. There is, therefore, the need for accelerating the efforts in this regard with renewed vigour. With this in view, the following action plans are recommended:

(1a) The Fourth Plan introduced a programme of functional literacy built round farmer's training in selected districts where high yielding varieties of crops were being cultivated. It is estimated that about 90,000 women received this training during the Fourth Plan and about 5 to 7 lakh of women are likely to be trained under this programmes during the Fifth Plan. This programme must be extended to all the rural areas.

(1b) Apart from imparting knowledge about farming, the curriculum for women should include courses of training, in occupational skills like kitchen gardening, food cultivation, poultry keeping, animal husbandry; household arts like cooking, nutritional values of foods locally available, sewing, knitting, etc.; and family planning.

(1c) Preference should be given to women belonging to Scheduled Castes, tribal women, widowed women and destitutes under this functional literacy programme.

(2a) For the non-student young girls without any education and school drop-outs - particularly for girls in the age group 11-14 years, the pre-vocational training programmes should be reviewed and strengthened by enlarging the scope of training and by increasing the number of trades.

(2b) In respect of girls in the age group 11-14 years, the objective of pre-vocational training should also be to train them to be self-sufficient in home management by organizing courses of training in sewing, cooking, nutrition, minor repairs of the house, motherhood, child care, etc.

(2c) Pre-vocational programmes should be extended to cover girls in this age group in the rural areas. In urban areas, preference should be given to girls in the slum areas and destitute girls.

(3) Condensed courses of education were started in 1958 with the twin objective of

(a) opening new vistas of employment to a large number of deserving and needy women, and

(b) creating a band of competent trained workers required to man the various projects in the rural areas in the shortest possible time. Under the scheme, women in the age group 18-30 who have studied up to classes IV and VI are trained for middle school/matriculation examinations within a period of two years. The scheme was found very useful but the statistics reveal that the beneficiaries have been mostly women belonging to the middle-class families. Preference should be given to women belonging to backward classes, widowed women and destitute women.

(4) Special efforts should be made to cover women belonging to Scheduled Castes and Scheduled Tribes through condensed courses. An incentive of Rs.1,000 (as recommended by the Review Committee), be given to the institution for every successful Scheduled Caste/ Scheduled Tribe candidate trained.

(5a) The condensed courses should be organized in a big way and for smaller groups of say 5 to 7 with the help of high schools and colleges for girls. Efforts should be made to cover about 215 lakh women under the condensed course programmes, during the Fifth Plan period.

(5b) Apart from imparting general education, condensed courses should also aim at imparting job-oriented training with the active cooperation of existing vocational training institutions.

(5c) Under this programme of condensed courses, short-term courses should be organized to retain women who have been temporarily out of job-market to fulfil child bearing responsibilities.

(5d) For the failed candidates, short-term course of six months to one year should be organized.

(5e) Special efforts should be initiated to follow-up successful candidates with a view to helping them in securing jobs.

(6) Pre-examination training facilities should be offered to duly qualified poor women with the objective of equipping them to successfully compete in examinations for public jobs. It is suggested that about 80 lakh girls in the age group 14-17 may be covered under this programme during the Fifth Plan period.

(7) The school curricula in various States in India should encourage the doing away of traditional prejudices of inequality of the sexes.

(8) Sex education should be introduced at the appropriate stage with the objective of also educating the young girls about the social and moral dangers they are likely to encounter.

(9) The value of physical training in the school curricula should be emphasized.

Promoting Voluntary Effort: The Role of Women: Voluntary welfare service organizations have been an integral part of the cultural and social traditions in India. Soon after independence, it was estimated that there were 10,000 voluntary organizations engaged in social welfare. In fact, all the schemes of Central Social Welfare Board are implemented only through voluntary organizations.

The reorientation given to social welfare in the Fifth Plan calls for more effort on the part of both voluntary organizations and the State agencies involved. The following action plans are, therefore, warranted in this regard:

(a) Efforts should be made to promote a large number of voluntary organizations throughout the country. They have a critical role in mobilizing public opinion in favour of equality among men and women, and eradicating superstitions, social evils and waste. The motivational strategy for encouraging voluntary organizations needs to be well thought through and support facilities provided. Women should be promoted to take the initiative and responsibility for organizing voluntary effort, for not only can they bring to the tasks the necessary dedication commitment and empathy; but their very presence will provide their socially handicapped sisters a source of inspiration and set in a cycle of social rejuvenation. All voluntary organizations particularly those concerned with social welfare vis-a-vis women must be encouraged to have women members. Women Panchayats, Mahila Mandals, working women, etc., should be encouraged to spearhead such voluntary activities. Mahila Mandals should be promoted in every village so that they can function as field level agencies for social and economic transformation.

(b) Most of the voluntary organizations have been operating independently of each other. They have, therefore, not been able to fully benefit the community. The role of existing organizations should be determined and measures should be initiated to coordinate/ supplement the efforts of various organizations at each district level.

(c) Many of the women's voluntary organizations are located in urban areas, while only a few organizations have endeavoured to work amongst rural women. Efforts should be made to promote a large number of voluntary women's organizations in the rural backward and tribal areas and urban slums to mobilize public support for different programmes and to implement them. This calls for liberation of the rules regarding the matching grant through voluntary contributions, simplification of the rules and procedures of obtaining the grant as well as administering the organizations, provision of trained staff, organization of leadership training programmes, etc.

Development of Human Resources: Administration of

various social welfare programmes have become increasingly technical. During the past two decades of developmental planning, lack of technically competent workers has had an adverse impact on the quality and success of welfare programmes. With a view to provide the necessary support to various agencies, the following action plans are suggested:

(1) Training facilities for the workers attached to all the voluntary agencies, like Mahila Mandals should be initiated immediately. The training needs of workers, however, differ from organization to organization depending on the nature of tasks required to be performed.

(2) Through a proper investigation training requirements of workers in each district should be assessed and suitable training programmes designed.

(3) These training programmes should, as far as possible be organized at each district level.

(4) Trainees should preferably be local candidates.

(5) Effective implementation of the various socio-economic programmes require two cadres of workers: the grass-root workers and supervisory staff. The grass-root workers should be provided training in the latest techniques and methods of production with the active collaboration of well established industrial units and Industrial Training Institutes. The supervisory staff, on the other hand, should be trained in advanced techniques of production, business management, personnel management, etc.

(6) In the case of handicrafts units under the socio-economic programme, practising craftsmen should be trained as instructors and appointed.

(7) Short-term orientation should also be given to the members of the managing committees of the units - socio-economic programmes - about the general working of such units.

(8) Senior level officers in charge of the socio-economic programmes should also be exposed to short-term orientation courses in business management and allied fields through Small Industries Service Institutes, University departments of business management, etc.

Administrative Set-Up and Coordination: Administrative traditions in India have tended to attach least importance to departments dealing with social welfare. This is reflected even in the training imparted to administrators. Only recently it has been realized that administration must also be welfare oriented. The federal nature of our policy vests a large responsibility for implementing social policy and programmes with State and local authorities. There is, therefore, the need for reorganizing the administrative set-up with a view to effectively implementing the various welfare programmes. The following action plans may be taken up for consideration:

(1) Orientation/training programmes should be organized for social welfare personnel, particularly at decision making levels, to sensitize them to social welfare needs and adopt the extension approach of reaching out to the clients. The new developmental and preventive concept, of welfare also needs to be imparted.

(2) Every State Department of Social Welfare should have a Women's Welfare Division with responsibility for planning, programming and monitoring the implementation of schemes of women welfare.

(3) The Central Social Welfare Board is one of the most important agencies for the implementation of social welfare activities. It should be reorganized and strengthened, and vested with larger funds and responsibilities for promoting and developing voluntary effort particularly in rural, backward and tribal areas and among the weaker sections of the community.

(4) The Central Social Welfare Board should launch a massive campaign for enlisting and developing a cadre of voluntary social workers who should be provided some normal assistance to enable them to carry out this work.

(5) State Social Welfare (Advisory) Boards should also be reorganized and strengthened.

(6) The State Board should also be made to function as liaison among the State Government and the local agencies.

(7) Suitable infrastructure should be developed at each district level and block level for implementing and expanding the programmes of Central Social Welfare Board.

(8) Trained social welfare workers should be associated with all the committees to be set-up by the Central Social Welfare Board.

Legislative Measures

(1) International experience indicates that evolving a sound social security system takes a long period of time. However, suitable enactment can be initiated to provide public assistance to select groups like destitute women and people above 65 years but without any means of livelihood. Assistance here need not be in the form of cash. It should be in the form of medical, housing, feeding and recreational facilities, etc.

(2) It should be open to the States and Union Territories to go in for taxation or special levy to finance such public assistance schemes without prejudice to any assistance made available to States and Union Territories from the Central Government under plan schemes.

(3) No child should be tried in adult courts nor should any child be sent to a jail.

(4) State Governments should enact legislation for apprehension, institutional treatment and rehabilitation of beggars, particularly women.

(5) Machinery should be set up for speedy and effective adjudication in all cases concerning the family, including the setting up of family welfare courts since the ordinary judicial procedure is not suited to handle such cases. Women, particularly in rural areas, should be protected against harassment.

(6) A vigorous campaign should be launched to educate women about their rights and the machinery through which they can seek their realization.

(7) Active public support should be mobilized by government agencies, voluntary organizations and public leaders against child marriage and dowry to support the legislative measures for the eradication of these undesirable practices. Ostentatious weddings and other wasteful social ceremonies should be banned.

Zone of Research

Primary data available with sources such as the Census and National Sample Survey, are insufficient and are very scanty for social welfare planning, particularly on the needs and requirements of handicapped women, destitute women, women under the purview of the suppression of Immoral Traffic Act, etc.: In view of this, the following areas of research are suggested:

(i) Studies on 'Social profiles' with district as unit' wherein information on the prevailing conditions of social needs and requirements, etc., are investigated.

(ii) Studies on the requirements of physically handicapped children and women.

(iii) Studies on the requirements of destitute children and women.

(iv) Studies on the training requirements of workers in voluntary welfare organizations.

(v) Studies on the socio-economic and psychological factors behind the problem of premarital pregnancies.

(vi) Studies on the magnitude of problems facing prostitutes and their children such as problems of children of prostitutes, particularly female children.

Work on Option

Voluntary action in India has always been an integral part of the cultural and social traditions. A variety of social services were provided by voluntary agencies prior to independence and in the first few decades' of planned development in India. Traditionally, voluntary agencies undertook a wide variety of activities in the areas of social reform in the pre-independence period. Independence resulted in government policy and commitment to support and strengthen voluntary agencies. Voluntary agencies have currently opted for several alternative roles depending on their objectives, location (rural/urban) and resources available.

The role of voluntary agencies in national development has been considered vital due to their direct and first-hand experience and knowledge of local needs, problems and resources at the grass-roots. Further the commitment and zeal of the voluntary action movement is considered effective as it is not bound by rigid bureaucratic systems and is more responsive to people. The voluntary sector is observed to operate with great flexibility and bases its activities on felt needs. There is a process of continually learning from past experiences in programme planning and implementation, etc.

The essential strength of voluntary agencies derives from the fact that they are closer to the community and people. They represent in many cases the needs and aspirations of the people. Voluntary agencies often function more effectively than the government managed agencies in areas such as motivation, problem identification and analysis, project formulation, innovative methods of service delivery and involvement of the community, due to their spirit.

There are a number of lessons to be learned in such areas such as the demystification of technology; de-emphasizing formal educational qualification in favour of experience, capabilities, aptitude and ability to work with people; expansion of activities without adding on cumbersome bureaucracy; and reliance on community based and non-institutional approaches. The unique strength of the voluntary sector is its ability to pressurize the government without succumbing to it and losing its identity and lobbying on issues and ideas to make them acceptable to government and the people. The decentralized administration in the voluntary sector not only facilitates effective grass-roots, delivery mechanisms but also ensures the participation of the beneficiaries in the programmes.

Voluntary agencies in India have evolved as a result of a historical process that has brought them to their present status and role in the country's development. In the 1950s, most of the organizations provided either relief work or were involved in institutionalized programmes such as schools, destitute homes, hospitals as well as welfare activities. In the 1960s, many of these organizations realized that families with a weak economic base would be unable to procure the benefits of institutional welfare and relief services. It led them to the conclusion that services should enable beneficiaries to be productive and self-reliant through income generating programmes. In the 1970s, many of the voluntary organizations began to feel that economic inputs alone could not overcome poverty and a critical roadblock to development was the unequal social structure. A new type of education geared to raising the consciousness of weaker sections on their situation and rights so that they become active agents of their own development, and change was considered essential. Activist groups built around these considerations, subsequently came into existence in the voluntary sector.

The organization of women by voluntary organizations has acquired importance as the need has emerged for organizational structures to ensure women's participation in the development process. Many old established voluntary agencies have undertaken the task of setting up welfare development services for women in the country.

New Trends: From the mid 1970s onwards there was an emergence of many newly established organizations and activist groups. A large part of the activities of these groups have centered around combating atrocities and violence committed on women, dowry murder, brutal forms of maltreatment and exploitation. In many cases, women in distress have approached such groups for assistance in registering and follow up of cases, providing shelter, etc.

These activist groups have identified themselves with oppressed, victimized, and harassed women and awakened new hopes, aspirations and consciousness among women on these issues. Recently many formal and informal groups have emerged throughout the country which have successfully mobilized women's awareness and have preferred to work directly with the women, relying less on material inputs from the outside and more on increasing the internal capabilities and resources-economic, social, cultural and political. These activist groups have also elicited the intervention of the State, especially of the judiciary and of the fourth estate, to project the rights of women and ameliorate their situations. At the same time, they have organized the women themselves for struggle.

Besides voluntary agencies and activist groups, there are many other functional groups such as Mahila Mandals, Youth Clubs, Nehru Yuvak Kendras, National Service Schemes, cooperatives and other people's institutions that have effectively taken up the issues of women in development with varying degrees of success.

Government's Stance on Voluntary Action: The Planning Commission has recognized the role of voluntary action in accelerating the process of social and economic development in most of its plans, particularly so in the Sixth and Seventh Five-Year Plans. Voluntary agencies at their best have played an important role in providing a basis for testing and devising innovative projects and new Models and approaches in programme implementation and in ensuring feedback, as well as in securing the participation of women living below the poverty line.

They have developed competence in many non-traditional areas and played a vital role in supplementing governmental efforts so as to offer the rural poor choices and alternatives. They have often served as the eyes and ears of the people at the village level. By adopting simple, innovative, flexible and inexpensive means to suit their limited resources, they have tried to reach a larger number of beneficiaries with minimal overheads and with greater community participation. In the process they have successfully demonstrated how village and indigenous resources, rural skills and local knowledge are grossly underutilized at present, in a cost-effective manner. Voluntary agencies have also managed to mobilize and organize the poor to some extent and to generate in them the awareness to demand quality services and improve accountability of the local level functionaries. They have helped to train a cadre of grass root workers that believe in professionalizing voluntarism.

The increasing interest of the government in enhancing the role of voluntary agencies in the development of women is quite evident. Considering the magnitude of problems faced by women the government has rightly felt that it cannot assume the entire responsibility of service provision and development. It has sought to associate voluntary agencies in the various programmes aimed at women. The thrust of the current programmes is more towards development of women's potential and their productive participation in development rather than merely providing welfare services to them. A meaningful partnership with the voluntary sector has thus been an avowed goal and an essential variable in government's attempts to integrate women in development.

Women and the Voluntary Sector: Voluntary agencies have contributed immensely to the new directions and impetus provided to women's programmes during the decade for women. A number of innovative features in several government formulated schemes / programmes are based on the experience of the projects run successfully by voluntary agencies.

The rationale for involvement of voluntary agencies in women's development is quite clear. Women in India suffer from multifarious constraints such as a low level of literacy, lack of access to resources and obstacles caused by the cultural and social customs and traditions that are discriminatory of women. In a situation such as this, the role of voluntary agencies in creating awareness among women of their rights and mobilizing women as well as developing in them appropriate motivation and leadership to realize those rights cannot be minimized.

The process of creating an environment conducive to the progress of women is dependent on a multitude of socio-economic factors, starting with a political will to enforce the development of women as a priority. The long-term objectives of the Seventh Plan spell out that raising the economic and social status of women is a critical goal of national development. The basic approach suggested is to inculcate confidence among women and bring about an awareness of their own potential for development. Within this framework, gainful employment to women is accorded the highest priority as an effective strategy. Various ministries and departments have formulated programmes for the development of women with an emphasis on the involvement of voluntary agencies as delivery mechanisms. The role of voluntary agencies in the mobilization of women in particular is seen as a critical factor for the development strategies of the future.

A higher involvement of voluntary agencies is thus envisaged in the implementation of such government programmes as the Integrated Rural Development Program (IRDP), Training of Rural Youth in Self-Employment (TRYSEM), Development of Women and Children in Rural Areas (DWCRA), Integrated Child Development Services Scheme (ICDS), and Adult Literacy programmes.

Besides their involvement in these schemes, voluntary agencies can also assist in effective enforcement of minimum wages, supply of safe drinking water, afforestation, social forestry, consumer protection, promotion of science and technology, rural housing, legal education, etc. With the new focus on women, some funds should be earmarked for implementation of these programmes in the concerned ministries/ departments for voluntary agencies. Further through the Central Social Welfare Board (CSWB), Council for Advancement of People's Action and Rural Technology (CAPART) and the National Rural Development Fund, the activities of and cooperation with voluntary agencies should be expanded and strengthened. To the extent that voluntary agencies are dependent on public funds, accountability has to be ensured but without cumbersome and rigid methods.

Voluntary Action in the Organization of Women: Empowerment of women cannot be ensured until they are enabled to organize themselves. Collective organizations spell strength. This is a prerequisite for initiating action, lobbying, pressurizing and bargaining. Grass roots organizations can greatly enhance the opportunities for poor women to participate in development programmes by providing an organizational base to operate from. By organizing, working together, sharing experiences and resources, building pressure groups and so forth, women can find independent access to opportunities for their betterment.

A large number of women are engaged in the unorganized sector working and living under precarious conditions and with no legal protection. The unorganized sector denies women all benefits of collective action. Dispersed and unorganized, they have no political power and no bargaining strength. As a result, it becomes much more difficult to implement protective labour laws relating to wages, conditions of work, insurance, provident fund, maternity leave, and creches, etc., and also to channelize economic inputs such as credit, technical training and marketing. In such a situation, the need for collective action becomes critical, and is dependent upon the organization of women in the unorganized sector. Many spontaneous and organized struggles have been launched by some voluntary organizations for the articulation of the needs of poor women, particularly the need to organize them for their interaction into the mainstream. For instance, the whole issue of women in the unorganized sector has been debated and seriously addressed through the awareness generated by certain organizations in different parts of the country.

Uncovered Territory: The issue of gender disparity at work is yet to be voiced effectively in the organized voluntary action movement. Of the vast masses in the category of the working poor, the unskilled ranks contain a larger proportion of females. These women are much less organized for any kind of market leverage or wage bargaining and even when organized, less inclined to redress gender inequalities at work sites. There is the need to replicate the success stories of voluntary action in organizing women in different parts of the country and to take up the issue to parity at work in a larger way.

The participation of women in development requires an all

round transformation in the consciousness of both men and women as also in the socio-cultural norms, the mass media and pattern of education all of which at present tend to perpetuate a passive unequal role of women in social, economic and political affairs. There is a need for a strong voluntary action involvement in order to evolve a specific strategy based on the local situation, in this area, of women. Any voluntary agency that is serious about promoting women's participation would have to seriously consider the challenge of recruiting and training women catalysts, extension agents and functionaries for reaching and eliciting women's participation.

Voluntary Action for Legal Aid: The majority of women have no knowledge about their rights and very few have resources to obtain legal redressal. It is now being strongly felt that laws by themselves cannot bring about the desirable change in the status of women unless women become aware of their rights. At the same time, it is also felt that since most of the women cannot afford legal representation in courts due to high financial costs and lack of access to knowledge pertaining to the legal process, the countrywide network of voluntary agencies can play an effective role in providing legal aid and legal education to women.

One of the priority areas for the legal aid movement in the country should be the mobilization of women through voluntary agencies. Voluntary organizations also have an important role in providing counselling, para-legal support and rehabilitation of women in distress. In fact, in the absence of such help, neither police nor courts can effectively help women. In many such cases, women are compelled to withdraw cases under the dowry prohibition act and compromise with unjust situations due to lack of alternatives. This situation could be remedied if women could be assisted through counselling support, employment training, and rehabilitation and development support by voluntary agencies.

The upsurge of interest in women's issues which characterized the decade, has left its mark on the legal scene. Voluntary organizations and activist groups are beginning to initiate action on various legal issues. It is felt that the Government should provide financial assistance to women's organizations for setting up legal aid cells. Evidently, there is a need for many more voluntary agencies to take up the issues of women and provide necessary legal aid to women.

Environment and Women: It is well recognized that the management of the environment requires the participation of people as they are closest to it and have a stake in its preservation. Active involvement of women and their organizations in environment protection is of paramount significance since women are most affected by the issue. There is a serious threat to the environment due to its degradation and pollution arising from various factors such as policies of government as well as the private sector, unplanned discharge of residual and waste, handling of toxic chemicals, indiscriminate construction of dams, large-scale deforestation, expansion of settlements and unplanned mining and quarrying work. Such conditions have pushed great number of women into marginal environment where floods, droughts, shortage of fuel, and excessive utilization of grazing land have deprived women of their livelihood.

Many voluntary agencies have taken up the issue of environment protection. Among these agencies are the Dasholi Gram Swarajya Mandal that has started the Chipko Movement in which women play a very important role. This movement has received international acclaim and was initiated by hill women. Women embraced (Chipko) trees to prevent them being felled and some women were killed while thus protecting these with their own bodies. Trees to these women and others are the source of life. The impact of environmental degradation and of soil erosion is first felt by women. Many grass root level women's organizations have begun to take up environmental issues in addition to their continuing concern for rural poverty due to the intrinsic link among environment, poverty and gender.

The responsibility for creating awareness, mobilizing public opinion and building a strong people's movement lies mainly with the voluntary agencies. The awareness generated by individual women pioneers/leaders and all types of women's organizations on environmental issues has focused on the fact that women and men have the capacity to manage their environment, and their access to productive resources should be sustained and enhanced. It is also recognized that the requisite knowledge and information can be disseminated by voluntary organizations to reinforce the self-help potential of women in conserving and improving the environment.

Demystification of Technology: A number of voluntary agencies are involved in commendable work in the, demystification of appropriate technology for the advancement of rural women. The programmes implemented by voluntary agencies in this area include, providing opportunities for gainful employment and self-employment for women, reducing the drudgery in their lives, ensuring adequate medical and nutritional facilities, improving sanitation and environmental conditions and protecting women from occupational hazards.

However, there is a need for further voluntary action in this direction that can develop and disseminate appropriate technology for women. Since the technological marginalization of female work is endemic in both the agricultural and the nonagricultural informal sector, voluntary agencies should be involved in overcoming gender differentials in the application and generation of technology. There is a need to actively deploy technology to reduce the drudgery of the poorest working women in back breaking tasks such as gathering of fuel, fodder and water.

Training constitutes another important input, particularly

for upgradation of skill and augmentation of earning capacities of women. There is a strong need for a diversification of training undertaking by voluntary organizations. Their role should be particularly geared to the sensitization of administrators functionaries and catalysts on the issues and needs of women in development and in the delivery of comprehensive training programmes that have a component of knowledge, attitudes and skills for women's development.

Suggestions

The increase in the number, expansion and diversification of activities of the voluntary agencies has not necessarily equalized the disparities between them. There are not only regional imbalances in the growth of the voluntary sector but within a particular state, the growth of this sector has not been even. It is also well known that a majority of voluntary agencies are urban based and that relatively few have taken up the issues of women. It is recommended that the focus of voluntary agencies move from urban to rural areas, as the situation of rural women warrants immediate support. There is also need for the government to encourage voluntary action for the development of women by provision of adequate financial and structural support.

There is an urgent need to improve the effectiveness of voluntary action. Improvement will have to be brought about both in the organizational structures as also in the quality of services offered. Voluntary workers need to be professionals, equipped with appropriate skills for managing women's projects and sensitivity towards women's issues. National and State level institutions and training organizations should provide adequate facilities for research and training relating to women's issues. They should take up activities guided by the felt needs of women and those that can make a qualitative difference to women's lives, rather than be confined to traditional areas of support and action. Their work should be related to contemporary issues and thinking on women. As a caution, they should resist the temptation of initiating more work than they can effectively manage.

Voluntary action should be directed particularly towards preventive rather than purely curative measures. Efforts of voluntary agencies should also be geared towards generating self-reliance rather than to create dependencies. To improve their capabilities in planning and implementation of programmes, voluntary agencies are in need of expertise and technical guidance as much as financial assistance.

Unfortunately, in the existing system of grants-in-aid, financial assistance to them assumes overriding importance vis-a-vis other forms of assistance such as technical guidance in the area of programme planning, project formulation, financial planning, administration, monitoring and evaluation. The proposed Resource Centre at the national level could also facilitate in the training needs of functionaries and in providing necessary managerial and technical assistance to voluntary agencies.

The process of grant-seeking and receiving is considered by a number of voluntary agencies as a frustrating experience. There is an urgent need to review the working of the grants-in-aid system. Wherever needed, modifications should be introduced to ensure that rules are simplified, grants released on-time and the amount provided is commensurate and proportionate to the needs of a particular programme. While a system of accountability for government funds is unavoidable, it need not be painful. Further, it should be ensured that financial assistance from the government does not seriously affect the basic character of voluntarism, its flexibility and innovativeness.

A number of programmes implemented by conventional voluntary agencies have emphasized imparting skills to improve the efficiency of women as housewives and mothers, and to improve their earning capacities. Voluntary agencies tend to neglect the participative potential of women in the development process as well as conscientizing women on their rights and roles. There is the need for such efforts that could increase the awareness of women and improve their participation as equal citizens in national development. Further, voluntary agencies should play a surveillance role and observe, explore and analyse the extent to which social legislations implemented for women have actually benefited them. They should also act as pressure groups to better enforcement of laws for women.

At present, there is no proper mechanism of coordination among different voluntary agencies working for the development of women. An effective mechanism for coordination between the government and the voluntary agencies is also to be ensured. CAPART and CSWB are appropriately situated to make efforts for more effective coordination and implementation of various programmes for women through voluntary organizations. For them to perform this role effectively, there should be a proper representation of grass roots women's organizations in CAPART and CSWB, that can serve as pressure groups. There is also the need for a continuous flow of information from government to voluntary agencies and vice versa through such mechanisms as a clearing house for information.

A focal point is desirable in the rural areas to encourage women's voluntary activities. Mahila Mandals and women's groups at the village or community level should be organized or revived and encouraged to register and function as women's institutions for undertaking socio-economic programmes. These institutions should be effectively linked with the various development and service agencies, offering training facilities for income generations as well as enhanced awareness among women. This linkage will enable women to absorb institutional finance for the development of viable economic activities.

Particular attention will need to be given to the training of the Mahila Mandal functionaries and women's group organizers and provide them an orientation to development perspective rather than purely welfare approaches.

The CSWB which has been the coordinating agency for voluntary action for women and children, must respond to the new thrust of government policy meant for women and recast its own programmes.

Greater coordination and cooperation among NGOs is called for to avoid duplication of services. Greater funding for networking among NGOs must be provided. This will ensure more efficient utilization of funds and greater coverage of programmes. Government support to voluntary agencies for providing assistance to women in distress, including the running of crisis centres and short stay homes must be expanded. Para legal training must be an integral part of such efforts.

Voluntary agencies must be increasingly involved in the provision of employment and supportive services for women. The National Literacy Mission must involve women's organizations in a big way.

The voluntary sector should increasingly be involved to act as a catalyst/intermediary in organizing women for collective action.

There is the need to document success stories of major NGOs in India and learn from their success and failures. Further, it is necessary to analyse the cost-benefit of NGO Projects versus governmental projects, i.e., both economic and social costs. It would also be critical to total the overall number of women reached by NGOs in India. The areas of activities and fields of success would also highlight their strengths and limitations.

In order to ensure that the security and integrity of the

nation are preserved, there is a need to adopt suitable policies to ensure that voluntary agencies abide by the rules governing the receipt and utilization of foreign grants and submit audited accounts, returns and reports periodically.

Identity cards should be issued to workers of voluntary agencies who are dealing with cases of atrocities against women, as is already being done in some districts.

In order to have sufficient infrastructure and facilities, there is need to mobilize more resources for voluntary agencies which are engaged in welfare and development of women.

There is a need to decentralize the planning process to stimulate local people's participation in planning, implementation, monitoring and evaluation of development projects. A suitable mechanism should be evolved to involve voluntary agencies and other people's institutions at various stages of developmental programmes /projects. Voluntary agencies should further ensure the participation of poor women in the development process.

In the preceding chapters recommendations have been made sectorally with a view to strengthening women's roles therein. Certain important issues, however, impinge on all spheres of women's lives and work. With a view to enhancing women's status and capacities to participate in the process of nation building, the following general recommendations are made:

The overall approach of this National Perspective Plan is to perceive women in a holistic manner. While the programmes for women will continue to be implemented by different ministries as part of their department plans, it is essential to have a strong inter-ministerial coordination and monitoring body along with its own supportive facilities service by the Department of Women and Child Development (Proposed infrastructure at Annexure 1).

All ministries must reflect the concern for the all round development of women. The concerned ministries must have women's cell which currently only exists in the Ministries of Labour, Small-Scale Industry, Science and Technology and Rural Development. It is essential that the new policy thrust for women's development should be reflected in the Planning Commission as well as the State Planning Boards. The National Commission on Self-Employed Women and Women in the Informal Sector, has also independently concluded that the Planning Commission and State Planning Boards need to focus their attention sharply on the realistic situation of (labouring) women.

An essential prerequisite for the implementation of these new policy directives would be a women's unit in the Planning Commission, to redefine categories of data collection for women, modify existing terminology and identify gaps in data collection relating to women and to give direction to plans and programmes for women's development. It is also essential to analyse the impact of the different macro policies on women while planning new endeavours.

Financial and fiscal resources should be apportioned and preferential allocations for women's employment in mainstream programmes and projects should be made. This would imply the rationalization on resource allocation within mainstream programmes so as to benefit women, rather than only seeking separate allocations for women. Critical emphasis must be placed on rate of investment in women preferred industries and occupations.

At the State level, the Departments/ Directorates of Women's Development should be initiated. Currently, there is no separate department of women in many States. Social welfare, handicapped, Scheduled Castes and Scheduled Tribes are subjects that are bracketed together with the development of women at the State level. This new department could also be the State level implementation body for the programmes/

policies of the Department of Women and Child Development of the Government of India.

In terms of programme implementation, the two major implementing bodies envisaged, are the Social Welfare Boards and the Women's Development Corporations. There can be a rationalization of service provision between these two bodies. The State Social Welfare Advisory Boards could eventually concentrate on implementing welfare/supportive programmes for women (homes for women in distress, working women's hostels, counselling centres for legal aid and paralegal training, condensed courses, etc.).

Women Development Corporations would be responsible for the implementation of economic programmes through non-governmental and governmental agencies/ departments wherever necessary, concentrating on technical inputs like credit, marketing, design development, etc., and reaching out to women at the district and village levels.

Women should be entitled to a package of services at the block level created by the convergence of schemes such as Development of Women and Children in Rural Areas (DWCRA), Integrated Child Development Schemes (ICDS), Adult Education, Health Care, etc., at the grass roots administrative level. Every district should have a coordinator to assist in the integration of these programmes aimed at the development of women.

The coordinator will also be responsible for motivating local planning of programmes and assist in their implementation and provide feedback for effective planning and evaluation. Since decentralization of planning monitoring and implementation of development programmes for women is suggested as also devolution of finance at district level, appointment of District coordinators for women's programmes would facilitate this process, and control over finance would empower them. The National Commission on Self-Employed

Women and Women in the Informal Sector has also recommended the appointment of District Coordination Officers to be responsible for planning, monitoring, coordination and evaluation of the programmes affecting women. Rationalization of functionaries at the block and village levels to ensure coordination of programmes affecting women at the grass roots level also needs to be undertaken.

There are today sufficient number of programmes in the Government of India as well as innovative programmes in many States and sectors. What is needed is not merely larger resource allocation but technical inputs for greater effectiveness of these programmes, to guarantee better resource utilization. Emphasis has to be placed on more effective planning, monitoring and evaluation of existing programmes through a result oriented mechanism operating at different levels.

Recognizing that a critical input for women's development would be a new thrust to training and wider dissemination of information backed by research data and documentation. It is proposed to set up a National Resource Centre for Women. This resource centre would translate national developmental needs of women into a systematic grid of programmes and schemes for training at different levels in skills/ knowledge/ attitudes.

The centre would identify and if necessary, strengthen existing governmental and non-governmental agencies including women's universities /women's centres and colleges through which the training, research/ dissemination could be carried out. The National Commission on Self-Employed Women and Women in Informal Sector has also recommended the need for a National Institute to cater to women's training as well as formulate guidelines and help the other constituent units at the State level, Divisional levels and district level to carry out training programmes.

Reorientation and sensitization of the administrative

machinery at all levels in the Government of India, the States, as well as specialized technical agencies (both Government and Voluntary) to the issues of women in development is essential. Three levels of orientation are necessary, i.e., at the policy and planning levels, at the district or intermediary level, and at the block and village levels. The training of functionaries and their orientation to women's issues must also be in the right perspective, i.e., women should be perceived as producers and participants, not clients for welfare. The dynamic role of women's contribution to the national economy as partners and equal citizens must be reiterated and translated into programmes and projects. The National Resource Centre would be responsible for revamping the existing content/ methodology and monitoring of training at all levels.

A special division should be created in the Department of Women and Child Development for the enforcement of law for women. The officer in charge may be designated Commissioner for Women's Rights and must liaise with the various Special Cells for women created by the police, the CBI as well as with the Departments of Public Grievances at Centre and State levels as also the Women's Cell in the Home Ministry. This division will be concerned with the enforcement of law to ensure women's rights, to facilitate action oriented research in needs such as discrimination against women, protection at work, etc.

This Plan recommends that the Census in future must take into account women's unpaid work in the household and outside as well as the value added in performing her many survival tasks for the family. A greater conceptual clarity has to emerge on 'work' and 'non-work' as well as a distinction between work that produces economic value and other activities that are Consumption oriented. Data relating to women, especially in the unorganized sector should be reflected in the data of the National Sample Survey and the Central Statistical Organization.

machinery at all levels in the Government of India, the States as well as specialised technical agencies (both Government and Voluntary) in the process of women in development is essential. Three levels of organisation are necessary at the policy and planning levels, the district or intermediate level, [illegible] and their [illegible] women's issues must [illegible] in the [illegible] perspective [illegible] programmes and [illegible] welfare. [illegible]

[illegible]

[illegible] sector [illegible] alone [illegible]

4

Women's Rights

The question is; What are the rights and obligations of a woman? It is a very complicated and delicate question of the modern age. The discussions and debates on this topic, both in the past and the current, if collected together would most likely fairly equip a small library. But all these discussions have failed to satisfactorily answer the question. Rather, it would not be wrong to say that they have further complicated it. In answering this question Islam too has taken a certain stand. It has not come as a reaction to the present day activity, but has existed from the earliest times. It was there yesterday, exists today and shall remain extant till the end of days. This stand of Islam was totally against that which had existed and recognized for centuries and was in vogue throughout the world.

Islamic Viewpoint

The Islamic stand has love, sympathy and help and cooperation for woman, her age and the nature of her relationship with man, recognition of her personality in her own right (separate from man), protection of her life, property, honour and dignity, her economic and political rights and also responsibilities in keeping with her strength and capabilities. It can be safely asserted that it provides fully for the development and perfection of her personality. And the complications by the present day stand on her position and status in the social life are also removed.

Basic Human Rights

In relation to Islam the behaviour of some people is irrational and partial. Owing to their peculiar religious and political thought and views, they cannot bring themselves to recognize excellence of Islam. They totally ignore the positive role of Islam in connection with woman. Prejudice and narrow mindedness are the two most dangerous diseases. Those afflicted with them fail to notice facts and realities of great importance.

And even after observation try to conceal them. But realities cannot be concealed. Facts must stand out in spite of our efforts to overlook them, and must get them recognized sooner or later. So long as the radiant truths and crystal clear teachings of the Quran and Hadith and the juristic and legal discussions of Islam which have been in practice for decisions on all sorts of problems for centuries, exist, the favours of Islam to woman cannot be denied.

Some people are of the opinion that Islam did correct and reform the miserable position of woman in the Jahili (Ignorant) society and conferred on her certain rights which had been denied to her earlier, but still it failed to do full justice to her. It denied to her the rights it conferred on man. Thus, failing to establish equality between the sexes.

Controversy

The rights conferred by Islam on woman are subjected to many objections from the point of view of the superiority of man in Islam. He is the guardian and supervisor in the household, he can marry more than one wife, has the right to divorce the wife, the woman receiving only half the share of man in the inheritance, she has been unjustly treated in the laws pertaining to evidence, Qisas (retaliatory punishment equal for equal), Diyat (blood money for loss of life and lesser injuries) -all these and so many other objections have been levelled against the Islamic Law.

Those raising these objections desire that those laws should be repealed, the superiority (higher position) of man be done away with and the woman be granted all those rights exercised by man in the household. Both should have equal authority in all domestic affairs. The woman should be brought on a par with man in her share of inheritance, she should have the power to divorce and she should be able to get rid of her partner as and when she is pleased.

In case of divorcing her, man should bear expenses of her upkeep life long. In the presence of one wife, man should be barred from marrying another. At times they do not hesitate in claiming for the woman the right to have more than one husband, the way man can have more than one wife. The woman should get all those political and social rights which a man enjoys. All these objections result from ignorance of the Islamic teachings. It is a pity so many of the highly educated and so-called intellectuals share this ignorance. The very wide and comprehensive concept of life given by Islam and the way it has helped build the edifice of the personal and collective life automatically removes the objections raised against it.

These objections are not of recent origin, they have been thrown on the face of the Muslims since long and the practice continues with greater fury now. During this period efforts have been made to remove them. And it is really deplorable and a contravention of intellectual honesty that these objections are being repeated as if they were being presented before the world for the first time and the Muslim thinkers have been dumb-founded. This leads us to think that at the back of this practice there is very little desire to understand Islam and the greater part of their interest is centred on making it the target of (destructive) criticism. What would have been the reasonable course for them was to have given serious thought to the Muslim rejoinders to their objections and any short-comings in them pointed out. This would have opened avenues for mutual understanding, removal of misunderstandings and Islam would have been understood in its proper perspective.

All these objections are raised by those whose minds are stuffed with the immoderate view of equality of sexes, presented by the West which has them in its tight grip. This is no more a view but has been under experiment for long and its results are before the world in the form of sexual vagrancy and ruination of the family and corporate life.

But overlooking these results of those experiments they are advocated in a manner to show that not only is it a harmless view but emancipation of woman from all ills is associated with it. If Islam cannot keep pace with it, it is the demand of our intellect to say good bye to it, although the experiment in the recent history of mankind has brought to light the value, utility and purity of the Islamic view. Whenever that Western view of the equality of sexes is reformed and its immoderation removed, it must approach very close to the Islamic view. Rather it would be more correct to say that Islam alone can reform it and remove its shortcomings.

The Islamic stand has been so violently attacked by its opponents that so many Muslims too paying lip service to Islam, have been influenced and are daunted by their objection and find many infirmities in the Islamic teachings.

This class of brow-beaten persons comprises various grades. It is not so easy to classify them. Some of them, they may or may not admit it, are those who want to get rid of these "decadent" and "impracticable" laws. To them the destiny of woman is pointed today by the West and not by Islam. She can never advance on the path of progress so long as she is confined to the "enclosure" of Islam. For such progress she will have to run about free among those 'meadows' prepared for this purpose by the West. A Muslim, so long as he subscribes to Islam, cannot subscribe to their wishes and endeavours. For him the laws prescribed by the Shari'ah are the limit which he is not permitted to overstep.

If ever he is guilty of breach in this respect, he regards himself a criminal and answerable to Allah and it will be his endeavour to retrace his steps for re-entry to this limit. It is the demand of his belief in the Divine Faith. At the moment all the laws of the Islamic Shari'ah are not the subject of our discussion. We are at the moment concerned only with those relating to familial life. The Quran has called these laws as the limits prescribed by Allah at various places in and has sternly forbidden the believers to violate them.

At one place, while mentioning divorce it has been observed:

> These are the limits ordained by Allah; so do not transgress them, if any do transgress the limits ordained by Allah, such persons wrong (themselves as well as others). [8] —Al-Quran II : 229

Laws of divorce are also mentioned in 'Sura-Talaq' (65) and immediately after that it is observed :

> How many nations that insolently opposed the command of their Lord and His Messengers did we not call them to account, - to severe account - And we chastised them with a horrible chastisement. Then did they taste the evil result of their conduct, and the end of their conduct was Perdition. Allah has prepared for them a severe Punishment (in the Here after). Therefore, fear ye Allah Oye men of understanding- who have

> believed ! -For Allah hath indeed sent down to you
> a Message, - [9] —Al Quran LXV: 8-10

After this menace can any Muslim think of opposing the right of women, familial laws or any law of the Shari'ah for that matter?

There are others whose minds are not so overwhelmed by the Western concepts and views that they may reject the Quranic injunctions as old and time barred. But they are labouring under the erroneous notion that gone are the days when the Islamic Shari'ah was revealed and conditions today are totally changed. Insistence on centuries old principles and traditions is unnecessary. This is the age of advancement and competition. The stand taken by Islam, relating to woman, is not the one that can let her compete in the modern age, and her lagging behind in this race means retardation of the entire nation. So what is needed is to amend the Islamic Laws to fall in line with the modern trends. To them it is *"ijtehad"*. And under the changed conditions 'ijtehad' is a must. Those who refrain from such 'ijtehad' have to put up with the taunts of ill-information and conservatism from these iconoclasts.

Movement in Society

And then there are those who go even further and say, wearing a mask of simplicity and innocence that Islam is a modern religion. It has conferred on the woman all the rights of the modern age, but the conservatives have interpreted the Quran and the Hadith in a way reminiscent of the days of slavery. So a modern and progressive interpretation of the Quran is badly needed. Who is there that will not applaud them for this understanding, insight and enlighenment? These simple-minded intellectuals of the modern age !

Those who desire amendment in the Islamic Law in the name of "ijtehad" most probably presume the Islamic Law to be like man-made laws which can be amended and repealed as and when the law maker so desires. The Islamic law on the other hand has been revealed by Allah and permits not of an iota's change by any one. It was not given even to the Prophet to whom it was revealed.

> But when our clear signs are rehearsed unto them, those who rest not their hope of their meeting with us, say: "Bring us a Quran other than this or change this." Say: "It is not for me of my own accord to change it: I follow not but what is revealed unto me : If I were to disobey my Lord, I should myself fear the chastisement of a Great Day (to come)." [10] —Al Quran X: 15

The other thing is that man-made laws are the product of time and the existing conditions. They are not free from the limits of time and space. They are very flexible and change with the times. Flexibility in the man-made laws is not their merit but a defect that makes them impracticable under changed conditions. But any one who has studied Islam even cursorily with an open mind cannot deny the fact that the Quran has presented itself as an eternally abiding faith which cannot change till the end of time. As for Ijtehad it is something altogether different. It does not aim at changing the evident Quranic injunctions but framing other new ones in the light of these (Quranic) injunctions. The work cannot be undertaken with unlimited freedom but will have to bind itself with certain strict limits.

Here a question persistently strikes us : why are these 'reformers' so much worried about the rights of women and social reform among the Muslims? There are many evils in the Muslim community, that of creed, action, morality, dealings etc., but why do they evince so much interest in and anxiety about Muslim women's aggrieved state? Why do other more serious problems not engage their attention with so much anxiety and compassion?

From a casual study of the minds of these "philanthropists" we learn that to them the end and object of man's life is and should be that appointed by the West. For this purpose they have adopted also the same course. A salient feature of it is that religion and faith are meaningless terms. They do not concern our life and have little bearing on it. If any one is interested in religion, he may follow it in his private life. The collective life should, however, be free from that "paraphernalia." So long as man is entangled in the bounds of religion he shall be rotting in the dark ages of the past. The avenues of progress shall remain closed on him. He has no right to live in the modern age.

They want to take the entire Muslim Ummah on this path. Towards this end perhaps they regard the social reform more useful. And with a hue and cry over this issue of Muslim women's right they probably expect to achieve greater success. For, to them, so long as the Muslim woman is held bound by the norms of old concepts, and is teaching and preaching to the younger generation loyalty to Allah and His Apostle, the strong bonds of religion cannot become loose enough to detach the Muslim Ummah from their faith and its practice, not withstanding their lack and zeal and strict adherence.

Their turning away from it is possible only with the woman changing her orientation vis-a-vis the faith, and holding aloft the banner against it in the struggle for her rights. Since they have so far not achieved any success in their endeavours and for that matter should not expect to succeed, they give vent to their pent up feelings of anger and grief against the standard bearers of Faith, calling them names like conservatives and old fashioned revivalists and fundamentalists. Every uttered and written word of theirs is an authority and the modern times have made arrangements for their wide publicity. Thus these "cultured outbursts" and "polite downpour" without hesitation or restraint!

Some of them are people with a religious bent of mind and in real earnest desire to keep away from the unhappy experiences of the Western civilization but its onslaught from every direction is so powerful that they themselves are not entirely free from its pestilential influence. Gradually and totally unawares, their ways of living are changing and the Western, civilization surreptitiously creeping into it, its grip is getting more and more tight on them every day. But even at this critical stage they are happy with the idea that in spite of their participation in the race of the blind pursuit of Western civilization their own culture is free from its evils and shall remain immune in future also.

But this is false self-assurance and sort of a pious wish which shall at best be short-lived. If they have not so far been forced to swallow the acrid fruit of the West, it is due to the counter-balancing effects of the Islamic Faith that its evils have not surfaced yet. When these salubrious effects disappear the Western civilization, with all its evils, shall descend into their courtyards. Those not roused to activity to guard their houses, on observing the first signs of a deluge, cannot escape inundation. Nobody can save them.

Significance of Rights

It is usually observed that a weak person has to strive hard and struggle against the opponents for obtaining his or her rights. Without fighting for them it is very difficult to get even the natural rights. They are not even recognized. The modern society recognized some of the basic rights after tiring debates and discussions, disputes and altercations and violent protests (the Suffragist Movement). This recognition and grant of woman's rights is accepted as a boon of the modern age whereas this is a blessing of Islam conferred on her (without her asking for it). To begin with Islam gave her those rights which had been denied to her and she had been silently suffering long as a result of this deprivation. They were not conferred on her in response to her demand for them. Her protest had continued and her cause was being advocated and promoted and representations were being made on her behalf. Rather, they were given to her since they were her natural rights, and she ought to have been enjoying them, without any body granting or any one else receiving them as charity. They have been and are free for all like light, air and rainfall. Islam was under no compulsion to confer them on her, but it granted them to her since she was the oppressed and aggrieved party and helping and supporting the aggrieved and the suffering, it regarded as binding on it.

We mention below some of the rights that Islam has granted to woman. Islam does not rest contented with the sanction of rights in so many high-sounding legal terms (usual with the stingy and petty natured man), but through persuasion and admonition, it also creates a congenial milieu for their fulfilment.

Human Respect

The women was in no better condition in Arabia than in the rest of the world. Certain tribes of Arabia buried their daughters alive. The Quran admonished them in very strong terms for this villainy and hardheartedness, granted her the right to live and declared that whoever lays hands on this right of hers (to live), will have to account for this felony of his. The Quran says :

> When the female (infant) buried alive is questioned for what crime she was killed; [1] —Al Quran LXXXI : 8-9

On the one hand, the perpetrators of the heinous crime of taking the life of the innocent girls were threatened with hell-fire and on the other, those abstaining from it and treating them on an equal footing with the sons given the glad tidings of entry to heaven. Abdullah Ibn Abbas reports the Prophet (S.A.W.) to have said :

Allah shall reward the Muslim with entry to heaven who neither buried his daughter alive, nor meted out ignoble treatment to her, nor treated the son preferentially compared to her.

Along with these moral backings Islam also instructed them to respect the right of woman to live, just like that of men, and for any breach of this ordinance armed her with Qisas (retaliatory punishment — like for like) for which the Islamic state was made responsible. Qisas means that if somebody is oppressed or suffers an excess, he or she has the right to seek redressal, so much so that if some innocent person is murdered, his or her relatives have the right to retaliate and take the life of the murderer. This law covers both man and woman. The Quran says:

> We ordained therein for them. - "Life for life, eye for eye, nose for nose, ear for ear, tooth for tooth and wounds equal for equal." But if any one remits the retaliations by way of charity, it is an act of atonement for himself. And if any fail to judge by what Allah hath revealed, they are wrongdoers. [2]
>
> —Al-Quran V : 45

Islam revived this Law of Torah (old Testament) and it became part of the Islamic Shari'ah. This law not only protected woman against tyranny but put a stop to all sorts of tyrannies and excesses against every weak individual and class and provided justice to them.

According to the Islamic law, every child is born with the natural right of being provided with the necessities. Upbringing of children and their proper care is a lengthy and tedious job and it is noticed that the extra loving care lavished on the boys is stinted or sparing in the case of girls. Islam branded this attitude as undesirable, inducing the parents particularly to her proper upkeep and loving care, declaring it as an act worthy of great reward. 'Ayeshah (R.A.A.) reports the Prophet (S.A.W.) to have said :

> Whoever is put to test with girls as offspring, and he treats them kindly, they will become a source of protecting him from hell-fire.

This tradition mentions 'Ehsan' in connection with the girls, which is a comprehensive word meaning, their upbringing, their education and training, kind treatment and loving care, all together.

Anas (R.A.A.) reports the Prophet (S.A.W.) to have said:

> The person who brings up two daughters until they attain maturity, on the Day of Reckoning, myself and he will be like this. And saying these words he brought his fingers together.

Now look at the legal aspect of the issue. According to the Islamic Shari'ah the support and upkeep of the offspring devolves on the father. Offspring includes both boys and girls (without any distinction). Therefore, he cannot deny any of them, this birth right of their's (proper upbringing). So we find in the Quran under the subject of breast-feeding the following injunction :

> And he (father of the child) shall bear the cost of their (mothers giving suck) food and clothing. [3]
>
> —Al Quran II: 233

The jurists have furnished details of the ordainment. The erudites of the Hanafite school have opined that the responsibility of support, care, education and training in case of the boys is up to the age of majority. And there it ends. However, the responsibility of upkeep of the female offspring shall remain liable even after her attaining majority, until such time as she gets married and has a home of her own. Others are of the opinion that this responsibility is to be divided between the father and the mother after the daughter's attaining majority. Two thirds is to be borne by the father and one third by the mother. Similarly, the responsibility of any major girl, if she is without means of support shall be the responsibility of the closest eternally prohibited relation. However, if any of them has property of her own, the expenses of her upkeep shall be met from that source. Nobody else shall be held responsible for bearing her burden.

The progress of man is associated with education. If he is not equipped with knowledge, he lags behind in the struggle of life. He is neither elevated in thought nor can he make any material progress. But a sufficiently long period of history passed by leaving her uneducated, for education was not deemed necessary for her. This field used to be the exclusive domain of man. And among men too only some particular classes were benefited by it. The woman lived in the darkness of ignorance, far from the high pedestal of knowledge and learning.

It was Islam that made the doors of education open on men and women alike. All the impediments of the way were removed and all sorts of facilities provided to promote its cause. It drew, attention towards female education in particular, creating inducements for it, declaring it an act worthy of reward in the Hereafter. Abu Saeed Khudri (R.A.A.) reports the Prophet (S.A.W.) to have said :

> The person who brought up three daughters, embellished them with education and training, married them off and remained benevolently inclined to them even after their marriage, (Allah Willing) paradise is ensured for him.

Islam addresses both man and woman. It had made each one of them duty-bound morally to devotional acts and observance of the Laws of Shari'ah. It is not possible to live up to these demands without knowledge. For the woman the relationship with man is of great importance, since the relations are very complicated and also of a delicate nature. They comprise woman's rights as well as her obligations. So long as she is ignorant of them, she can neither discharge her duties nor can she protect her own rights from usurpation.

The jurists are of the opinion that for both man and woman basic knowledge of the faith is essential. If the woman is ignorant, it is the husband's duty to inform and educate her or make some alternative arrangement for her education. If the husband fails in this duty she would herself seek and attain that much needed knowledge, for, it is her legal right. For this purpose she can go out of her house too if necessary, but of course within the moral limits prescribed by Islam. The husband has no authority to stop her from such pursuit of knowledge.

This attitude resulted in the early phase of plan in the education of men along with the female education. Among the companions of the Prophet (S.A.W.) we come upon a fairly large number of the female companions well-versed in the knowledge of the Quran and the Hadith. Deduction of religious principles and practices and pronouncing religious verdicts in the light of the Quran and Hadith is not such an easy job. But there were also women who were capable of it. Among them 'Ayeshah, Umm Salmah, Umm 'Atiyah, Safiyah, Umm Habibah, Asma' bint Abu Bakr, Umm Sharik, Fatimah bint Qais, Khaula bint Tawait (R.A.A.) and others are most prominent.

Just as the woman was denied the right to speak and express her opinion on any important issue or problem of life, she could not give utterance to her own will or desire in the matter of being given away in marriage. Her parents or elders of the family made such decisions and married her off to whomsoever they liked. And she could not refuse or even protest. Her objection or opinion in this particular matter was considered extremely undesirable and most improper (violation of feminine decorum). The society interpreted it in ways reflecting on her moral character. Any remark on her part relating to her marital arrangement and rejecting the selection of the elders was considered a sign of her dissoluteness.

It is usually said that giving her a free hand in the matter of matrimonial arrangements is against her own interests. She is likely to take faulty decisions due to her immaturity and lack of experience. Her parents or guardians more experienced and having better knowledge of men and matters, are less likely to err in their decisions. Moreover, they are her well-wishers and cannot deceive her.

Undoubtedly there is truth in it that her guardians can make a better selection of the partner in life for her, but it cannot be denied either that the guardians are guilty of excesses in this regard, and so often they make these matches a means of serving their own selfish ends. At least, it is difficult to deny the fact that the parents or guardians do not keep before them norms to which their daughter attaches great importance. Therefore, it would not be in the fitness of things to leave the selection of partners for girls entirely to their guardians.

It is a fact that the entering of a girl in a contract of marriage with some man is an important event. Both of them start a new phase of life and the match had better be in order with the mutual consent of the principal parties concerned (instead of leaving it entirely to the seconds). It would not be proper and reasonable to impose upon the girl the decision about her future life against her wishes.

Islam has certainly attached importance to the guardian of the girl being given in marriage, but it has also stressed the point that her permission is essential in a marriage tie. If the ward happens to be a widow or a divorced woman her explicit consent (spelt out in so many words) is necessary. In case of a virgin, however, her silence is to be deemed her consent and concurrence. Abu Hurairah (R.A.A.) reports the Prophet (S.A.W.) to have said :

> The widow or a divorcee shall not be given in

marriage without asking for her opinion (about the match) and a virgin without her consent.

The companions submitted that a virgin shall not give utterance to her opinion. How are we to obtain her permission? The messenger of Allah (S.A.W.) said, "Her silence is her consent."

If a guardian of a woman gives her away in marriage and she disapproves of it, it would stand null and void. So we find that when Khansa' Bint-e-Khizam was given in marriage against her wishes (she complained) and the Prophet (S.A.W.) nullified the contract.

Many more such cases have come for mention in the Hadith literature. A minor girl can be given in marriage by her guardian. But the jurists are of the opinion that on attaining the age of majority she may retain or reject it at will.

Islam has ordained man that the woman, he marries, must be paid her dower, without which *nikah* is not valid. The concept of dower (*mahar*) existed during the period of Jahiliyah also before the advent of Islam. But the Arabs had practically deprived her of it in various ways:

1. The guardian of woman regarded her dower as his own property and took possession of whatever she was given as dower. The Arabs regarded the daughter as a disgrace to themselves, and the news of the birth of a daughter overwhelmed them with grief and shame. But from this angle it was a source of happiness also to them that her dower would increase their wealth. That is why they called the daughter Al-Nafijah.—The means of increase, and in her birth they were congratulated : 'Happy birth to you of one who will increase your wealth'. Since they accepted only camels as dower, this meant that on marriage she will get camels for them as her dower and they will thus increase their wealth of camels.

2. It was also a common practice that on the death of a person, his son from a different mother would cast a sheet of cloth over the widow (not his real but a step mother) and declare himself the owner of that widow also along with the father's inheritance. This declaration confined his claim over that woman. Neither any other person could claim her nor she could herself do any thing against the step-son's will and claim. If he was serious about marrying her, he did so against the dower earlier paid to her by his deceased father. And in case he consented to give her in marriage to any other person, her dower would be his, depriving her totally of her legitimate right.
3. At times taking advantage of the week position she was given less than the usual dower in vogue. 'Ayeshah (R.A.A.) says that an orphaned girl under the care of a person, if she was beautiful and had property of her own and the guardian wanted to marry her, he would do so in preference to other suitors, and against much less dower than others were ready to pay her. The Quran put a check on this practice, instructing them to either pay their full dower according to usage or marry some one else (and not their poor helpless ward).
4. During the period of Jahiliyah (Ignorance) there was yet another stratagem for getting rid of a woman's dower which has been called 'Shighar' in Hadith. This was a clever trick played on poor helpless women in as much as a person gave his daughter in marriage to another person on condition that he in turn would give his daughter in marriage to him. And in this cross-marriage neither of them paid either woman any dower (one cancelling the other).

Islam put an end to this unjust practice. Abdullah bin 'Umar R.A.A. says:

The Prophet has prohibited 'Shighar'.

In another report it has been said:

There is no 'Shighar' in Islam. In the report quoted by Bukhari the exchange of daughters without dower has come for mention. In another report quoted by Muslim, exchange of sisters too has been narrated. Both these are as examples, otherwise as remarked by Imam Navavi the Ulama are unanimous on it that exchange of nieces, paternal aunts and cousins like uncle's daughters also come under the same prohibition.

There is consensus of the Ulama that this practice of Jahiliyah has been declared unlawful by Islam. But they differ on the issue that the marriage contracts made on this basis shall be lawful or declared illegal and shall not hold.

A report of Abu Daood says that Abbas son of Abdullah Ibn Abbas (R.A.A.) gave his daughter in marriage to Abdur Rahman bin Hakam and he did in turn marry his daughter to Abbas, making this cross-marriage the dower (they cancelled each other). When Mu'awiyah (R.A.A.) learnt about it, he wrote to his governor of Medina, Marwan, that they should be legally separated as it is Shighar and prohibited by the Prophet (S.A.W.).

Imam Malik, Imam Shafi'i and Imam Ahmad R.A. and some others declare such a marriage illegal. Imam Abu Haneefah and Sufyan Thauri (R.A.) are of the opinion that the *nikah* is valid but both women shall be entitled to dower according to usage. To them the fault lies here in usurpation of dower which can be removed by its payment to both of them, according to the usual practice among the women of their class and status.

Thus, Islam declared dower to be the exclusive property of the woman and removed all the false and unjust claims on it one by one. It openly declared :

> And give them, the women, (on marriage) their dower as an obligation. [4]
>
> —Al Quran IV: 4

Allamah Abu Bakr Jassas says in its exposition :

> Dower is her property. She alone has a right to it. Her guardian has no claim to it.

The Islamic Shari'ah has prescribed no limits on the amount of dower. It can be increased or brought down according to the financial status of the person entering the marriage contract. However, it certainly is its inclination that it should be an amount that the man can easily pay. The jurists differ on the issue of fixation of the minimum amount of dower. Those belonging to the Hanafite school of jurisprudence put it at ten dirhams and not less than that.

Before her marriage the responsibility of the up-keep of the girl devolves on the father. After marriage her maintenance becomes the concern, and a binding one too, of the husband. According to the Shari'ah, the maintenance of the wife is compulsorily the responsibility of the husband, without consideration of his financial status. The Hanafite school says that if the husband and wife are both wealthy, the maintenance of the wife shall be according to her status in life. In case of the wife being at a lower level financially, her maintenance shall be the mean between the rich and the poor. But if the reverse is the case, he shall spend on her according to his means and any deficiency shall become a liability as credit due from him to be paid to her at his convenience.

If the woman is rich, a servant shall be provided to her. If the wife does not want to live together with the husband's relations, she can demand a separate house (or an apartment in the same house but affording her privacy). It is her legal right and the husband has to meet it.

In this connection it would not be improper to mention

here that according to the Hanafite Fiqh service to her husband and doing household chores is not the duty of the wife. If she undertakes it, it is courtesy from her and the urge of her moral virtue. She cannot be compelled to it.

Islam has granted the woman freedom of economic pursuits in the form of business, profession and work (any of the public services). She is permitted to undertake trade, agriculture, financing, industry, service, teaching jobs, journalism and writing and compilation of books — in fact all permitted trades. For this purpose she can come out of her house too if necessary. However, it imposes certain restrictions on her in this connection. There are two objectives behind these checks on her. In the first place, her activity outside should create no confusion and interference in the order of the household and the normal life of the family circle and its stability and harmony should not be disturbed. And secondly the woman should be able to do an existence of modesty and chastity. Her economic effort and work in this direction should not put her under conditions which can hazard her strict adherence to moral limits.

There were many nations of the world that had denied right of ownership to their women. She had no share in the family property. Rather, even her own earnings were not left to her. Whatever she got through her own efforts was regarded the property of the father, husband, sons or other members of the family. Islam recognized the right of woman to ownership of the property and any meddling with it was declared wrongful and unlawful. According to it just as a man has a right to honestly earned wealth so has a woman right to own and use her lawful earnings.

> To men is allotted what they earn and to women what they earn. [5]
>
> —Al Quran IV - 32

Whatever a woman gets from her parents, husband or the

offspring under the law of the Islamic Shari'ah or whatever she obtains through her own economic effort, she is the rightful owner of it all, and is entitled to spend it as she likes. She can spend on her own person, her husband and children, parents and other members of the family of her own free will. She can also invest it in charitable acts. She has also the right to the sale and purchase of property, forming trusts, gift it to others and can bequeath it at her own discretion. Nobody can interfere in these matters.

Honour and dignity are a valuable asset of man. Playing with it and high-handedness cannot be allowed. Attacks on the honour and dignity of a woman have been a common practice and due to her weakness she has not been very successful either in protecting them. There are two forms of attack on her: Qazaf (slandering) and fornication. Qazaf means to question the honour and dignity of some woman and tarnishing her fair name by accusing her of dissoluteness and fornication. According to Islam it is a great crime and a moral sin. The Prophet (S.A.W.) has mentioned one of the seven mortal sins in these words:

> It is Qazaf or slandering chaste innocent believing but indiscreet woman.

As a legal measure against it Islam imposed the severe punishment of eighty cuts of the lash for calumniating a woman with illicit sex and such a person shall be debarred from appearing as a witness. Allah says:

> And those who launch a charge against chaste women and produce not four witnesses (to support their allegations), -flog them with eighty stripes - and reject their evidence ever after : for such men are wicked transgressors, except those who repent thereafter and mend (their conduct); for Allah is Oft-Forgiving. Most Merciful. [6]
>
> —Al-Quran, XXIV: 4-5

Now taking the issue of fornication and molestation of women, under the Islamic law, any person found guilty of raping a woman forcibly, in case he is unmarried shall receive hundred cuts of the lash and shall be stoned to death if he is married. However, if the woman as his partner cooperates with him she shall be liable to the same punishment.

Undoubtedly Islam has exempted the woman from collective and political responsibilities. (The issue shall be taken up at length later on). But this exemption does not mean that she shall remain totally unconcerned with these affairs and evince no interest in the collective welfare. The Quran has ordained both man and woman to enjoin good and forbid evil:

> The believing men and women are one of another: they enjoin what is just and forbid what is evil. [7]
>
> —Al-Quran IX: 71

Enjoining good and forbidding evil has very wide and far-reaching demands. Call to Faith and preaching is also a part of those demands alongwith the reformation of the ummah and criticism and calling people to account, the rulers being also included in it. It is the responsibility of a woman to meet all these demands within her own limits of action. History bears testimony to the fact that women of the early phase of Islam realized this responsibility and fulfilled it.

In the pre-Islamic day's, Arabian society rights and privileges were totally denied to woman, being exclusively a man's domain. Their argument in this behalf was that she was weak incapable of enhancing family's resources and a hindrance rather than an asset in the defence against the enemies, her own and that of the family. She could not bring in spoils of war home to improve the economic condition of the household and the tribe. And so she could not be the recipient of a share in the family's substance. Similarly boys of tender age were denied any portion of the bequeathal of the family on those very grounds. Only able-bodied young men (war-worthy) who could' face the enemies in the field received their share of inheritance.

The Arabian society was not alone in keeping the woman deprived of her share in inheritance. The other social orders of the world on the basis of these and other pretexts kept her out of it, only the male offspring and the first born getting away with it in its entirety. (Even in this so-called age of enlightenment with elaborate charters of woman's rights, children's rights and human rights and what not, the nations regarding themselves the most sensible and just, believe in and act on the self-invented principle of primo-progeniture. It can be witnessed in broad daylight in all the vestiges of monarchies of the world. And all feudal societies do the same unashamed in this democratic age).

Islam raised its voice against this gross injustice to the weaker sex, proclaiming aloud that woman had as much right to her share in the inheritance. The Quran declared:

> From what is left by parents and those nearest related there is a share for men and a share for women, whether the property be small or large,- a determinate share. [61] —Al Quran IV: 7

And along with this instruction on principle it also appointed the share of men and women. Some details are to be found in Hadith and Fiqh (Islamic jurisprudence). The objection raised here is that equality has not been maintained between the sexes and man has been endowed with greater right to it than the woman. But this is a baseless objection levelled against the Islamic Law because of the ignorance of its underlying wisdom and intrinsic value. So long as one does not have the details of this law of inheritance and their wisdom before him, it is difficult to understand it in its proper perspective and misunderstandings are most likely. Here we shall try to present some details of the Islamic Law of inheritance and later an attempt will be made to bring out some of its underlying wisdom.

Islam has restricted the inheritance strictly to the family, and has specified the rights of the members the family with gradation depending on closeness to the deceased. The first and the foremost among the shareholders is the progeny of the person leaving behind property. Allah says in the Quran :

> Allah (thus) directs you as regards your children's (inheritance) : to the male a portion equal to that of two females :[62] —Al Quran IV: 11

This brings out the following points for our consideration: Progeny includes both boys and girls. The inheritance is not the exclusive share of the boys. The girls also have their right to it. One boy's share shall be equal to those of two girls. Suppose the deceased has a boy and a girl. The property left by him shall be divided into three equal portions, one third going to the daughter, and two thirds to the boy. With two girls and one boy, the property shall be divided into four equal parts two parts (2/4) or half going to the two girls and the remaining half to the boy. Allah says :

> If only daughters two or more, their share is two thirds of the inheritance. [63]
>
> —Al Quran IV : 11

This is about a situation where there is no male progeny and there are more than two girls. The girls here shall get two thirds. Here more than two daughters have come for mention, but if they are two their portion remains the same, two thirds.

If there is no male progeny and only one daughter she shall be entitled to half the inheritance. Allah say :

> If only one, her share is a half. [64]
>
> —Al Quran IV : 11

This leads us also to the point that if there is only one boy he must get the entire property of the dead since his share is twice that of the girl. When an only girl gets half of it, the only boy, common sense demands, should get twice that or full property. However, in case of more than one boy, it will get divided among them since there is no basis for distinction between one brother and another.

After the progeny the parents have priority in the matter of rights to the property of the deceased. The Quran has stated their rights thus :

> For parents a sixth share of the inheritance to each if the deceased left children; if no children and the parents are the (only) heirs, the mother shall get a third. If the deceased left brothers (or sisters) the mother has a sixth. [65]
>
> —Al Quran II

The following principles can be derived from the verse: In the event of the deceased having progeny, even if it is an only boy or a girl, the parents shall get one sixth. Grandsons and grand daughters and even their descendants come under progeny. And in the absence of the progeny of the deceased, the mother shall get one third and the father two thirds. The deceased has no progeny but two or more brothers (of whatever relationship), the mother's share shall become one sixth, the rest going to the father. Brothers and sisters shall have no share whatsoever. And after stating the rights of the parents, it has been said :

> (The distribution in all cases is) after the payment of legacies and debts. You know not whether your parents or your children are nearest to you in benefit. These are settled portions ordained by Allah: And Allah is All-Knowing, All Wise. [66]
>
> —Al Quran IV : 11

That means legacies shall be attended to on a priority basis and debts shall be paid (before distribution). When these two liabilities are fully settled, then only what remains of the inheritance shall be distributed.

The rights of the husband and the wife have been declared in the Quran in these words:

> In what your wives leave your share is a half, if they have no child, but if they leave a child, ye get a fourth, after payment of legacies and debts. In what ye leave, their share is a fourth, if ye leave no child; but if ye leave a child, they get an eighth; after payment of legacies and debts. [67]
>
> —Al Quran IV : 12

The verse brings out the following: The husband shall get half of the inheritance of his wife in case she has no children (from this husband or any other before that). Grandson is also progeny. There is consensus on it. The husband shall get one fourth of the wife's property if she has children (from the same or some other husband). The wife shall get one fourth from the property of the deceased husband if he leaves no children. The wife shall get one eighth if the husband leaves children after him (no matter whether borne to him by this wife or any other wife).

The children, parents, husband and wife shall be inheritors in every case. Others follow suit. Among them brother and sister have precedence. Brothers and sisters are of three kinds: *'aini, 'allati* and *akhyafi*. Among these three 'aini (real) brothers and sisters have precedence over the rest. If they are absent 'allati brothers and sisters (same father but different mothers) shall be the inheritors. The shares of akhyafi brothers and sisters (same mother, different fathers) are specified, on which there is consensus of the ummah and they have been stated in the following verse :

> If the man or woman whose inheritance is in question, has left neither ascendants nor descendants, but has left a brother or a sister (Akhyafi), each one of the two gets a sixth; but if more than two, they share in a third, after payment

> of legacies and debts; so that no loss is caused (to any one). Thus, is it ordained by Allah; and Allah is All Knowing and Most Forbearing. [68]
>
> —Al Quran IV: 12

This means that Akhyafi brother or sister, each, will be entitled to one sixth. If they are more than two, then they all will be entitled to one-third equally. There will be no difference in the share of brother and sister.

The rights of real and step brothers and sisters have been stated in these words :

> Say: Allah directs (thus) about those who leave no descendants or ascendants as heirs. If it is a man that dies, leaving a sister but no child, she shall have half the inheritance : If (such a deceased was) a woman who left no child, her brother takes her inheritance : If there are two sisters they shall have two thirds of the inheritance (between them). If there are brothers and sisters, (they share) the male having twice the share of the females; Thus doth Allah make clear to you (His Law), least ye err, and Allah hath knowledge of all things. [69]
>
> —Al Quran IV: 176

This shows that if the deceased has a son (grandson and male progeny in the descending order) or father, grandfather, and others in the ascending order, the brothers and sisters shall have no share in the inheritance. If they (progeny or parents) are not there, the inheritance shall be divided among them like this: If only one sister she will get a half. If only one brother, he will be entitled to the entire property. If two or more sisters and no brother, they will get two thirds. If brothers and sisters both are there, the share of a brother shall be equal to that of two sisters.

If the deceased has daughters only their predetermined shares (half if only one, and for more than one two thirds' for them and the rest shall go to the brothers and sister according to the predetermined principle of one man's share equal to that of two women). If there are only sisters with the daughters, after apportioning their shares the rest shall be given to the sisters.

These are the broad principles of inheritance which the Quran has enunciated. Their details are to be found in compilations of Hadith and Fiqh. We are not going to discuss them here.

Now, we shall try to briefly explain the bases on which the Islamic Law of inheritance rests, which will bring out some aspects of their underlying wisdom. Inheritance is divided among the members of the family. Blood relationship and that through nikah have been made the basis of consideration in the apportioning. The family is a definite unit, kept intact by heritage and blood ties.

The natural feelings of love, sympathy and cooperation exist among them. They are practically partners in all matters involving benefit and detriment of the family, help in promoting their interests and come to their aid in solving knotty problems. That is why the family attachments of a person are very firm and strong. He or she keeps its well-being upper most in all the benefits accruing to him or her individually. His economic effort too is to a large extent for the family. Therefore, normally he regards the family as partner in his substance and its rightful shareholder. Usually, husband and wife are not blood relations of each other. However, they are so close that they become part of the unit of family. Hence, they inherit from one another and this is certainly natural and justified.

The members of the family directly related to the deceased must and do get their share in his/her property, never deprived of it under any circumstances, be they men or woman. The following come under this category: The children of the deceased, both boys and girls. The parents of the deceased. Either of the husband or wife who survives.

Among them, As'habul-Fara'iz shall receive their due shares. The remaining portion shall go to 'Usbah.

The reason behind precedence of these members over others is evident enough. A person regards them too close to himself and factually too it is they who are closest to him. All his life, directly and intermediarily it is they, he has to and does deal with. In spending on them, his hard earned wealth, he feels a pleasure and sort of mental peace and tranquillity. It is his earnest desire that even after his passing away they should inherit his property and none other than they should take possession of it. It is a natural sentiment and cannot be declared wrong or misplaced. And all that the Quran has done is to give it legal sanction.

Even among these most closely related family members Islam has given precedence to the right of offspring over those of the parents. Their needs and financial demands on them have been kept in view in this regard. The children are the rightful successors of their parents. After their passing away they shoulder many of their responsibilities and promote many of the projects left unfinished by them.

And over and above these there are many responsibilities of their own with which they have to grapple and have to find means to meet them, planning their future in the light of the existing conditions. Apparently enough their needs of wealth are far greater than those of the parents of the deceased. And the parents (grandparents of the children) themselves are inclined to help the children (their grandchildren) in every possible manner in preference to others. However, if there is no offspring the parents gain importance and their rights have priority.

If the man and woman stand on an equal footing in the matter of relationship to the deceased, one man's share shall be equal to that of two women, like son and daughter, brother and sister. It does not at all reflect in any way on the inferiority of woman and superiority of man. Had there been any such concept woman's share would have been permanently kept at a minimum or none at all and she would have stood totally deprived of any share in the inheritance, whereas in fact none of these things is true. The reason behind it is that Islam has associated inheritance with financial responsibilities. According to Islam man has to shoulder all the financial responsibilities, whereas woman has been totally exempted from them. To illustrate let us take an example of a young man and a young girl.

The boy (young man) spends on the support of his wife and children. May be he has to support his parents, both or the surviving one. There is a likelihood of his extending help to his poor brothers and sisters and some other relatives in need of help. Thus, whatever he earns is drained through these channels. As compared with him the girl (woman), if she is well off she may be spending on herself at the most, since she has not been burdened with anybody else's responsibility. And after marriage the expenditure on self too ends, the husband taking over her maintenance. The fact is that if the responsibilities of both are kept in view, neither the boy gets more (than necessary), nor the girl is given less than her need. A just balance has been maintained between them.

Similarly, the share of the wife is half that of the husband. Here too the woman is free from liabilities. Moreover, she gets *mahar* from the husband and all the ornaments and other gifts she receives on marriage and other occasions add to her property. In the event of the husband's death the wife gets her share of inheritance and vice versa. If after the wife's death the husband wants to remarry, he will have to pay, the second wife her mahar and take over the responsibility of her maintenance. But if the widowed wife intends to remarry she will get her mahar from the second husband and he will have to maintain her also. Thus, wouldn't it be just and proper that the woman should get in the inheritance half that of the husband? And wouldn't it be gross injustice to the husband that his share be kept equal to that of the woman ? That is exactly what Ibn Katheer has said in the following words :

> Allah, the exalted, has fixed the share of man equal to that of two women because he has to bear the burden of maintenance of the woman, the difficulties of trade and earning his livelihood and other hardships of this type, it is in the fitness of things that he should get twice that of woman.

Allamah Rasheed Raza Misri says:

> The underlying wisdom in allowing man a share equal to that of two women is that he has to spend on his own support as well as on the maintenance of his wife and so two shares for him. The woman spends her substance on herself and after her marriage her maintenance too has to be borne by her husband. For consideration of the burden of maintenance under certain conditions the share of woman becomes greater than that of man.

In this way lightening the burden of woman in the matter of financial responsibilities, in some cases of inheritance woman's share has become reduced to half of that of man. Under the circumstances neither man complains that he has been overburdened with responsibilities, nor can woman question why her share has been reduced to half. As against this, if they had been placed on an equal footing in their shares in inheritance, man would have been justified in making a demand that a woman should also be involved in financial responsibilities. This division of rights and obligations is exactly in keeping with the natures of both of them. A better division is unimaginable.

Hafiz Ibn Qayyim, along with the financial responsibilities of man, points to yet another aspect that since man during his life-time is benefited much more by man, in the event of his death man's share should be more than woman's share in his inheritance. He says:

> Man receiving greater share in the inheritance is manifest enough. He stands in greater need of substance than woman since he is the supervisor in the family (he has to shoulder the responsibilities of woman's maintenance). Moreover, man is benefited much more from man in his life-time. Allah, often specifying the rights in inheritance and keeping them at different levels, pointing to this fact has said : you don't know which of the two, your parents or, your offspring is more beneficial to you. When during the life-time of the deceased he had been benefited by man more than by the woman, and he also stands in greater need of money, he deserves precedence in his share from inheritance.

Where the financial responsibilities of man get lightened, Islam does not discriminate between the sexes. In case the deceased has children the shares of both mother and father are the same. One very evident reason is that the right of the progeny has precedence. The second reason is that a person whose progeny has come to have progeny of its own, his financial responsibilities get minimised. He, at this stage comes to take the position of the patron of his grandsons and grand daughters. However, if the deceased has no children who have priority in his property, the father in that case having children (brothers and sisters of the deceased) will have greater right to inheritance than the mother of the deceased since his responsibilities too can be greater.

Islam has based the division of inheritance on the principle that among the blood relations the closer to the deceased the greater his precedence over others. Those far removed shall be entitled to it only in case close relations are absent or after their having received their shares, there is still some property left. Under the principle the woman closer to the deceased may be entitled to' greater share than male relatives not so closely related. Suppose the deceased has a daughter and a brother, the property shall be equally divided between them. If only one daughter and two brothers, the daughter shall have half and the remaining half will go to the two brothers. If two or more than two daughters two thirds shall go to them and one or more brothers shall get only one third.

These detailed discussions refute outright the objection that justice has not been meted out to the woman in the distribution of inheritance. Neither there has been any partiality or biased treatment in dealing with man, nor has the woman been let down in the form of iniquitous treatment. Islam on the one hand has attached importance to woman's close relationship with the deceased and on the other it has kept in view the financial responsibilities of man.

On these bases the woman is the recipient of greater share in the inheritance in certain situations and not so great in others. And in certain other situations they stand on the same plane. This is unparalleled equilibrium between closeness of relationship and financial responsibilities. And this exemplary balance is that outstanding characteristic of the Islamic Shari'ah which bestows on it a unique characteristic not enjoyed by any other religion or ideology.

There are several verses in the Holy Quran that say in a clear cut way that kindness to one's parents is next only to Allah. But there should be no Shirk (polytheism) under whatsoever a banner. In this respect Quran tells us amazingly:

> "We have enjoined on man kindness to parents; but if they (either of them) strive to force thee to join with Me anything of which thou hast no knowledge, obey them not ....," (Quran 29: 8)
>
> "Thy Lord hath decreed that ye worship none but

> Him and that ye be kind to parents. Whether one or both of them attain old age in thy life, say not a word of contempt, nor repel them, but address them in terms of honour. And out of kindness lower to them thy wing of humility; and say: "My Lord ! Bestow on them thy Mercy even as they cherished me in childhood." (Quran 17: 23)

If there is conflict between our duty to Allah and our duty to our parents and those in authority, we are to obey Allah and disobey them in a kind, considerate and courteous way. We should never be arrogant, We learn this from the coming verses of the Quran:

> "And We have enjoined on man (to be good) to his parents. In travail upon travail did his mother bear him and in years twain was his weaning. Show gratitude to Me and to thy parents. To Me is thy final goal.
>
> "But if they strive to make the associate in worship with Me things of which thou hast no knowledge, obey them not; yet bear them company in this life (and consideration....)." (Quran 31: 14-15)

The mother is the one who suffers more than the father especially at the early stages of the child. The child remains in her womb for nine solid months. At this period she undergoes several physical and psychological changes. Some of the mothers become sick and anaemic, while other pregnant women suffer in different ways.

After that she gives birth. Here she can get some sort of material aid from others such as nannies, baby sisters and a hundred and one other evils of our twentieth century Jahilia. The only person to look after a baby is the mother. Feeders are the worst things to use. They are the carriers of all the diseases that attack our children especially in a backward society. Worst of all is that the bottle feeding media lacks the

Heavenly maternal feeling that a child feels when he suckles from his mother's breast. That is why some of our scholars say that if a child does not complete a 24 months suckling period the father is to compensate him (giving him a share from property).

Because of all the troubles that a mother faces, the Holy Quran teaches us to be very kind to them. Let us read the following verse:

> "We have enjoined on man kindness to his parents, in pain did his mother bear him, and in pain did she give him birth. The carrying of the child to his weaning is (a period of) thirty months. At length, when he reaches the age of full strength and attains forty years, he says: "O my Lord ! Grant me that I may be grateful for Thy favour which -Thou hast bestowed upon me, and upon both my parents ...." (Quran 46 -.15)

The Messenger of Allah (may Allah give him peace) is quoted as saying what it meant:

> "Paradise is under the feet of mothers."
>
> "It is the generous in character who is good to women., and it is the wicked who insults them."

It is reported that a man came to the Apostle of Allah (peace be upon him) and asked him the following :

> "O Messenger of Allah, who is the most worthy of my company?"

The Prophet said, "Your Mother."

The man asked, "Who is the next?" with the same answer, "Your Mother." It was repeated with the same reply, only in the fourth time did the Prophet change his answer and said, "Your Father."

We learn from such Ahadith (Sayings of the Prophet-may

Allah give him peace) how Islam honours and respects the mother.

> "........ But consort with them in kindness, for if ye hate them it may happen that ye hate a thing wherein Allah hath placed much good." (Quran 4: 19)

May I repeat here once again the three Ahadith (Sayings of the Prophet). It is reported that he said :

> "The best of you is the best of you to his family and I am the best of you to my family."
>
> "Lo many women came to Muhammad's wives complaining against their husbands beating them; those are not the best of you."
>
> "A male Muslim should never hate a female Muslim (wife) because, if he hates some of her manners he is sure to like others."
>
> "Truly a woman is like a rib. If you try to straighten it, you are sure to break it, but if you leave it as it is, you will enjoy with it while it is a bit bent."

The husband is told to be more patient and should not be angry with her quickly, as she is more emotional; he should therefore be somewhat rational.

> "The most perfect believers are the best in conduct and the best of you are the best of you to their wives."

No husband is to spy on his wife. He should not tell her for example; that: "I shall not come back tonight. I shall go to such and such a place." And he comes at midnight knocking at the door spying on her.

The husband is to maintain his family in its wide and narrow sense of the word (family Husband, wife and children and the Eastern type of joint Family).

He is to provide his wife with all the necessary means of leisure according to his means. He should cut his coat according to his length.

He should consort with her and respect her feelings. If she did anything unbecoming, he, is not to reprimand her before visitors or anyone else (especially before their own children).

He should take good care of her personal property and should never spend a penny without her consent.

Both of them are required to preserve personal secrets of the other. Neither of them is to tell people anything of their intimate family life. He is to allow her to visit her parents. It would be better if he sent her to visit them now and then.

The Messenger of Allah (peace be upon him) told Abdullah b. 'Amr bin al-'Aas, who was fasting daily and spending his nights in prayers: "...Do not do that, fast and break fast (do not fast for some days) and sleep. Truly your, body has rights, on you, your eyes and your wife has (her legal) rights on you .... Give each its rights."

Islam fully acknowledges the woman's right of an independent ownership in her money, real estate or on any other properties. This right does not undergo any changes whether she is single or married; whether she acquired the property before marriage or after it. She retains her full rights upon her property whether selling, buying it or other wise.

A woman used to be an object of inheritance. This went on, in some cultures, as late as the nineteenth century, while Islam gave her the right of inheritance 1,400 years ago. She has the full right on her share of inheritance, it is completely hers. Neither her father, husband, mother or anyone else could make any claim on her share of an inheritance. It is hers.

The Holy Quran says:

> "Unto men of the family belongs a share of that which parents and near kindred leave, and unto

women a share of that which parents and near kindred leave :-whether it be a little or much a determined share." (Quran 4: 7)

Her share of inheritance is governed by certain factors, whether there are sons and daughters, or the only child in the family etc. etc.

We shall appreciate this more if we remember that as late as the twelfth century a wife was sold in some cultures soon after the death of her husband. Her luck was not even better in Arabia, because she did not inherit anything from her parents or her husband.

Women's Importance

Over and above all this, she must retain her full identity: her maiden name. Suppose a Fatima Mohammad ar-Riyamy marries a Khalfan Moosa an-Na'asaany. She never changes her name and becomes a Mrs. Na'asaany. No and never. Her doing so (change of name) is regarded by some of the scholars as completely un-Islamic, that is a sin. The wife retains her identity while she is with her husband, and when he dies or divorces her and she marries another man there is no such nuisance of rechanging of names for the third or fourth times. Her first maiden (father's) name is hers till she dies.

Going back into history we find that nearly all Christian women lose their maiden names soon after marriage as she has to sign her maiden name for the last time in the Church register after the wedding ceremonies. It was only, of all that I know, Lucy Stone, one of the most famous speakers on the movement to emancipate women, that retained her maiden name as a protest against the unequal laws applicable to married women. She became known as Mrs. Stone and not as Mrs. Blackwell.

It is also said that some of the Slavonic tribes gave the woman a choice of whether to retain her maiden name or change it to that of her husband's.

Throughout the history of Islam, we find a Muslim woman is given full political rights. Women took part in serious discussions and argued even with the Messenger of Allah himself (may Allah give him peace). Through our reading of the following verses of the Holy Quran we know how Islam gave her political rights :

> "Allah has indeed heard (and accepted) the statement of the woman who pleads with thee concerning her husband and carries her complaint (in prayer) to Allah, and Allah (always) hears the arguments between both sides among you: for Allah hears and sees (all things). (58 :1)
>
> "O ye who believe, when there come to you believing women refugees, examine (and test) them Allah knows best as to their faith: if ye ascertain that they are Believers then send them not back to the Unbelievers. They are not lawful (wives) for the Unbelievers, nor are the (Unbelievers) lawful (husbands) for them. But pay the Unbelievers what they have spent (on the dower....)."
>
> (60: 10 see also 66: 11)

It is reported the Caliph 'Umar said what it meant: "We never paid any attention to whatever was said by a woman before Islam, nor did we ask her any advice. It was only the teaching of Islam that gave her full rights as reasonable being."

> "I was once thinking and pondering over something important when my wife suggested that I had better do this and that. I told her to stop that as it was none of her business.'
>
> "She told me: 'What is wrong with you O Ibn al-Khattaab? You do not want to be given any advice while your daughter argues with the Prophet till he becomes angry.'

> 'I went straight to Hafsa and asked her: 'Tell me; daughter; what is it that you discuss with the Apostle till you make him angry?'
>
> She responded, "Yes, father ! All his wives do. It is natural. (He sometimes remains angry for the whole day because of our arguments with him)".

Caliph 'Umar was once discussing with Muslims in a Mosque (as it is not only a place of worship, but also the Parliament, the Court, the Army Headquarters, the Muslim Government itself) certain problems. A woman corrected him and made him declare before the public: "The woman is right and 'Umar is wrong."

One might argue pointing out that there is a Prophet's saying which mean that no country will prosper if it were led by a woman. It has nothing to do with the dignity of women, neither does it hinder her rights. It is rather, due to the natural differences in the biological and psychological set up of the two sexes. According to Islamic Law the Head of the State is not just a figure head. He is the centre of all activities. He is the chief justice. He must lead people in prayers, especially Friday prayers (Juma) and on religious festivities. He leads people in Jihaad (religious wars) against non-Muslims for the well being of humanity).

During the monthly periods and during pregnancy, women generally undergo frequent psychological changes; let alone the monthly changes of her hormones (which generally happens twice a month) the kind which makes a woman become more emotional than rational.

Had mothers brought up their children themselves and without the help of nannies, maids or baby-sitters, I am sure that most of the mental hospitals, psychological clinics, would have to close down because there would have not been cases that needed their utmost care. The psychotherapists would have to find some other jobs to do.

A child needs maternal care more than anything else especially during his early infant stage if we really need a good and mentally healthy society. And that is why Islam regarded the woman's role in a society as that of a mother and a wife, which is the most essential one in any healthy, society. The society whose members are upright, complex free and carefully reared members.

Hence the best jobs for a woman are those pertaining to Health and Education. I said, "the best" and I did not say "the only". She can do good in any other field as well, but these are the two fields which satisfy her nature more; therefore, she can contribute better to the well being of humanity in general. Not only that, but also she learns more about human nature.

Islam does not restrict a society from benefiting from any exceptionally talented woman in any field.

The Elites

Abu Jahal was torturing Sumayya at the point of death forcing her to abuse Prophet Muhammad and Allah and praise the gods of Quraish Tribe: He told her if she did not do what he asked her she won't see the evening of that day any more as she was going to, die before sunset. Sumayya answered him in a very low and separated and interrupted voice: "Fie to you and your gods and misfortune, befell on you. Is their anything better for me than death that will release me from seeing this ugly face of yours?" Her words and the unexpected outburst of laughter from both 'Utba and Shaiba bin Rabii'a made Abu Jahal so furious that he could control himself no longer. He thrust her with a lance. She became the first martyr in Islam.

We have seen in the Introduction that two members (Nusaiba and Asma'a) out of the 75 Yathrib (Medina) delegation to ask the Prophet (peace be upon him) to migrate to Medina were women. We shall appreciate it more if we remember that these things had happened during the sixth and seventh centuries (of the Christian Era) at the time when in other parts of the world (in Europe) conferences were being held to discuss if a woman was human or not, whether she was with or without a soul and whether she was to worship god or otherwise.

We see Muslim women taking part in Jihad (the religious wars against non-Muslims for the well being of humanity) during the period of the Apostle of Allah (S.A.W.) and after. Their main task was in the following fields: Ambulance, mending and making clothes for the army, preparing food for them, giving them water, nursing and all other essential needs.

Aisha bint Abu Bakar and 'Umme 'Aiman al-Habashiyya and some other Muslim ladies took part in the battle of Uhud. They were giving water to the soldiers, taking care of the wounded and consoling them.

When the Prophet (peace be upon him) was wounded it was. Aisha who ran looking for straws and old mats. She burnt them and took the ash to heal wounds of the Messenger of Allah.

Nusaiba led a women's delegation to the Apostle of Allah asking him to give them permission to take part in the Jihad as men do. He asked them: "What can you (women) do, O Nusaiba?" She responded:, "We can mend clothes, take care of the injured and 'wounded by tending and comforting them, cure the sick and, give water to all."

She even took part in the actual fighting, to protect the Prophet.

In the battle of the confederates, Safia bint 'Abd Al-Muttalib (Hamza's sister) killed one of the Jews who were spying for the enemy of Islam,

Zainab the daughter of the Holy Prophet (peace be upon him) mediated or asked her father to protect Abul 'Aas bin ar-Rabi" (at the time when he was still an infidel) from Abul

Baseer and it was granted after he consulted Muslims. No sooner had this stroke of kindness fell on Abul 'Aas heart and he embraced Islam.

Safia (Zubair bin Al-Awwam's mother) was one of those who took part in the Khybar battle. She was afraid for her son Zubair being killed. The Prophet told her that Zubair was going to kill his foe.

In the battle of Yarmouk some Muslim ladies were taken as war prisoners. They wanted to fight for their freedom. They had no weapons with them, They fought with ordinary poles, sticks and pegs from the tents. The freedom battle was led by Khawla bint al-Azwar.

The Muslim woman played a very important role in Islam. Her life was not confined to the house. No, she went out taking part in different walks of life under the banner of Sharia protecting her chastity, and not forgetting her primary role in life is that of wife and mother.

Islam always benefits from the exceptionally talented Muslim woman in any field;

Ali Yahya Mitammar in his book *al-Abadhiyya fi Mawkibit Taarikh* (Ibadhi through History) mentioned many Muslim women of North Africa who played very important role in shaping Islam. You could find this in a chapter heading; al-Mar-atul Muslimatu fi Libya (Muslim Woman in Libya).

Let us quote just one example from Mu-ammar:

> "(7) Ummu Yahya; the pious, highly educated and most able teacher lived at, Amsiyin between Jailaat and Timjaarah, somewhere in Jebel Nafusa (Libya).
>
> She felt that girls education was not complete if she learnt in boys' schools. She thought that had she been able to open a girls' school, that would have provided opportunities for girls to study upto the final stages of education She opened a girls school

and opened also what is now called 'A Girls' Hostel' for those girls who live in far different places. She directed her students into a variety of walks of life. She found employment for some, and arranged marriage for others, and further studies for those who wanted to go on with their studies.

Let us sum up with what Dr. Inamullah said in his articles: The Holy Prophet: A Blessing for the Teeming Millions:

> "He (the Prophet) came to grant woman her rightful place in the society of man, raising her above the position of goods and chattels and granting her a respectful entity and a personality to herself. She was considered an independent social and economic unit functioning in her own individual right, if she so desired. For the first time she was given the right to education, the right to hold property in her own name, the right of inheritances and above all, the right to vote, and pray. What is the right to vote, but to have the legal right for a free expression of opinion or choice. Human history fails to give that place of pride which the Holy Prophet gave to woman. His words: 'Paradise lies at the feet of thy mother' are eternal, a sparkling and glowing tribute to the status of woman."

The chapter of the Quran called 'The Woman' (al-Nisa) details in a just manner the share of inheritance that is due to each individual, male and female. According to this chapter, women are not only no longer allowed to be inherited like chattels but, as individuals, they have a legal right to inheritance. 'Men shall have a share in what their parents and kinsmen leave; and women shall have a share in what their parents and kins men leave; whether it be little or much, it is legally theirs'.

This verse was revealed when an Ansari lady came to the Prophet and complained that after her husband's death she and her daughter were prevented from inheriting any of his property. Her husband's brother justified the action by stating that, 'Women do not mount horses, do not endanger themselves and go .into battle', therefore they could not be allowed to inherit.

Before Islam, women were not only deprived of their right to inheritance, but also had no impact over their own destiny, which was a matter between the men of the husband's clan or her own relatives. During the Jahiliyya, when a man lost his father, brother, or son, and that person left a widow, the heir, taking advantage of the fact that her dowry was paid by the dead man, rushed to the widow, covered her with his cloak, thus claiming (unjustly) to himself the sole right to marry her. When he married her, he denied her of her right to the part of the inheritance constituted by the dowry. But if he decided, for one reason or another, not to have her as a wife, he could then ask another person to marry her in return he would take (for himself) her dowry.

However, if the widow (at the time of her husband's death) managed to get to her own clan before the arrival of the heir, he would lose his rights over her in favour of the males of her own clan. New laws regarding women challenged the social structure of a society that had given males the upper hand over females in matters related to inheritance. Therefore, it was inevitable that it would create an uproar among sections of the male population who felt threatened by them and questioned the validity of granting women a share in the inheritance. So, they decided to ignore these laws and continued to apply the customs of the Jahiliyya, hoping that as time went by the Prophet would change them. But the matter was brought to the surface by women themselves who continued to suffer from the Jahiliyya mentality.

For pre-Islamic Arabian society, it was outrageous to allow fatherless children who could not fight or earn a living to have shares in the inheritance. Therefore, they were denied any rights to inheritance. Moreover, they were mistreated and not looked after well, especially young girls who were also the object of sexual abuse. For example, the guardian very often decided to marry the prettiest ones thus securing two things for himself.

(1) controlling their share of inheritance;

(2) setting away from or escaping: paying a dowry for them. If a fatherless girl happened to be ugly or not pretty enough to persuade him to marry her he would use her ugliness, to oppose any marriage for her. In doing so, he did not have to pay her share of inheritance. If a fatherless girl was ugly, her guardian did not give her her share. He forced her not to marry and waited for her to pass away so that he would assume control over her inheritance. Islam, would not tolerate such inhumane practices, with its egalitarian message which aimed at redressing the injustice of society. It began by affirming the legal right of fatherless children to have a share in their own inheritance and ended by cautioning against depriving them of their due.

Although Islam granted woman the right to inheritance, her share is by no means fair and equal to that given to man. The critics refer to the verse that allows the brother to take twice as much as the share of their sisters. Therefore, they view this as detrimental to the dignity of women. By giving women half the share of men, they say, there is a clear implication that women are inferior to men. This argument has been used by both Muslims and non-Muslims. But it is based on a fallacy. If it happens for one reason or another that one sex receives a greater or lesser share than the other, this does not mean that the recipient of the lesser share is regarded as inferior. The whole issue of inheritance in Islam depends entirely on the social and economic context, and the role or function of a particular sex within it. If this crucial contextual factor is borne in mind, a proper understanding of the verses related to inheritance in the Quran would ensue.

The Quran has ensured that women could get their shares of inheritance not only as daughters, but also as mothers and wives. The fact that women have been given half the share of male heirs has to be looked at within its social and economic framework. In Islam the wife is to be cared for by her husband, even if she is wealthy enough to maintain herself. By law she is entitled to claim maintenance from her husband. At the same time she is not obliged to spend any of her wealth on the household.

In addition a Muslim woman receives at the time of her marriage a considerable sum of money. This money, which the husband is obliged to pay, constitutes her dowry, or Mahr, which belongs to her alone. She is free to use, spend or invest it in any way she likes. Therefore, as a wife she adds to whatever she receives through inheritance in her capacity as daughter and that, too, without any legal commitment to support either herself or her children.

The position of women is secure as far as inheritance is concerned. Although women have been given half the share of men, their financial situation in the long term is guaranteed. This is due to the fact that the marriage contract gives her the right to ask for Mahr as well as claim maintenance, both of which entail no legal commitment to anybody including herself.

But it may be objected, what about women who cannot marry for one reason or another? What about the ones who cannot work and earn a living, especially in the rural areas where women have been denied the chance to gain a decent education? How would they live and maintain themselves?

The Quranic injunctions make it clear that male relatives, especially brothers, have the obligation to care for women and meet their financial needs. At the moment, in most Muslim countries this issue has been left to the individual conscience, which has led to many cases of abuse and desertion. Therefore, in order to secure and protect these women, governments need to legislate and make it legally binding on those male relatives to pay for the upkeep of their needy women.

The Quran makes it clear that a person is entitled to make a will. Indeed, it is highly recommended by the Prophet that a person should prepare a will as early as possible and not wait until it is too late. Contrary to the misconception held by large sections of the Muslim public that a person has no right to make a will, both the Quran and the Sunnah encourage people to do so. There are even some misguided jurists who argue, contrary to clear principles in the Quran, that Islam does not recommend the making of wills. This negative attitude advocated by a small band of jurists has confused ordinary Muslim people and has led many to abandon the idea of making wills.

The Quran, on the other hand, has specifically asked for the distant relatives, the needy people and the orphans to be treated kindly and to be helped if they are present at the time of the division of inheritance:

> If relatives, orphans, or needy men are present at the division of an inheritance, give them, too, a share of it, and speak to them in kind words.

So, if the Quran is so kind even to distant relatives and needy people by virtue of the fact that it encourages people to give them some share of the inheritance, we see no problem, in keeping with this spirit of Divine Justice, that a bequest be made in favour of a needy person, particularly if this person is a close member of the family. The point here is emphasised that if parents think that their daughter is unable to get married for whatever reason and she is in a disadvantaged position, they can write a will in her favour in order to secure her future. This accords with the spirit of the Quran and the Sunnah.

The position of Muslim women as far as inheritance is concerned is secure and guaranteed by the Islamic Law. But in practice this is not the case. Constantly, the Divine instructions concerning women's rights to inheritance are violated and overlooked by Muslim societies. Social, political, economic and cultural factors play a major role in determining who does and who does not take a share. In such situations the weak have always been kept at bay when it comes to their right to inheritance. This takes place in both the cities as well as the rural areas.

Very often, strong social pressure is applied on women to renounce their shares for the benefit of the immediate male members of the family. This is particularly the case when women are well off or married to wealthy men.

Their due is automatically written off and transferred to their male relatives. Whether they like it or not they are all too often forced to accept the loss of their shares; if they refuse, they are accused of being selfish, greedy, inconsiderate and irresponsible.

Often this has led to tension, friction and conflict of interests among the members of the family, shattering the whole concept of caring and sharing which lies at the heart of the Islamic faith. Here are a few examples which illustrate the evident disregard for the Divine decrees regarding women's right to inheritance.

The Islamic concept of broad and equitable shares which take into consideration the interests of all persons concerned has been transferred into a prerogative for males, outrageously disregarding the Divine Will. There is no doubt about the fact that in most parts of the Muslim world the Islamic Law concerning women's rights to inheritance is not in operation; instead it is the social and cultural rules which dominate. It is crucial that something has to be done to rectify this situation, and women themselves have an essential role to play.

Legal Rights

One of the objections levelled against the Law of Evidence in Islam is that it equates the evidence of two women to that of one man. This is insulting to the woman and negation of equity to her.

There is no doubt about it that Islam has, in many affairs, made a distinction between the evidence of man and woman. But taking it as an insult to the woman is unjustified and against the teachings of Islam. Islam has not arbitrarily made this distinction.

The reasons for it are to be found in woman's nature, temperament and her sphere of action. To appreciate this attitude of Islam in this particular regard one has to understand fully the Islamic point of view in some detail.

Islam has classified evidence under three heads: Evidence in Divine Limits and Qisas. Evidence in matters relating to rights and dealings. Evidence in matter exclusive to her and her sex.

Order of God

To enforce a divine limit on somebody or for the purpose of Qisas evidence of two men is essential. However, in a case of fornication, four men witnesses are needed without which the allegation of illicit sex shall not be established and the prescribed limit cannot be enforced. The Quran has mentioned the number of witnesses in a case of fornication in the following verse :

> If any of your women are guilty of lewdness, take the evidence of four reliable witnesses from amongst you against them. [76] —Al Quran IV: 15

At another place it has been said :

> And those who launch a charge against chaste

> women and produce not four witnesses (to support their allegations), - flog them with eighty stripes. [77]
>
> —Al Quran XXIV : 4

In these verses (four men from amongst you, and four male witnesses) are the words showing that for the establishment of the charge of fornication evidence of four men is essential.

That means that in matters relating to the divine limits and Qisas only men are considered reliable as witnesses. Evidence of woman shall not be accepted. The well known tabi'i, Imam Zahiri says that during the period of the Prophet S.W.W. and Abu Bakr and 'Umar R.A.A. this was the principle in practice. He says :

> From the time of the Prophet S.W.W. and then first two caliphs immediately following him (Shaikhain-Abu Bakr and 'Umar R.A.A.) the Sunnah or the principle in practice has been that in matters relating to the divine limits and Qisas the evidence of women has not been acceptable.

Islam has provided divine limits and Qisas for the protection of life, property and honour and dignity of man. For deliberate murder of some body the murderer has to pay with his own life in Qisas. Unmarried person implicating himself in fornication has to be flogged. The married person is to be stoned to death for illicit sex.

Theft if definitely established deprives the thief of his hand, it has to be smitten. And similarly there are punishments for slander and drinking. The crimes for which Islam has prescribed limits or ordained Qisas. are so serious in nature that even if man survives their perpetration, his honour and prestige in society are shamefully dragged into mire. For these crimes nonacceptance of the evidence of women is apparently because of their peculiar nature and importance. Woman is basically the organizer and manager of her home. She has an intellect and temperament of her own and is brought up and educated and trained in a particular (purely domestic) atmosphere. She seldom comes in contact with those conditions and causes responsible for these heinous crimes.

Therefore, about them her knowledge and observations cannot be so perfect as that of man who is mostly in the world outside. Again, for a woman, due to her mild temper and greater sensitivity, it is not easy to keep in mind all the major and minor details of the individual and collective crimes of murder, theft, robbery and those related to sex (including rape), and put them up before the court exactly (without any omissions or additions). Her statement relating to these matters cannot satisfy the court as does that of man, firm and strong. The aspect of uncertainties and wavering shall dominate in her statement. Islam insists that the limits should not be enforced without firmly establishing the crime and no effort should be spared in saving the accused from the punishment. The Prophet S.A.W. is reported to have said:

Keep away enforcement of limits from the believers as far as possible.

In another tradition it has been said :

In the presence of doubts try to avoid enforcement of limits.

There may be some women whose observation can be regarded reliable even in the most formidable forms of murder, theft, robbery and criminal assault on women, and they may be capable of presenting their observations accurately before the court. But the sex as a whole is not suited to this job (weak nerves, sentimentality, careless observation and taking of mental notes). Apparently pronouncing judgement on any particular sex, a few exceptional individuals cannot make the rule. A considerable majority or bulk of a kind (woman kind) has to recommend itself as capable and competent.

PREVAILING RIGHTS

Barring limits and Qisas in matters concerning rights and dealings, woman's evidence shall be accepted. One reason for that is the exclusive importance of the limits and Qisas, not attached to other matters. Secondly, they are related to every day life. Not withstanding her limited sphere of activity, her home, she comes in contact with these day to day common happenings around her.

However, in face of her peculiar circumstances and also due to her frailties, two precautions had to be taken. Firstly, no case should be decided on the evidence of woman alone, but with the evidence of two men or one man and two women. The reason put forth by the Quran for replacement one man by two women is this that it is possible for a woman to forget the details of some incident and in that case the other may remind her companion.

Allah says:

> And get two witnesses out of your own men. And if there are not two men, then a man and two women such as ye choose, for witnesses, so that if one of them errs, the other can remind her. [78]
> —Al Quran 11 : 282

The verse may give an erroneous idea that women witnesses are to be accepted only in case men are not available. But this is far from the fact. It simply means that for evidence either, there should be two men or one man and two women. Where woman is acceptable as a witness, even in the presence of men, one man and two women can be called for evidence. It has also been inferred as an argument that the women shall not be separated, making statements in isolation. They will appear before the court together so that if one forgets any fact or some important detail, the other may remind her.

The verse under reference occurs in connection with the

rules and regulations and ordainments of debts so the majority of the Imams of jurisprudence have consensus on it that in matters relating to debts and in other dealings the evidence of women shall be accepted.

According to the Hanafite school of Fiqh, the evidence of one man and two women shall not be accepted only in matters relating to Hudood and Qisas. With this exception all other matters like, trade, debt, financial dealings, temporary loan of articles, monopoly, security, nikah, attorneyship, divorce, legacy, inheritance and other matters relating to rights and dealings, their evidence shall be accepted.

The argument brought forward in its support is this that there are three essentials for evidence. Firstly, accurate observation of the incident. Secondly, the observation should be clearly and carefully kept in mind. And thirdly and finally to state these observations just as they are, neither less nor more. The infirmity of woman as stated by the Quran is that she can forget the details and therefore, the corrective provided is two women together instead of one. So barring limits prescribed by Allah and Qisas or retaliatory punishments, in all other matters concerning human activities, woman's evidence shall be accepted.

At this juncture a question can be raised that taking the evidence of two women equivalent to that of one man, in matters that can be decided on the evidence of two men, that of four women should also be decisive. The jurists have answered it on the ground that though our intellect accepts it as reasonable, but if it is permitted, the movement of women outside their homes would be much enhanced, whereas it is the considered plan of Shari'ah that their movement outside their houses should not be too frequent and free. (Perfect freedom of such frequent and unrestricted movements gives rise to evils and corruptions too dangerous to be allowed in Muslim society. They are before us in such a formidable form).

Particular Rights

The Jurists are unanimous on the issue that the evidence of women is sufficient in all matters relating to themselves, such as the evidence of the new born showing signs of life at birth, since in case of live-birth, there will be funeral prayer for him and all other matters relating to inheritance which ceases in case of a still birth, or evidence relating to a girl coming of age (majority in the juristic sense -commencement of the menstruation) or confirmation of a woman's virginity or otherwise, or evidence in connection with the genital defects and diseases peculiar to women. All these matters have a bearing on nikah and related matters.

In this connection Imam Zahri says:

> The Sunnah or the usual practice has been that the evidence of woman (alone) is permitted in matters with which none else (men) can be conversant (due to strict restrictions), namely the condition of the babe at the time of delivery, (living or still-birth, or the physical defects of the female genitalia or development of secondary sex characters at puberty).

'Abdullah ibn 'Umar, Saeed bin Musayyib and 'Urwah bin Zubair's R.A.A. sayings are available on this issue. It is reported about 'Ali R.A.A. that he decided a case on the evidence of a mid-wife. 'umar R.A.A. is also reported to have accepted the evidence of a mid-wife about a live- birth.

The jurists are at variance about the number of women whose evidence is essential in matters relating exclusively to women. Generally four is the number accepted for such evidence to be effective and conclusive. Imam Malik and Ibn-e-Abi Laila say that decisions can be made on the evidence of two women only. Imam Thauri and the Hanafite school regard the isolated evidence of one woman sufficient for legal purposes.

The Hanafite school has offered two arguments in support of their opinion. Firstly that the number has not been touched upon in the report (quoted above), and hence one woman's evidence should suffice. The second argument is that the exclusive evidence of women is considered enough in matters related to women alone, and men's evidence was not deemed necessary for the simple reason that men's observations or examination of the private parts of a woman is more undesirable than the same undertaken by women. (Difference of the degree of undesirability only).

It can be asserted on this basis that observation and examination by more than one woman involves greater degree of undesirability. But in spite of that the precaution demands that there should be more than one-two or three -women for furnishing evidence.

The Equality

Qisas or the law of equality (equal for equal) pertains to life as well as injuries and wounds. Qisas for life is that any one murdering an innocent person the murderer shall forfeit his life and be killed in return for that murder. That for wounds and other injuries is that if somebody inflicts a wound on some one or injures some organ of his body, the injured or wounded person shall be avenged accordingly. This law of Qisas is meant for providing protection to the life and limb of man. The question arises whether the law is applicable to man and woman alike or there is some discrimination where woman is the offender. The question has raged in our Fiqh since long. And lately with the voices raised in support of the rights of woman, it has once again surfaced to engage our attention. Here we shall try to present only the needful details of the problem, the most acceptable and preferred by the generality of the jurists, being brought forward.

The Quran has ordained Qisas in the following words :

> O ye who believe! The Law of equality is prescribed to you in cases of murder: [70]
>
> —Al Quran 11 : 178

And the underlying wisdom has been stated thus:

> In the Law of Equality there is (saving of) life to ye men of Understanding. [71]
>
> —Al Quran 11 : 179.

With reference to the Torah it has been said :

> We ordained therein for them "Life for life." [72]
>
> —Al Quran V : 45

Under this law if a man murders a woman the man shall pay for it with his life. And if a woman murders a man, a woman shall be put to death for her crime. The Hadith supports it. It has been expressly said in a report from the Prophet S.A.W. :

> If a man were to murder a woman, he shall be killed for his crime.

This is further supported by other reports. A report of Sihah-Sitta (the six most reliably correct Hadith collections — Bukhari, Muslim, Abu Da'ood, Tirmizi, Ibn Majah and Nisai), says that a Jew, to snatch her jewellery, crushed the head of an Ansari girl and threw her dead body into a hole in the ground. In her last moments she was brought to the Prophet S.A.W. When the probable murderers were named she denied by just shaking her head. But when that particular Jew was named within her hearing she confirmed it by a nod (of assent). When the accused Jew was questioned about it, after some resistance he broke down and confessed his guilt. And so he too was stoned to death in Qisas (equal for equal). Imam Navavi says : So many issues arise from this report :

One of them is that man shall be put to death in return for the murder of woman. There is consensus on this issue of all those that count.

In a lengthy report quoted by Abu Da'ood, it has been said:

> The blood money of murder by a woman shall fall due to her 'usbah. But in case she is murdered her blood money will have to be distributed among them all without any distinction of As'habul-Faruz and 'Usbah. And if they decide on Qisas they would be permitted to take the life of the murderer of their related lady.

Here in the text of the report "they can take the life of their murderer" means the murderer of their kins woman. Nisa'i and Ibn Majah have reported it with the words "her murderer". That makes it amply manifest that a man shall be put to death in return for the murder of a woman. In calling the woman's murderer that of her relatives indicates that the legal position that he is not only the murderer of the woman but that of all her inheritors. They would be in their rights legally to have him put to death for his crime or accept blood money in lieu of it or even consent to forgive him.

The great stalwart among the Tabieen, Saeed bin Musayyib says:

> Man shall be put to death for the woman, if he is found guilty of her murder.

Imam Bukhari says:

> The learned men have said that the man shall be put to death for the murder of a woman.

And this is the opinion of the four most outstanding Imams of jurisprudence from the point of view of their following, Imam Abu Haneefah, Imam Malik, Imam Shafi'i, Imam Ahmad R.A. and other great erudites of the Muslim Ummah.

Allamah Ibn Abdul Bar says that there is consensus on it that man shall pay for his crime against a woman, worth his life and the woman shall likewise be put to death if she has taken his life. Among the companions 'Ali R.A.A. and among the tabi'een Hasan Basri R.A. are said to be of the opinion that if man murders a woman and her inheritors want him to be put to death they can do so after payment of half the blood money since a woman's blood money is half that of man. If they do not pay half the blood money, they will get the blood money of the woman. But this does not stand confirmed from 'Ali R.A.A. As a matter of fact this is the opinion of 'Uthman-al-Labatti, a jurist of Basrah. We are also told that Hasan Basri and 'Ata R.A. are also of the opinion held by the majority.

That the blood money of woman is half that of man is no strong argument and hence man will be liable to Qisas or forfeiting his life, when half the blood money has been paid to him since the punishment for Qazaf or slander is the same for both. The woman calumminating a man with involvement in fornication shall be liable to the same punishment as for the man slandering a woman. Man shall not be the recipient of any amount as return before being put to death. No discrimination is made between the murderer and the murdered on the basis of their positions. That is why an entire body of men joining hands in the murder of an individual, shall all be put to death for their participation in the crime.

Imam Shaukani says' that the purpose and underlying wisdom of Qisas also supports the opinion of the majority of the jurists. The wisdom behind Qisas is to prevent shedding of blood of man and oppression and excesses may not torment him. If the man is not put to death as Qisas for a woman, for several reasons is to deprive her of her share in inheritance. The person who does not want to give her anything from inheritance may very likely murder her and thus getting her out of the way. The other reason may be the sense of shame and degradation of the days of Jahiliyah which may prompt him to murder a daughter, particularly incase of a minor slip on her part may be made the excuse for it. Female offspring was buried alive during the period of Jahiliyah for this reason alone is a shame and disgrace. The third very strong reason is her frailty. The intending murderer does not expect the same resistance from her as from man. Therefore, any leave or relaxation in Qisas will enhance oppression and tyranny and taking her life shall become an easy job.

These details reveal that there is consensus of the ummah or at least the four well known imams of Fiqh and the majority of the jurists are unanimous on the issue that a woman shall be put to death for taking the life of a man and vice versa. Now the question that remains is whether the punishment shall be enforced even if the murderer and the murdered are both women. The answer to this query is clear enough. When a man can be put to death for the murder of a woman why a woman cannot be put to death for the murder of a woman. The Quran is explicit about it:

> And woman shall be put to death for woman. [73]
> —Al Quran 11 : 178

So there is no contention on this point among the jurist that a female murderer can be put to death for taking the life of another woman. The statement of the Quran is general and the Hanafite Fiqh has also reasoned on its basis that a free woman murdering a slave girl shall also pay for it with her life.

Social Justice

Let us now take up the punishment for the physical injuries to a woman. It also takes the same forms discussed earlier under loss of life: A woman shall pay for her crime against man. Man shall be put to death for the murder of a woman. A woman shall be liable to punishment for any crime against a woman.

The following Quranic verse has ordained Qisas :

> We ordained therein for them 'Life for Life, eye for eye, nose for nose, ear for ear, tooth for tooth, and wounds equal for equal.' But if any one remits the

> retaliation by way of charity; it is an act of atonement for himself., And if any fail to judge by what Allah hath revealed, they are wrong-doers. [74]
>
> —Al Quran : 45

The question arises whether in case of men and women injuring one other, like man taking the life of woman or vice versa are put to death, the injuries, wounds and other types of damage shall be avenged or there is some difference between the two (life and injuries).

'Abdullah Ibn Abbas R.A.A. says that the Arabs did not inflict capital punishment on woman in Qisas for murder committed by her. They punished woman for a crime against woman and a man for murder of an individual of his own sex. In the verse above it was pointed out that Muslim man and woman if they are free (not bonded) are peers or equal in status. One taking the life of another intentionally or causing a damage of a lesser degree (than murder), shall have to pay for it on the basis of equality.

Imam Navavi says that the majority among the companions, tabi'een and latter day 'ulama reasoned from the verse that the ordainment of Qisas shall be enforced among the men and women also and murderers of each other shall pay with their lives. And physical injuries shall be avenged accordingly in a just measure. For example, a man fracturing the hand of a woman or vice versa, the hand of the culprit shall be fractured likewise. But in case of an injury in which avenging on the basis of equality is not possible, compensation will have to be allowed for it. Anas R.A.A. reports that his paternal aunt, Rubayyi broke a tooth of an Ansari girl. Her people wanted her to be forgiven or compensation demanded of her. But the family of the Ansari girl appeared bent on being avenged. When the case was brought before the Prophet S.A.W., he ordered Qisas (tooth for tooth). The uncle of Anas, brother of Rubayyi' said, "O Messenger of Allah ! By Allah Rubayyi's tooth shall not be broken." Now he had outspokenly opposed the decision of the Prophet but due to his faith in Allah's mercy and confidence in himself that he would ultimately prevail upon the parents of the complainant to remit retaliation or accept *diyat* (compensation).

The Messenger of Allah S.A.W. said to Anas that the Book of Allah ordains equal for equal which cannot go unavenged. A little later the party insisting on Qisas consented to accept diyat instead. Seeing this change in their attitude the Apostle of Allah remarked that there were slaves of Allah who, if they take an oath with trust in Allah, He proves them true.

This is a report carried by Bukhari and others which goes to prove that a woman injuring another must pay in the form of Qisas. The report by Muslim tells us that sister of Rubayyi', Umme-Harithah wounded a certain person. When the case was brought to the notice of the Prophet S.A.W., he said, "She will have to pay for the injuries."

At this Rubayyi's mother intervened saying, "Shall umm-e-Harithah be subjected to retaliation ? By Allah ! It will never come to pass." The Prophet said to her, "Allah be glorified ! What manner of talk is that ! The Book of Allah has ordained Qisas."

But the people of the wounded person later accepted diyat. The Apostle of Allah at this change in the situation remarked that there were slaves of Allah who, when they swear in the name of Allah, are not disappointed.

Imam Navavi says the report reveals several things. One of them that is proved by it is that there will certainly be Qisas or retaliatory punishment between man and woman if occasion arises for it.

Now we are presenting here some sayings of the companions R.A.A. and Tabieen R.A., which go to prove that woman has to pay for her crime against man and vice versa.

Imam Bukhari says that 'Umar R.A.A. is reported to have said:

> If a woman murders a man intentionally or in lesser degree causes some hurt to him, she will be called to pay it with her life or retaliatory punishment equal for equal.

When woman will have to suffer for her crime, man is all the more liable to such retaliatory action. And we find 'Umar R.A.A. saying on another occasion :

> The wounds of man and woman hurt equally.

'Umar bin Abdul Aziz R.A. says :

> The ordainment of Qisas shall be enforced between woman and men, even in the matter of life.

Abu Zanad says about seven well-known jurists of the period of Tabieen and such other 'Ulama and jurists :

Women will have to pay for the crimes against man, eye for eye, ear for ear and various types of wounds equal for equal. (In a similar manner man will have to pay for his crimes against woman) and if man murders her he will be put to death.

Imam Malik reasoning from the verse quoted above (Q.V : 45) says:

> The ordainment of Qisas as it is applicable to cases between men and men, so also it is binding on men and women in their crimes (of one against the other sex).

Allamah Ibn Qudamah Hanbali says that the persons (men and women) between whom Qisas is applicable to the matter of life, retaliatory punishments for lesser damage, physical injuries, will also be enforced. And this is also the opinion of Imam Malik, Imam Thauri, Imam Shafi'i, Is'haq bin Rahuwaih, Abu Thaur and Imam Ahmad. Under this principle since for the life of man, woman is put to death and for the life of woman, man is put to death, so if they cause injury to each other, they will pay for it on the principle of equal for equal.

According to Hanafite school of jurisprudence, retaliatory capital punishment for the lives of men and women is permitted in case of wilful murder of one by the other, but it ceases where lesser damage, injuries and hurts of various kinds come in between them. For example man murdering a woman or vice versa shall be put to death for their crimes. But if a man smites the the hand of a woman or the other way round, none of them in Hanafite jurisprudence shall be punished with like for like, but will have to pay diyat for it.

Murder shall be the cause of loss of life to the man as well as to the woman, loss of life being common between them, and so retaliatory action or Qisas is justified. But the matter of body organs is different. They are in the nature of property. Property is also meant for the protection of life. And body organs are also meant for this purpose (protection of life). Qisas relating to them can be permitted only when their value is the same. The Shari'ah has evaluated woman's organs a little lower than those of man. (We shall take it up later). When there is a difference in their value, there shall be no Qisas or retaliatory action for one against the other.

The ordainment of Qisas in Surah Ma'idah (Q. V : 45) is not absolute. It is accepted on all hands that there is no Qisas for a Harbi and Muslim (a citizen of a country at war with the Islamic state is Harbi and one temporarily offered refuge is Mustamin). When they have been exempted from the coverage of the verse, the women can also be granted immunity on the authority of this Hadith.

If it is asserted that the hands of men differ in length and so they differ also in applying energy and power of grip, but there is no consideration in the application of the ordainment of Qisas. Measured by this yardstick no distinction should be made between man and woman on the difference of size of their hands, etc. The argument offered against this reasoning is that since difference between the diyat of man and woman has been recognized, it will have to be taken into account. But the difference between the hands of one man and another cannot be given any consideration since there is no rule for it. So for all practical purposes they will be regarded equal.

One of the objections raised is this also that if equality of diyat between man and woman is not made the basis of comparison in the matter of Qisas of limbs and organs, it would not be wrong to punish woman as a retaliatory measure for crime committed against man, since diyat of man's organs is greater than those of woman. Why Qisas for something more valuable cannot be imposed on a comparatively cheaper object ? For example, if a woman smites the hand of a man, it would be right to have her hand cut off since diyat of man's hand is not only on a par with woman's hand but greater, although Hanafite Fiqh does not regard it justifiable.

The well-known opinion and usage of the Hanafite Fiqh is also this. However, there is also in this school an opinion permitting it. According to it, if the woman were to smite the hand of man, her hand too can be cut off as a measure of equal for equal. If this opinion is accepted the objection vanishes.

Concerning the wounds of head and face, there is an opinion in Hanafite Fiqh that Qisas between man and woman cannot be allowed in such cases since equality must exist for Qisas in value and utility, and it does not factually exist between man and woman. But there is a different opinion also in this regard which permits Qisas between man and woman since there is some difference between the Qisas of limbs and organs compared with that for wounds. Cutting off limbs and organs ends their utility and the defect abides. But wounds inflicted on the face, though causing deformity and defect, do not affect utility. And on this point man and woman are at the same footing.

The wounds of the face are not alone in causing disfigurement. The loss of limbs and other organs also causes deformity and defects. When on the basis of disfigurement due to facial wounds Qisas is justified, the damage to limbs and other organs too deserves the same consideration and treatment. Apart from the point of utility if consideration is given to the aspect of defect the opinion of Hanafite Fiqh necessitates further thought and discussion. In this matter the opinions of other Imams of the well-known and recognized schools of Fiqh and that of the majority of jurists appears to be stronger — that in the Qisas for organs and limbs, there is no distinction between man and woman.

The Monetary compensation for wilful murder of lesser harm in the form of physical damage imposed by the Shari'ah is known as 'Diyat' (Blood Money). One of the objections raised against the Law of Diyat in Islam is also this that here too as in other fields of activity, it has failed to maintain equality between the sexes. The objection, however, does not hold water.

This is a juristical discussion and individuals and schools of thought differ in their opinions. Below we are going to furnish some details and an analysis of the issue under attack.

According to the Hanafite Fiqh, diyat of woman is half that of man whether it be for loss of life or damage to limbs and organs.

This is also the opinion of Imam Shafi'i, Sufyan Thauri, Imam Laith and Abu Thaur. The argument brought forward in support of it is that according to Mu'az bin Jabal R.A.A. the Prophet S.A.W. said :

> The diyat of woman is half that of man.

This report is not based on strong authority.

However 'Ali R.A.A. says:

> The Diyat for the injuries of woman is half of those

> of man, whether they (her injuries) are extensive or limited.

Ibrahim Nakha'j reports from 'Umar and 'Ali R.A.A. both

> The diyat of woman is half that of man whether it pertains to loss of life or a physical damage of lesser degree.
>
> And this opinion is also said to be that of 'Abdullah Ibn 'Umar and Abdullah Ibn Abbas R.A.A. Hafiz Ibn Hajar, however, informs us that he failed to find this opinion of these two companions.

The question arises why woman's diyat should be half that of man The answer offered is that since man is the bread-winner of the family and bears the financial burden, his death causes greater loss to his family than that in the event of woman's death. Therefore, his diyat has been fixed twice that of the woman. Allamah Rasheed Raza Misri says:

> The basic consideration in this matter is that due to man's death the family is deprived of greater benefits than their deprivation through the death of woman. So on the grounds governing man's share in the inheritance his diyat has also been kept double that of woman.

Another thing that has been brought in support of it is that according to the Islamic Law it is the man who has been declared fit for holding positions of authority like Imamat (leadership) of prayer and Hajj as also heading the Islamic state and positions for the collective responsibilities like military services and guarding the frontiers. In purely mundane affairs also, the industries and professions essential for the survival of man, he has a much larger share. So man's loss of life extends further, causing damage to the society in addition to his own family, in a much bigger way than that caused by woman's loss of life. Naturally his diyat has been fixed double that of the woman.

Undoubtedly these arguments carry weight. But the ordainments of the Shari'ah do not stand on reasoning alone. Strong and convincing arguments of the Quran and the Sunnah are needed to confirm an issue. The reports from the Prophet S.A.W. and sayings of the companions that have been presented in support of this issue, as stated earlier, are not strong enough.

According to Imam Malik and Imam Ahmad and others, there is no difference between man's and woman's diyat upto one third. However, after one third, woman's diyat becomes half of that of man. It finds support in the report by 'Abdullah Ibn 'Umro bin-al-'As. He reports the Prophet S.A.W. to have said :

> Woman's diyat is equal to that of man until it (her diyat) becomes one third.

This report is not strong in the matter of authority.

In support of this *maslak* (way or code of conduct) the following words of Zaid bin Thabit R.A.A. are put forth. He says :

> The diyat of man and woman is the same up to a certain limit. After crossing that limit it will become half that of man.

A more or less similar report has come down to us from 'Umar R.A.A.

Saeed bin Musayyib R.A. says that up to the limit of one third, the diyat of man and woman will be equal whether it pertains to a finger, a tooth, a wound on the body, or a head injury; beyond that the woman's diyat becomes half that of man.

Imam Malik R.A. says that Imam Zahiri R.A. and 'Urwah bin Zubair R.A.A. also hold the same view as that of Saeed bin Musayyib R.A.

It is said that this is also the opinion of the majority of the jurists of Medinah, the outstanding jurists among the Tabieen, the seven well-known jurists, 'Umar bin Abdul Aziz R.A., Imam Laith and Qatadah.

Qazi Ibn Rushd is a Malekite. He opines on these arguments: The first of these groups-Malik and others have reposed their confidence in merely some Mursal reports.

This much about their supporting authority. Now, let us take them up at the intellectual level. A very pertinent question arises: what is the wisdom (reason) behind the statement that up to a certain limit man and woman are made to stand at the same level but after one third (limit) the woman's diyat becomes half that of man ? The answer given to this question is that if one third also is halved it becomes very small and cannot compensate the loss incurred by the woman. So upto one third it was kept on a par with man, but after crossing that limit reduced to half that of man.

If the reports quoted above are accepted as in order and reliable, this answer appears reasonable enough. But another question crops up and it is this that the injuries and wounds for which the woman receives one third diyat, for much more serious injuries it gets reduced to less than one third, whereas common sense demands that proportionate to the damage caused to her, she must be allowed enhanced compensation. So we find that according to the report of Mu'atta, the following discussion on this issue took place between Rabiah bin 'Abdur Rahman R.A. and Saeed bin Musayyib R.A.:

> ***Rabiah :*** "Sir, tell me about the diyat of one finger of a woman."
>
> ***Saeed bin Musayyib:*** "Ten camels."
>
> ***Rabiah :*** "And that of two fingers?"
>
> ***Saeed bin Musayyib :*** "Twenty camels."
>
> ***Rabiah :*** "And what about three?"
>
> ***Saeed bin Musayyib :*** "Thirty camels."
>
> ***Rabiah :*** "What do you say about four fingers?"

Saeed bin Musayyib : "Twenty camels only since the diyat of the life of man (with his entire body) is a hundred camels. The diyat of woman exceeding one third, became half according to him."

Rabiah : "When the woman suffers pain and trouble due to greater loss (damage) will diyat in that situation come down?"

Saeed bin Musayyib : "Are you an Iraqi that you are given to belief in reasoning in every thing, even where an injunction (Sunnah) comes in ? Guess work against definite ordainment!"

Rabiah : "No. I am a student and anxious to learn about the nature of the issue."

Saeed bin Musayyib : "My son ! This is the Sunnah."

Among the latter day jurists Imam Shaukani held this opinion that after a third amount of diyat, woman's share becomes half that of man. But he is conscious of the weight of the objection that in this way after a third, woman's diyat gets much reduced when common sense demands that it should be enhanced. According to him up to one third, the diyat of man and woman are equal. Only in the excess after one third, it will become half. For example, where man will be entitled to forty camels, woman's diyat shall be thirty five camels. He says that the report of 'Abdullah bin Umro bin-Al- As, that is put forth there, is no deterrent to construe it this way. As for that of Saeed bin Musayyib, it is a Mursal report and hence, unacceptable. And this is not all. He writes that it is necessary to construe the Hadith like this :

So that man may not find himself lost in a narrow gorge against all that justice and equity, reason and conjecture demand.

Significance of Women

There are differences of opinion and contentions based on

reason. Those who hold the opinion that after the limit of a third, woman's diyat becomes half, have this contention among themselves whether one third is that, one third as such forms a part of it or not. One opinion is that before reaching one third, man and woman will have equal diyat. But as soon as it attains that value, one third, it shall become half. The other opinion is that it becomes one third. Ibn Qudamah a Hambalite, has preferred this opinion. He says that the words of the report "until it reaches one third" tell us that the equality of man and woman is limited to less than one third.

Some of these learned men do not believe in the equality of diyat of man and woman even up to one third. 'Abdullah Ibn Mas'ood R.A.A. says that in the diyat of tooth and *'muzihah'* (a wound exposing the under lying bone), man and woman will be equal, but after that woman's diyat shall become half that of man.

A tradition of the Prophet S.A.W. says that the diyat of a tooth is five camels. And this is also the diyat of 'muzihah', namely five camels. That means up to five camels, there shall be no difference in the diyat of man and woman. After that the diyat of woman shall become half that of man. This also is said to be the opinion of Qazi Shuraih. There is one opinion to this effect that up to 15 camels the diyat of woman shall be equal to that of man and half after that.

As against this Hasan Basri R.A. says that upto half (fifty camels) man and woman shall be equal in the matter of diyat. After that, woman's diyat shall be half that of man.

More or less the same opinion we come upon among the learned men of the latter days. Allamah 'Abdur-Ra'uf Manavi, a Shafi'ite, says that upto one third the diyat of organs and limbs of woman is like that of man. But when it becomes half, the woman's diyat shall be half that of man. Exactly the same thing has been said by Allamah Muhammad bin 'Abdul-Hadi Sindhi who subscribes to Hanafite jurisprudence.

In this way that majority of the jurists though unanimous on it that woman's diyat shall be only half that of man, differ widely in details. Every diyat of woman, big or small, shall be half that of man or half of that excess over one third of the total diyat when it becomes half? And there are other contentions too besides these. The reason is to be found in the fact that there is no definite instruction in the Quran to this effect.

The traditions of the Prophet S.A.W. brought forward in this connection are not strong enough in authority on whose basis there could be some decisive derivation that could remove all doubts, and end contentions once for all. The sayings of the companions and their followers (*tabi'een*) are not also in harmony and are differing widely in details. And that naturally caused greater differences among the jurists. There is room for all these opinions and any one of them can be given preference also. And keeping all these contentions and discussions, further thought can also be given to them.

We also come upon yet another opinion, that of Asam and the exegetist, Ibn-e-'Atiyah. He says that the diyat of man and woman is the same. He reasons for it from the Quranic verse:

> And who ever kills a believer by mistake, it is ordained that he should free a believing slave and pay blood money to the deceased from it. [75]
>
> —Al Quran IV: 92

There is consensus of opinion that in this Quranic verse the murder of both man and woman is meant and so their diyat should also be the same.

Allamah Rasheed Raza Misri says that the Quran has mentioned diyat absolutely without any specification of man or woman. The word has been used in a general sense. It demands that to whatever quantum of diyat the heirs of the murdered person agree would be in order and acceptable, no matter whether it is too low or too high in the estimate of the opposite party. But the Sunnah has put a limit on it, keeping the diyat of a free Muslim who is not guilty of any crime to forfeit his blood, is a hundred camels, or their value in cash. And that of a woman is half that (fifty camels or their market price in the form, of cash). After that he goes on to say :

The Quranic verse makes it clear that there is no discrimination here between man and woman. Undoubtedly the well known jurists have not adopted the opinion that the diyat of man and woman is the same, and as such it is an isolated and rare opinion.

5

Women's Role in Society

Education and Nation Building

Earlier, education in India, for a long time was dissociated from the idea of nation building. It was viewed as a process for infusing piety during the ancient period. It was then seen as a cultural process, to transmit the accumulated wealth of knowledge, to impart classical values and to build the character of the individuals. It was essentially for a privileged few and hence was not really contributory to the development of the nation as we understand today. When the demand for women's education started in the 18th century it was more in the light of women's rights, for the access to knowledge and not as a national economic asset.

Slow Start : According to the statistics available regarding professional education of women in 1901-1902, the number of women students in training schools was 1412, medical schools was 166, technical and industrial schools was 468 and commercial schools 26. Of all the careers then open to women, teaching was obviously the most popular. Next to teaching, medical career, such as nursing, midwifery and medicine were popular. The necessity of women doctors began to be felt very early as Indian women were naturally averse to consulting male doctors. The best achievement during the first quarter of this century was that there was large number of women teachers in general and trained teachers in particular. In 1921-22, the number of women in training schools rose to 4391 as against 1412 in 1901-02.

A great social and political awakening unequalled by that in any preceding period occurred among women in the two decades following the first world war and this led to a great improvement in their social position. In the social field, the age of marriage was now rising fast particularly among the upper classes of Hindus in urban areas.

Political Power : In the national field, women had already obtained the right to vote in elections to local bodies and they could also be elected as representatives of local bodies. Another factor which helped the development of education among women was the new leadership that was now rising in their midst. Gandhiji's contribution to the emancipation of women also was phenomenal. He was a staunch advocate of the equality of men and women and this had a great impact in all walks of life. The freedom struggle under Gandhiji's leadership attracted many women to enter politics and this also did considerable service to elevate the status of women.

Women took part in the Non-cooperation movement of 1921, the Civil Disobedience movement of 1931 and the Quit Indian Campaign of 1942; they fought shoulder to shoulder with men and won their emancipation as a tribute of gratitude. A specially important feature of their emancipation was the emergence of middle class women from the shelter of their homes. Constitutional directives of non-discrimination on grounds of sex in employment and the specific directives to promote with special care, educational and economic interests of the weaker sections of the people had a direct bearing on the employment of middle class women. Greater opportunities to obtain higher education increased the employment opportunities in the organised sector and there was greater demand for women professionals, especially teachers, doctors and nurses; there was great pressure on middle class families in urban areas for enhancing, the family income; these are all features of post-independent India. The emphasis on women's equality that emerged during the freedom struggle had also influenced the attitude and aspirations of the educated middle class women.

The processes of modernization, industrialisation and urbanisation also had their impact on women's employment. One of the most important features of the developed and technologically advanced societies of the present age is the high rate of mobility and social change. In the developing countries also, societies were changing but gradually and slowly, because of the dead weight of traditionalism and social-cultural barriers. The processes of modernisation have accelerated social change and have been forcing Indian women into new social roles.

Modernisation refers to an inherent change in the mode of life. It involves not only changes in the material culture of a nation but also its beliefs, values, norms and way of life as a whole.

In traditional Indian societies, women were economically and socially dependent on their fathers till marriage, on the husbands after marriage and on the sons later. They were mostly confined to household affairs and they were not allowed to participate in the political and economic affairs of the society. But with independence and attempts at modernisation, sex bias and discrimination have been done away with, and the concept of equality of the two sexes have been widely propagated and honoured.

The rapid industrialisation also created general employment opportunities from which women have benefitted. Though they are mostly employed at the lower levels, in unskilled occupations, it has helped them to become economically independent. There has been an increase in the number of home-based women workers. The process of urbanisation enabled girls to get exposed to education, information, health care, drudgery reduction and employment opportunities.

After independence, the possibility of employment under government provided a great stimulus for women's higher education. The demand for equality gradually broke the resistance of educational authorities and engineering, technical and vocational institutions which have been the monopoly of men till now, were opened out to women.

In short, industrial expansion, migration to urban areas, technology changes, western education and awareness of better standards of life etc. enabled women, especially middle class, urban, educated upper caste women to take up work outside in significant numbers and this economic activity outside home helped them to experience financial and psychological independence to a certain extent. But it must be accepted that with a very few exceptions in the higher strata of society, majority of women took to working outside the home for economic reasons; men supported women's employment to augment the family's income. Rising prices, increasing cost of housing and education, aspiration for a higher standard of living increased the economic pressure on the middle class women.

Success Rate

Since independence, there has been a steady increase in over all enrolment of girls in schools as well as improvement in gross enrolment ratio.

Enrolment percentage of girls in the age group 6-11 years

which was 24.6 in 1950-51 increased to 66.4 in 1973-74. In the age group 11-14 years, the percentage of girls increased from 4.5 in 1950-51 to 22.2 in 1973-74. The following figures taken from the census reports on percentage of literate women give insight into the development of women's education.

Years	*Percentage of Literate-Women*
1891	0.5%
1901	0.7%
1911	1.1%
1921	1.9%
1931	2.4%
1941	6.9%
1951	7.93%
1961	12.95%
1971	18.72%
1981	24.88%
1991	39.29%
2001	43.62%

Women's literacy is still way behind male literacy which has increased from 39.51% in 1971 to 64.13% in 1991.

In 1971 more than three fourths of the children who were not enrolled in school were girls. It has now decreased to 60% but it is still a very unsatisfactory position.

There has also been a rapid increase in higher educational opportunities and female enrolment in higher education has gone up by more than thirty points since 1951. The number of women in higher education in 1951 was 40000 and by 1988, it increased to 12 lakhs, an increase by 30 times. In the last four decades, the proportion of women to every hundred men at the university stage has increased from 14 in 1951 to 46 in 1988.

In the colleges of general education, in 1950-51, there were only 14 girls for every 100 boys students, in 1960-61, it was 17 girls for every 100 boys and in 1965-66 it went upto 25 girls for every 100 boys. Of all students enrolled in higher education, 32.5% are girls today.

There has also been a change in the trends of the courses taken by women. More and more women have started taking up science, commerce and other professional courses.

According to figures available for 1991, enrolment of girls in science courses has increased to 33.3% and in commerce to 20.8%. In 1971, out of a total of 45000 science graduates, 81800, i.e. 18% only were women. In professional courses at college level, there were only 5 girls for every 100 boys in 1950-51; in 1961, 14 girls for every 100 boys were getting training in professional courses. One sector of higher professional education where women have come in large numbers is medicine.

In 1971, 20% of the total number of medical students were women. The total number of girls enrolled in Engineering and Technology in 1971 was hardly 1051 students, i.e., less than 1% of the total enrolment. 8.5% of the law students, 4.6% of the agricultural college students and 5.2% of vaterinary college students were women.

In 1988, 31% of the total enrolment in medical sciences were women and women practicing medicine were 26%. Today, 35% of all physicians in India are women. Girls started to enter engineering institutions in significant numbers only after 1980. In 1988, 7% of the total entrants into engineering colleges were women and in law, it was 8.5%.

In ten years, i.e., by 1987, enrolment of girls increased by three times in engineering and one and a half times in medicine. The 1991 enrolment figures of women are 32.3% in medicine, 7.9% in Engineering, 8.2% in veterinary science, 7.2% in agriculture and 10% in law.

Occupational Distribution

A significant trend in women's occupational pattern since independence is the increasing entry of women workers into non traditional services and professions.

Non-discriminatory opportunities for higher education, equality of opportunities in employment, changing social values, rapid industrial expansion, better economic development etc. gave opportunities for urban literate women to take up employment outside the home in considerable numbers.

The number of women in the various professional categories has been continuously increasing since 1960. Women administrators, executives, managerial workers also increased from 10000 in 1960 to 18000 in 1966. Women in clerical cadre in government registered a phenomenal increased from 37000 in 1960 to 79000 in 1968.

Concentration of women in profession of teaching and nursing continued to increase and according to 1966 census, 70% of the educated women were teachers, 7% were nurses, 11.8% were clerks, and only 1% were physicians. According to an I.L.O study made in 1970 only 1.7% of the professional and technical workers were women of which, three fourths were teachers.

Since 1970, there has been a change in the trend of the courses taken up by women. New job opportunities were opened up in industries, such as pharmaceutical, food processing and other chemical industries and women started going in for science; the classification of occupation of women according to 1971 census was that there were 60000 teachers, 2000 physicians, 1700 lawyers, 700 engineers and 2500 were medical technicians in nurisng and health care. In relation to men, the proportion of women in their selected occupation were as follows :

Physicians	7.1%
Teachers	30.3%
Lawyers	1.2%
Health Technicians	72.2%
Scientists	10.9%

The data supplied by the Ministry of Social Welfare for 1978 is that for every 100 males, were the number of women was

Supreme Court Judge	0
High Court Judge	2
I.A.S.	9
I.P.S.	0.09
Indian Education Service	5
Engineers	12
Doctors	25

Out of 23700 persons working as proprietors, directors and managers in business, in 1971, only 5300 were women. In 1991, women executives are still a miniscule proportion, less than 1%. In Government services, the proportion of women is only 6% in all civil services, 7.5% in I.A.S. and 10% in the foreign services. In the Indian Police service, women's employment has increased from 1% in 1971 to 21% in 1988. In the judicial service at the level of judges, sub judges and magistrates for every 40 men, there is just one woman.

Among the university teachers, there is one female teacher for every 10 male teachers; in the research institutions the ratio is 1 : 9, in colleges of professional education the ratio 1 : 6 and in college of general education, the ratio is 1 : 4. Among professors in the universities, women constitute about 2%; out of 179 vice-chancellors of universities and institutions deemed as universities, there has not been more than 10 women at any one time. The proportion of seats won by women to the Lok Sabha in 1988 was 46 out of 537 seats. The Rajya Sabha had 28 women in a house of 245 seats. The pattern in similar at the state level also. In 1991 general election, women accounted for just 33 of the 503 members of parliament elected, which is a dismal 6.6%. Thus women's participation in politics has been quite poor.

If we take working women in general, 80% of the working women are in the primary sector as agricultural labourers and cultivators, 18% are factory workers and only 2% constitute professional in higher salary brackets. Self employed women entrepreneurs, managers in business etc. are very few as women have little control on the productive resources. Thus very few women happen to be in a position to influence political thinking or decision making process.

In the Indian Police Service, employment has increased from 1% in 1972 to 21% today. Women have entered all the so called male dominated professions including military services, police forces, aviation and piloting and business management. All adminsitrative positions are open to them on a competitive basis. The guarantee of the rights envisaged in the Constitution have enabled the women of modern India to enter all walks of life and make an imprint of her presence.

Occupational Pattern : Woman is man's oldest beast of burden. From time immemorial there has been a certain sex division of labour. In all societies of the world women not only bore and nursed children, but also did the entire household work of cooking, cleaning and washing. In the pre-historic age women could not participate in hunting. However they were required to work "as hard perhaps even harder" than men. There were early matriarchal societies in which women were

(i) home-makers and also

(ii) economically active income earners in trade and

commerce, and producers in agriculture and industry. Men in such societies were nomadic or warriors with little or no economic responsibilities.

Embedded in the social division of labour is the sex division of labour. Compared with the differences in social patterns across the globe, the similarity of the sex division of labour is very striking. Apart from, and in addition to, their different roles in the biological process of reproduction, males and females have had different traditional or customary occupations and are subject to different inherited duties and rights. They develop distinct personality characteristics befitting the status assigned to them by the culture to which they belong. The criteria for male-female division of labour are based on local customs and traditions rather than on real differences between them in terms of physiological or mental capacities. Their slender build has given women the title of weaker sex. But that has not precluded them from being carriers of burden or from doing relatively heavy agricultural labour and other strenuous and protracted physical labour.

Midwifery was universally a female vocation from pre-historic times and it was handed down from mother to daughter. Many taboos are associated with it. "Healing the sick and wounded accorded well with creating new life" and women were also believed to possess in some social groups, special magical powers. Other than these two, viz., midwifery and healing (sometimes by witchcraft too) women had little else to do as a vocation, except the allotted tasks in or/and nearer home. Preoccupation with prolonged child bearing, and associated health and physical conditions for most part of their lives kept women "tied" to their families.

The greater physical strength of males, as against the energy consuming reproductive functions, and the attendant limitations on females' time disposition resulted in many other social and cultural differences with the notable male dominance.

Notwithstanding modern industrialisation and technological changes these social practices are perpetuated and developed. Despite the concept of equality of sexes enshrined in a few modern constitutions, and especially in the Indian Constitution discrimination against women is continued even today.

Traditional Roles : Passage of time has brought in many changes. Personal achievements determine "achieved status" in contrast to "traditional status" on the old criteria of age, sex, family membership and allied factors. Social transformation has gradually made individual's status - male or female - to be based on achieved roles rather than traditionally assigned roles. In the competitive society his or her personal merit matters, more than the age-old stratification and order. And yet very few women, educated and sophisticated alone, can claim this social recognition. For the rest of them, there is not much difference from the olden days; and sufferance is still their badge, with or without sacrifice.

Achieved Roles : There has occurred the transition from primitive subsistence living to industry based production, as a consequence of a continuous increase in specialization of functions and division of labour as it obtains today. In spite of the long history of human development, the age old sex division has not changed fundamentally, because domestic duties and child care are the inescapable responsibilities of women and in addition to these responsibilities women may opt to work. The occupational pattern of women the world over is woven around this basic fact of family living. This sharp division of labour was apparently rational and labour saving in a self-sufficient community. Customs have become so ingrained and is perpetuated, even after production became specialized. Though the rationale for it has disappeared, sex division of labour continues to remain in many more avoidable forms.

Many attempts to foster agricultural development have failed because men refused to weed a crop, which women had no time to weed. Or the introduction of cash crops was retarded because women refused to help with a new crop, and insisted on cultivating only the usual food crops which were considered proper work for women. Such refusal by both men and women to change traditional sex roles in the labour market occurs not only in India but also in many parts of the world. African men arc often unwilling to cultivate food crops as cash crops because food production is supposed to be a female task, and men in many parts of Latin America are unwilling to engage in commercial poultry production because it is traditionally a female work.

Sex Division : The sex division of labour has extended from the household work, to work outside in the industry. Occupations are divided into male and female occupations. Large industries and modern enterprises predominantly employ male workers. But in industries like textiles and food processing a comparatively high proportion of women is taken. Clerical and secretarial work is considered mainly a female job while higher level management and administration are male dominated. The labour market when classified job-wise, gives a clear demarcation between male and female jobs. Strict domestic responsibility of women, low levels of literacy and training drive majority of women altogether to the tail-end jobs.

Sex division of labour within the family, community and the society is structured largely "by the inter-section of economy, demography and family. With entrenched social stratification arising from socio-economic inequality, there results a stratificatory significance of each type of work. Three related and yet distinct approaches are used in examining the women's work patterns and variations in them:

(i) The first approach explains the pattern of allocation of female time in terms of selected economic and non-economic determinants. The economic determinants are paid work for market wages, family income, family enterprises, domestic work of varying ranges and labour intensity based on local amenities and commerciali-zation, extent of land holding, the caste based social status, and allied characteristics.

(ii) The second approach identifies the forms of occupations and wage differentiation. These are called sex-discrimination based market imperfection or exploitation. Wage differentials unrelated to productivity differentials result in wage discrimination.

(iii) The third approach examines the link between work participation and the other conditions that affect the status of women. Higher levels of work participation has been noticed among the 'land-poor, low caste and tribal women', and their common denominator is economic distress. Besides, in the case of most of Indian women, working and earning do not entitle them to control over their earnings. Earnings are pooled together and the male head of the household controls the earnings and in only exceptional cases, women excerise control over their earnings. When incomes are pooled, control could also be jointly shared, according to the relative ability of the partners.

The Characteristics : Depending on the differing social values from country to country, and region to region there are variations in the male-female job polarisation. Teaching and nursing remain mostly feminine occupations. Clerical jobs which are predominantly in the female domain in most of the advanced countries remain in a male dominted sector in Korea. While women in most countries, except India, would consider it unsuitable to be an assistant to male brick layer, men in most European countries find typing and stenography as unsuitable jobs for them. However, the idea that specialization of the labour market, rigid sex division of occupations and male and female tasks are related to biological differences between men and women is proved wrong when we compare the labour markets of different parts of the world. We find that the same jobs are male as well as female tasks. No doubt the concept of sex division of labour was based on physiological and psychological differences between the sexes but the key to comprehend these patterns is in the fields of culture and socio-economic development level rather than in human physiology and anatomy.

In each economy at its different phases of development there appears a certain segregation of the labour market. Based on the location of industries, skill and training requirements and educational levels, there obtains a grouping of labourers into certain occupations. The effect of sex division of labour is that in majority of cases women workers tend to concentrate in the low paid tail-end jobs. Owing to the slow, and at times little change in the educational levels of women in most countries, women employment market has been static and stagnant.

A Committee of the Department of Employment in the United States of America which studied the occupational segregation between men and women, reported a particularly gloomy picture of "no change". Even in modern and advanced societies, far from greater equality between the sexes at work, there is a "complete stalemate".

There does not appear any strong and consistent trend over the country towards greater integration of the sexes in the labour market. The small inroads made by women into typically male occupations could not imply the occurrence of significant changes in the existing sex division of labour. There is little change since the turn of the century. The large increase in the number of women in the labour market does not necessarily mean they cover a wider range of functions. Irrespective of the stage of development, women workforce concentrates in the lowest grades of white collar and blue collar jobs. Women find themselves often in "occupations that closely mirror functions carried out on an unpaid and non-specialist basis"

Women on Progress

Migration has become a major factor in economic development providing improved prospects to labourers of all categories. The ability to migrate is based upon social customs and conventions, and the economic prospects in the new region of residence. The influence of sex factor in the migratory nature of a population is different for different cultures and human groups. Males or females migrate depending on the opportunities for either sex. Migration of heads of the families invariably results in families migrating in search of pastures anew. Indian women are registered as the most migratory of the population. But their migration is sociological, resulting from marriage, and 'marriage - related migration'. Whatever new work opportunities available are made use of by the women of the migrant families.

In search of occupations, however, women have a tendency to cover shorter distances than migrating men. Pursuance of a career is a social compulsion for men but not yet so for women. Despite modernising influences in recent years, career based migration necessitating long distance movement' is considered less important for women than for men. All variations of migration, tribal migration, forced or induced migration, free migration, chain migration, mass migration and rural-urban migration, arc mostly male induced and for male advantage. Occupation-wise, women may or may not be benefited as a member of the migrant family.

In India, rural-urban migration has posed quite a few economic and social problems. In times of distress and to seek better fortunes the poverty ridden rural youth and families migrate to urban areas. The differences in urban-rural incomes in most cases are more imaginary than real. This migration has assumed enormous proportions in India. Rural women have less tendency to migrate for occupational reasons but the common practice is for the whole family to migrate for shorter or longer periods depending upon the prosperity of the village. When agriculture does not offer livelihood for the labouring families, migration to nearby urban centres takes place. Only marginal cases of migration from rural areas to urban centres are induced by job availability in the organised sector of the labour market while majority of rural migrants find themselves in the unorganised sector.

Classification of Occupations : The classification of population into three broad groups of main worker, marginal worker and non-worker has already been discussed in its conceptual context. This threefold classification in the 1981 census has been evolved from the deficiencies and limitations of the classification in the earlier censuses. The worker category includes cultivators, agricultural labourers, workers engaged in household industry and other workers.

The first two categories cover the entire work spectrum in the agricultural operations. The third category of household industry refers to a home based industry cither in rural or urban area, engaging a large proportion of members of the household including the head. What are grouped as other activities are in fact more significant in the non-agricultural sector of an economy. The service sector is gaining importance with economic development. To put all non-agricultural and non-home based activities as a hotch-potch of other activities appears an inadequate and inappropriate approach to classification of activities of the population.

For considering the specific issue of women employment in the Indian scene, census categories are not really useful for proper assessment either of the nature and extent of women's participation in the labour market or of their problems and disabilities. The ICSSR study classifies occupations into two broad categories of organised and unorganised sectors. The organised sector is characterised by modern relations of production and is regulated by protective taws for the security and working conditions of labour as well as labour organisations engaged in collective bargainng.

The unorganised sector, with its main component in agriculture, is characterised by the absence of these protective measures and machinery. With 94% of the women in India in the unorganised labour market, a mere 6% is in the organized sector. The difference between the two is not functional but lies in the degree of penetration of public control and regulation and recognition by the data collecting agencies and scientific investigators.

Sectoral Classification : Another classification of occupations is on the basis of manpower requirements, in relation to the core sector, sectoral characteristics and level of education. Mostly on the basis of level of literacy there is a division into white collar and blue collar jobs. However, the overall pattern of occupation by education level is not clear. As far as occupational distribution by industry is concerned, it is in terms of the production structure of industry and classified as primary, secondary and tertiary sector occupations. From the Census data the Registrar General of India adopts sectoral classification. The primary sector includes cultivation, agricultural labour, mining, quarrying, livestock, forestry, hunting, plantation, orchard, and allied activities. The secondary sector has household industry manufacturing and construction under its head and the tertiary category consists of trade, commerce, transport, storage, communication and other services.

Rural Education

India fives in its villages and a meaningful classification

focussing on this rural context of the employment pattern is to classify as rural and urban employment. However, the activities listed under sectoral classification are not mutually exclusive between rural and urban divisions. In the analysis of women employment rural-urban distinction is of value since there is higher rural female participation rate compared with urban female participation rate. Owing to definitional changes, the 1971 Census returned the main activities of housewives as non- workers even if they made additional contribution to economic activity working as cultivators and agricultural labourers. Most of the non-workers of 1971 census have fallen in the category of workers in 1981.

Based on the duration and continuity of work, another classification was attempted by D.T. Lakdawala in 1978. His distribution of labour force by usual activity matrix gives at the same time, stable or unstable work categories as well as rural-urban division of the work. Work was available to 68% of the working population and the unemployment figure was a low percentage of 1.7 but in absolute terms the total unemployed numbered 4.1 million. This exercise did not focus on female employment vis-a-vis male employment. It may be inferred, however, that the majority of female workers in India were under the categories of 'casual work' and 'no work'.

Secondary Activity : As for the employment prospects both on a stable and casual basis, it is the rural economy which has higher employ ability. Wage earner no work for only (one) 1% of rural and 5.2% of urban labour force. These are more optimistic than the figures given by the census report. The category of secondary activities of 1961 census gave a better deal to the women's work participation in India than the changed approach in 1971 census to workers and non-workers.

Leela Gulati who has made commendable contribution to the analysis of women employment in India makes use of the

1961 census data to analyse women's participation in work as secondary activity to their household domestic duties. This is a methodologically sound approach in the background of the social system and work culture as obtaining in India. Work outside home is primary to males and household work is primary to women. With all the years of progress and modernisation this ingrained social value is indelible and cannot be erased from our way of life. Gulati's findings arc noteworthy. They are:

(i) There is one male agricultural-labourer for every five male workers whereas women agricultural labourers are 50% of the female workers,

(ii) For women who participate in work only as a secondary activity almost nine out of every ten are engaged in cultivation in their remaining timings allocated for other work including household industry.

(iii) The proportion of women engaged in work as secondary activity is as high as that of women engaged in work as main activity.

(iv) A sort of regional pattern can be observed in the participation in work as main activity and there too, for cultivators and agricultural labourers as compared to other workers.

(v) A movement from north to south and from east to west seems to be accompanied by higher female participation with exceptions like Himachal Pradesh and Kerala.

(vi) The frequently mentioned relationship between concentration of small holdings and more intensive cultivation is not borne out in so far as it refers to the inter-state comparison of the employment of women as cultivators, whether as main or secondary activity.

There has been a marked change in the sectoral distribution of workers both male and female in the last two decades. There is a decline of workers in the primary sector and increase in the secondary and tertiary sector. But this has been very marginal for female workers who still predominate the primary sector with 82%.

Female employment is concentrated in the primary sector except in Punjab where women workers were found in the tertiary sector. Barring the states Gujarat, Haryana, Orissa, Punjab and West Bengal women workers are in higher proportion in the secondary sector compared with the tertiary sector. There is imperative need to change the present sectoral distribution of female labour in favour of the secondary and tertiary sectors.

Unorganised Labour Market : The several classifications outlined above approach occupational analysis from different angles. In the proper context each becomes meaningful and purposeful. It is easy to divide them into a number of groups. But when it comes to empirical exercise the real difficulties emerge. The major stumbling blocks in any serious study are the non-availability and inadequacy of data and particularly disaggregated data. While relatively more information is available on organised work force, that on the unorganised sector is very much wanting. The unorganised labour markets consist of contract labour market and daily rated market. Within the unorganised sector, compared with data on agricultural workers, there is practically no reliable information on non-agricultural occupations. The census classification of workers by primary activity ignores the overlapping nature of agricultural and non-agricultural occupations and the seasonal and fluctuating nature of these occupations.

Unorganised Labour in Agriculture : In contrast to contrast labour market the most striking characteristic of the daily rated market for farm work is its essential impersonal nature. Employers employ anyone capable of work regardless of caste or other socio-economic relationships. Similarly workers are willing to work for any employer. Workers work for a large number of employers in the course of the year (i.e.) the daily rated market gives everyone a chance to participate on nearly equal terms. Stemming from the impersonality of relationships a daily rated worker cannot under any circumstance get a loan or an advance from an employer on the basis of a promise that he will work for him later. Without collateral, no loan is possible. Tenants and family members do not provide labour on a preferential basis in the landlord's farm. With the exception of harvesting, agricultural tasks are sex specific. There are some regional variations in the sexual division of labour. Attempts by farmers to collude to fix wages are common. But delays in agricultural operations by labourers make such collusions unsuccessful.

Concentration of Women : With all the difficulties in estimation, the number of women in the unorganised sector is many times more than that in the organised sector. They are pushed invariably into the many occupations in this sector because of their helpless dependence caused by lack of employment opportunities, limited skills, illiteracy and restricted mobility. The occupation of women in most cases and particularly in the rural set up is linked to that of her husband or father.

The unorganised sector is not governed by Minimum Wages Act, 1948, Factories Act, 1948, Contract Labour (Regulation and Abolition) Act, 1970, etc. Hence it offers no guarantee of minimum wages, or security of tenure, or gratuity, or pension or paid leave. The employer-employee relationship is always tilted in favour of the former. Bulk of work force in rural and tribal areas, and mainly the lower income groups in the urban areas form the unorganised sector. Taking advantage of the loopholes in the several acts the employers manage to be in the unorganised sector, whatever, be the occupational category. The unorganised sector comprises two parts viz.

(i) the pseudo unorganised sector and

(ii) the unorganised sector proper. With a tightening of

governmental control over enterprises and improved business ethics more and more occupations, could come under the organised sector.

Apart from collection of fuel, fodder and water for the household, which work happens to be the lot of most of the Indian women, they have to earn for household expenditure. In many households what little is earned by men is spent on drinking and smoking. Artifacts of modern living are making their headway into poor families as well. For millions of women, selling of firewood earns them a livelihood. In terms of the volume of firewood consumed in the urban areas, it is estimated that at least two to three million people must be doing head loading. Firewood trade is the largest employer in the commercial energy sector of the country. Landlessness and unemployment have driven many more into this trade. The head loaders are mostly women. Despite the back-breaking work and very little earning, this work is generally available round the year. Even this opening for women employment is under threat what with the ruthless deforestation and destruction of environment which more than affecting the quality of life, pose the question of survival.

Shifting of Enterprises : The case histories of many enterprises show shifts from organised to unorganised sector with adverse effects on remuneration and working conditions of employees. Coir industry, Cashew industry, Bidi industry, Brick industry etc. have enormous market potential and the first two are important foreign exchange earners. Garment making is a modern development in urban centres. Construction industry is an area with enormous potential for employment. Innumerable such enterprises are mostly in the unorganised sector. Whenever and wherever the workers' movement is effective and strong, employers make the immediate shift to the unorganised sector by breaking the scale of operation.

The coir industry of Kerala produces 95% of total output employing 5 lakh women. 80% of the coir factories is in the private sector and 20% in the cooperative sector. All anomalies of the unorganised sector are present in these industries. The cashew industry of Kerala is a foreign exchange earner. But the big factories are closed to avoid unionisation and units are all moved into the employer's homes. 90% of the entire labour force in this industry is made up of women. This industry thrives on the cheap female labour force which is' exploited despite a fair level of union strength. Bidi industry employs considerable number of women workers in Kerala, Tamil Nadu, Andhra Pradesh, Madhya Pradesh, Maharashtra and West Bengal. Through these occupations women contribute nearly 40% of the family income.

Casual employment and contractual construction work fall within the organised sector of the economy. Several labour security acts are technically enforceable. Yet, the statutes are thrown to the winds and women get a raw deal with lower and differential payments. In the urban areas women are concentrated in unorganised sector of which quite a few occupations are literacy level based. Nearly 75% of all urban working women are in about 19 occupations in the non-modern sector. Lower middle class and poor income group women predominate in this sector. Several surveys in urban centres show that between 30% and 40% of women of these groups are in the unorganised sector about 25% of those women workers are domestic servants. We need a human needs" approach to solve their dependency.

It is surprising but true that employed women in organised sector, specially in urban areas, pay lip sympathy to the poor domestic servants, but seem to have done nothing to 'organise' them into trade unions, though almost a century back Dr. Annie Besant started in England a movement to unite them. Women earners in organised sector can be the willing exploiters of women in unorganised sector. It is an old story of cruelty of men to fellowmen, except that what injustice men perpetuated then, women do now.

Generally speaking women's labour force participation is by and large random, casual, low paid and highly unorganised. Let alone the deficiencies and anomalies of employment in the unorganised sector, these have their impact on organised employment as well. Random female employment destabilises the organised sector and depresses wage rate throughout the economy to a considerable extent.

The poor working class women do a wide variety of traditional and new kinds of jobs. These employment avenues are likely to be significant enough to "disturb the equilibrium of the job market and wage structure. The Commission on Self-Employed Women in its Report submitted in 1988, reiterated the "poor occupational diversifications" of female labour force, the high incidence of canalisation, erratic and intermittent availability of work to sum up the multiplicity of activities that confront the women in India with multiple status. An overwhelming 93% of women in the total female population are engaged in the unorganised sector as self employed, wage earners, non-wage or casual labourers. The Commission, the first of its kind, in an indepth in critical area of female self employment situation in the informal sector made a strong case for reconsidering priorities in employment policy and emphasized the need for coordinating formal and informal sectors of employment.

Agricultural Women

Systematic research on employment trends of rural agricultural labourers commenced from the 1950's onwards with the Agricultural Labour Enquiry. Earlier studies by a few individual researchers have limited approach and coverage." The three all India surveys of agricultural labour and certain rounds of the National Sample Survey throw valuable light on the conditions of agricultural labourers. Village and area studies undertaken by the Agro-Economic Research Centres provide material for inter-temporal studies for certain regions.

The Agricultural Labour Enquiry of 1950-51 was the largest socio-economic enquiry of its kind in India and South-East Asia. Following Enquiries in 1956-57 and 1964-65 assessed the changes in conditions of agricultural labour since the fifties. Differences in definition, concepts, coverage and methodology used in those enquiries have restricted the usage of their results. To improve the comparability of the enquiries several methods were suggested by C.H. Shah and others who established that the conditions of agricultural labourers were not as gloomy as they were presented in the reports.

In the measurement of working population two alternative methods are made use of, viz. 'gainful worker' approach and the 'labour force' approach. In the former, the 'activity status' is determined by the gainful employment of the person. But the period of employment is not made specific. The Census and N.S.S. upto 5th round adopted this method. Labour force includes all persons in the age group 15-58 employed or unemployed during the reference period. Further the concept of worker's 'usual status' or 'current status' is used to classify employed and unemployed. The dominant pattern of activity of the worker over a long period determines the usual status whereas the activity during a short reference period such as a day or week determines the current status.

The first agricultural labour enquiry has over-estimated employment, and the second enquiry gave a picture in the reverse, viz. underestimation of employment and over estimation of unemployment. Between the two Enquiries (1950-1956) employment of female labourers showed a market uptrend. Women labourers were mostly in casual agricultural work like weeding, transplanting and harvesting. Despite the fact that many comprehensive studies have been undertaken in the past two decades, there is no systematic effort to present comparable data for long term analysis. Particularly ignorance about every aspect of women employment is appalling and conspicuous.

Women Cultivators

The work performance of women in rural areas shows that the work they do on the farm and in their household contributes at least half if not more to the economic development of the country. The largest number of women workers is engaged in farming operations as cultivators and agricultural labourers. They account for 80% of women workers and constitute 87% of the female work force in rural areas (1971 census). Within the two types of agricultural employment, viz., cultivators and agricultural labourers, there is a general pattern of downward movement in the agricultural labourer category. There is upward mobility only for a very small number caused by improved productivity. But the downtrend is quite visible apparently caused by rising land values and declining ownership, increasing pressure of growing families on small holdings, indebtedness leading to loss of land etc.

There has been a sharp decline in women cultivators from 18.3 million in 1951 to 9.2 million in 1971. Women agricultural labourers have increased from 12.6 million in 1951 to 15.7 million in 1971 and to 28.83 in 1991 amounting to a shift from one third to one half of the total women force." This does not indicate increasing opportunities for women. Between 1961 and 1971 the decline is marked in spite of the benefit of the first two five year plans with their thrust on agricultural development. There has not been a change in employment pattern of women even at the turn of the 1990s. Nearly 45% of the total women workers are agricultural labourers and non agricultural occupations provide employment to 20% of the female work force.

This growing concentration of women as wage earners as against independent self employed cultivators is characterised as female proletarianisation. Rural women employment thus has the twin problems of marginalisation and proletarianisation. As long as women remain illiterate and ignorant severe problems arising from such consequences are inevitable.

The occupational mobility that was available in the rural sector in India became limited with the decline of village and cottage industries. Women have become more vulnerable than ever before when the husband or head of the family is reduced to the status of an agricultural labourer working on other's land. Modernisation of agriculture has also displaced women more than men from their traditional jobs. With unemployment as the only alternative more and more women have become agricultural labourers.

In his study on *'Women in the Working Force in India'*, D.R. Gadgil puts the maximum number of working days in the year for male workers as about 186 days in lands with assured water supply and only 112 days in the year in the dry zone, and the maximum number of working days for women as 180 days in the wet zone and 85 days in the dry zone. Thus, 29m female agricultural labourers and 46m male agricultural labourers are in fact working for less than half the year as per census figure of 1991. Shakuntala Mehra has made an impressive attempt to estimate surplus labour in Indian agriculture in 1966 based on the Sen model.

Assuming the supply curve for labour to be flat, she calculated how many could be withdrawn from Indian agriculture without affecting total output. Her estimates were in line with the other estimates in considering female-male labour together as farm labour (family labour). A similar exercise is called for at present to focus on the policy imperatives for employment of women. Due consideration of the time pattern of the labour inputs is necessary for better results than taking merely the number of days per year per person.

In areas under paddy cultivation, agricultural system continues to be heavily dependent on female labour. Even in wheat growing areas with fewer jobs for female labourers, there is a substantial proportion of women workers. In south India paddy cultivation is the main activity. With male rural-urban migration, females remain behind in villages as agents of their husbands and help not only in male occupational mobility but also provide continuity in the agricultural process.

Besides support to farming in rural areas, women work on plantations, in quarries, and on public works mostly as unskilled labour. Some work in cottage industries in their own houses or outside. Women workers in plantations have better working conditions. In tea plantations women form half the total workers. Coffee plantations and Rubber plantations employ women to the extent of 44% and 35% respectively. All plantation workers are governed by the Plantation Labour Act of 1951 which regulates the working conditions and provides certain facilities to the workers. Unlike in other industries, in plantation industries there is very little difference between wages for men and women.

Agricultural Occupations : Non-agricultural workers are found partly in the rural areas and mainly in the urban areas and cities. Of the total number of 57 million non-workers grouped together under the head 'other workers' in the 1971 Census, only 9 million or under 16% are women. This number has gradually increased to 11.42m in 1991. The ratio of employment of women to men is lower in the categories of cultivators and agricultural workers but higher in that of agricultural workers and household industry workers. In other workers' category, male-female employment difference is the largest. Among educated women the proportion of women to men is even lower still. In jobs which require higher education there are less than 10% women in public and private sectors.

No authentic information is available on this category of 'other workers' except that work in most enterprises other than large and small scale industries fall under non-agricultural occupations. It includes employment in all unregulated industries and services, traditional cottage industries, household and village industries, and unregulated services like manual work of all kinds to petty trade and vending. Lack of organisation and failure of public regulatory control over the employers have led to undermining of workers' interest and exploitation in these areas. Several attempts were made by the government to regulate working conditions in this sector through the Contract Labour (Conditions of Employment) Act, 1966, and the various state Acts to regulate conditions of employment in shops and commercial establishments. Without strong labour organisations and vigilant enforcement machinery the statutes are futile.

Organised Sector : Organised sector includes all public sector establishments and non-agricultural private sector establishments employing ten or more persons. Though total employment is increasing steadily in all industries, employment of women in this sector has shown a decline. Between 1951 and 1971, the rate of women employment in organised sector decreased from 11.43% to 9.1% which is a decline of 21.7%. In mining, the decrease is very sharp from 21.1% to 11.9% for the same period, i.e., a decline of 47.4%. In coal mines particularly women employment is reduced to almost nothing from 55,000 to 5,000 persons. In all mining industries the decline was the sharpest. Between 1952 and 1962 the rate of women employment declined from 14.8% to 8.9%, in iron ore mines from 35.6% to 26.7% in mica mines, from 12.1% to 8.4% and in manganese mines from 42.4% to 39.9%. One has to be cautious in reading these falling percentages. When the health, and safety conditions preclude massive entry of women in these hazardous mining activities, women's health and safety are protected by legislation. Since 1962 the decline has been arrested and the trend reversed.

The Industry : After rationalisation of textile industry, the women workers were retrenched on the ground that very few women could receive training under the Craftsman Training

Scheme. While 121,879 men are trained, the women who underwent such training by 1971, were 1018. Systematic retrenchment in the textile industry has thrown out women to the extent of reducing their proportion from 9.2% in 1952 to 5.8% in 1962. In the fifties and sixties women was deprived from industrial employment.

This downtrend is attributed mainly to the adverse effects of protective laws for women labourers, and structural changes in the economy resulting from modernisation and rationalisation of production methods. The Report of the National Committee on the Status of women (1975), however, pointed out that the statutory provision of maternity benefits and welfare facilities like creches and separate sanitary conveniences constitute a negligible expenditure to the establishments.

Most industries do not implement the policy of equal wages by some escapist method or the other. The bulk of women employment was in textile and jute industries and mines. These have closed their doors to women employees with their switching over to capital intensive technology. Unlike, men, women workers are not given job-training. Low literacy level, ignorance and lack of union support have all contributed to the fullest displacement of women from these enterprises.

Services and Professions : A significant trend in women's occupational pattern since Independence is the increasing entry of women workers into non-traditional services and professions. Non-discrimination and equality of opportunity arising from women's education, changing social values regarding paid employment among urban middle class and the rapid expansion of tertiary sector as a direct consequence of economic development, have produced opportunities for urban literate women to take employment in considerable numbers.

The number of women in the public sector in the category of professional, technical and related occupations has been continuously increasing since 1960. Women administrators, executives and managerial workers have also increased from 10,000 in 1960 to 12,000 in 1966. There is a phenomenal growth in the category of clerical and related workers whose numbers have registered an increase from 37,000 in 1960 to 79,000 in 1968. The number in transport, storage, sports, recreation etc. also record a steady progress, from 5,000 to 13,000 for the same period. Under this category most of the women are in the lower rungs as maids, cooks, housekeepers, cleaners and sweepers. Women employment in private sector for all the above categories shows a steady increase. Many new industries have sprung up in recent years offering increased opportunities for women employment in the management cadre, in advertising, market research, hotel management and cottage industries with export prospects. Two perceptible trends in the employment scene of women in recent years are

(i) concentration of women in the professions of teaching and medicine which could well be called the traditional organized sector of occupation for women and

(ii) polarization of women in the organised sector into low paid low prestige jobs in the secretarial and clerical services.

Sex Discrimination : Notwithstanding the spectacular increase in opportunities in a few professions, the Indian pattern of occupational distribution of educated women is the same as the pattern in many other countries of east and west. The segregation of sex is so universal that the office structure itself is viewed as the extension of the natural situation of the household viz., men in authority and women in subordinate position, reflecting their place in society as a whole. Women whose educational levels are mostly skewed at the lower levels of literacy are given the "dead-end-jobs" where wages do not rise as much as in clerical and typing categories of office work. Women prove to be good workers at economical wages of nearly one half or two thirds of the wages paid to men.

The Causes : The reasons for sex discrimination are historical, sociological, and economic. Attitudes of men and women are equally significant and important in influencing sex discrimination. As employers and heads of households men's attitude is mostly responsible for preventing women from seeking employment by treating that as a social taboo, or as a competing factor in the labour market with adverse consequences on the wage structure, displacement of male workers, and destruction of family life. In scientific, executive and on job-training work there is hesitancy about encouraging women.

Women and Career

Discontinuity of women employment is a barrier to career development. With the primary commitment to household responsibility, women themselves seek such employments that are neither 'upward moving nor success oriented. Locationwise they do not prefer jobs far away from their residence. Despite talents and potential for higher pursuits, women's careers are universally of 'limited ambition'. However, when employment is skill-based and education-oriented, sex discrimination in the form of lower wages is ruled out except in very marginal cases. Equality of wages and opportunity to work increases with training and sophistication. But such cases are in the small minority of educated employment which is insignificant in volume compared to that in the unorganised and rural employment.

In agriculture and many other occupations in the unorganised sector, women get lower wages than men, the difference ranging from 10% to 60%. This is in spite of the fact that in certain types of work like transplanting, cutting, harvesting etc. in agriculture and in many processes of food industry, garment making and the like women workers are considered to be more skilful than men.

The sad state of affairs is that both in rural and urban employment, market forces are afoot to push women to a marginal employment status. If the unavoidable decline of female work from traditional activities is compensated by employment of women in modern production activities, there is no room for discrimination and dissatisfaction and there will be positive contribution to the national income. But as fast as technology liberates women from hard chores of traditional lives, so fast it displaces them from the employment market as well.

It is true that two thirds of all work in the world is performed by women. Yet, the classical role definition of women is 'non-working housewives'. This itself serves as the necessary precondition for the unlimited exploitation of their labour in the household and in the informal sector. With the mystification of non-working housewife-women concept, the unorganised sector is atomised to get the benefit of discrimination. The age long conviction that it is the prerogative of men to be the bread winners has obscured women's productive work even within the household as the crucial agent in development process.

Universal Pattern : As regards work participation by women there emerges a universal pattern with certain characteristics which are more or less the same in all the developing countries. The participation rates everywhere is less than 30% of the total labour force. Women are predominantly in the lowest occupations. They are paid comparatively lower than the male workers. In the women labour force, married women form a major part. Women employment is discontinuous. Except in skill and education based occupations there is no equality of wages and everywhere the different attitudes of men and women together determine the work characteristics of women's occupations. In the service and professional sectors, women's participation rate is high in western countries. This is mainly due to certain non-significant occupations being kept exclusively for women (e.g.) waitresses, secretaries, receptionists, typists, etc. When it comes to more challenging avocations, be it a lawyer or engineer, a scientist or administrator, the participation and performance of Indian women are no less than in other countries.

International comparisons of women employment and their occupational pattern are mostly based on data at aggregative levels. Whatever differences could be discerned they arise form broad non-economic factors like differences in education levels, cultural patterns, family ties and welfare facilities. With an economy like India, interstate differences have to be explained at less aggregative level. Leela Gulati has made an attempt to identify some relationship between economic and demographic factors such as per capita income, cropping pattern, literacy levels, male work participation rates, proportion of scheduled castes and tribes and ratio of female work participation. She could not arrive at any strong conclusion that the various factors mentioned above explained inter-stale differences in participation rates. Inter-state comparison themselves appear to be loo aggregative. The need for a more disaggregated approach of studies at district and taluk levels should be taken note of.

In inter-country studies, a more appropriate approach would be in terms of a sector-wise examination of women employment and occupations. Such an analysis indicates the major causative factors affecting women employment and their occupational pattern as stemming from structural changes within the economy as a whole from the intensification of socio-economic inequalities. Such structural changes arise when economy changes from a traditional to a modern market economy, from laissez faire to deliberate planned development, from unorganised to organised production, from unregulated to regulated relations of production or from labour to capital, intensive technology.

Women are in a vulnerable group with fewer opportunities and are affected more adversely than men when transformation of one kind or other occurs. Whether their position is improved or aggravated further, depends upon the level and extent of social and economic infrastructure made available and utilised by them. The National Committee on Status of Women has rightly stressed on the imperative need to provide education, vocational and technical training facilities and to devise specific measures to adjust women employment to their special needs as housewives and working mothers.

Choice of Job

The limits to the freedom of choice of employment varies essentially from woman to woman. If some broad generalisation could be arrived at in the Indian context, women in different income groups and correspondingly women from different social and communal groups react differently to employment stimuli. Lower strata women who invariably are in the low income groups have no choice between employment and leisure. Pure economic reasons override any other social restrictions. Sustenance and survival of the families necessitate men and women and quite often children to grab any opportunity to work, however, low paid it is. Large numbers of school dropouts in India arise from the phenomenon of employment of children to a large extent. Middle class women who are many shades better than the low income category, have no serious compulsion to work if they choose not to. But the household work is entirely theirs and if they do choose to work, provided jobs are available, it is for the economic relief they get from additional income for a better living. Freedom of choice to work is meaningful only in the case of high income upper class women.

They are free to take up work and if they do, they are motivated by job satisfaction, self-protection, prestige, and to a certain extent, by service to society. The middle and upper class women are invariably educated women at various levels and compete effectively with equally educated men in the employment market. For the women in the lower income groups, employment opportunities are limited and narrow and educational qualifications (which are mostly not there) become quite redundant. A maximum percentage of working women are with less than primary education and the participation rate decreases as the educational level of women increases. There are a number of case studies to support this generalisation.

Training and Vocationalisation : It is normally held that women workers are victims of the process of economic development, industrialisation, modernisation and technology. Instead of liberating them from drudgery of work, it has in fact displaced women from employment. Increasing unemployment of women is attributed in general to structural changes in the economy. But these contentions are open to certain modifications. There is a general overview of female unemployment. Certain essential rural and urban sectors employ women in large numbers. When traditional jobs are lost, women have to seek alternative channels elsewhere. A farm labourer when migrating to an urban centre takes up any job and adjusts to working environment. Movement into newer spheres is gradual. Acquiring skills takes time.

But to infer that women are losers in the developmental programme does not give a full image of Indian working women today. From the point of view of economies in production, women do provide the limitless quantum of cheap labour essential for both national and individual economics. Whether it is entirely exploitative, is quite another question.

Women's role in economic development has to be strengthened and the hitherto wasted women power should be channelised for better results. An employment strategy for women cannot but be rural in its approach. Little can be expected of urban women or urban educated women as "agents of change" in rural areas. Rural women are to be trained to work in the various agro-based rural industries. They need not be brought out of their rural setting to be trained in city-style institutions. But the institutions of training have to be taken to their rural environs. Institutions of professional and vocational training are remote from the grass roots of Indian womanhood, and therefore, they do not produce the potential change agents. Urban trained workers can hardly show preference or willingness for village life. Then communication is inhibited. Rural women when properly trained and guided, could improve their own environment from within.

Male - Female Differences : Adam Smith had the firm conviction that labour is the sinews of the Wealth of Nations. An economy revolves around people and they contribute to the economy. The differential contribution of men and women is a known fact. But the treatment of all women as unproductive economic agents is raising doubts and a good number of studies have addressed themselves to this specific issue of differences in their economic contribution.

There is a view that physical differences between men and women determine the psychological difference of intellect and temperament that largely account for the differentiation in social roles. Women's intellect is held inferior to that of men. A Tamil proverb is 'Women is wise after the event' and with equal emphasis there is another saying that everything can be done or undone by women (the maker and unmaker is woman). And so they proceed to argue that biological elements acquire importance only when they are socially recognised and established and that there are in fact great variations between societies and historical periods.

But these differences vanish in modern times. Moreover, the existence of innate psychological differences between men and women is not well established." On the other hand, these differences are explained away as arising from social and cultural influences and not biological inheritances. The relative importance of nature is made good by nurture. All the same, the physical differences between men and women need not lead to economic and social inequality. The inequality between sexes needs analysis in the "broad context of economic inequality arising out of differences in access to property, to work, to skill formation and education".

Participation in Economy

Many studies on this theme reveal that participation in economic activities does not necessarily enhance the social status of women. Regardless of the economic systems or the form of economic production, the social forces, norms and mores affect the status of women. Employment of women does not necessarily lead to economic independence or control over earnings. What exactly determines the male-female differences in the work field is yet to be ascertained and most studies have not helped in understanding the processes. And economic explanations are but partial. This, however, should not make one shy away from making an attempt at highlighting the male-female work contribution to throw light on the known as well as unknown and often undermined facts about the economics of female labour. For a proper assessment it is not necessary to hold on to any "ideology vital enough to sort out the muddle." Many writers, particularly of the women activist section, even claim that neutrality is a limitation to such exercises. They demand that the entire spectrum of women be studied in relation to sources of power. It is also noted with equal justification that women are just as capable of action as agents of an exploitative power machinery as their male counterparts.

Excellent Women

Participation or activity rate is the proportion of a whole

number in the age or sex group. The ratio of females of certain age group, say, 15-55, who work to the total number of women in that age group is called the participation rate. In certain age groups the labour a participation rate is limited. In modern urban centres men and women, below the age group of 20 are fewer than those in the age group 20 and above. In the former age group both girls and boys are either students or too young to work. As the age group reaches higher the activity rate increases. Similarly, the age group 60 and above also has fewer workers what with retirement, disability and old age.

Women form a large contingent (nearly 50%) of persons of working age. But in the labour force, they do not reflect this strength. There has occurred gradual changes in the latter half of the nineteenth century and the second World War has changed this pattern considerably with more and more women opting for paid employment outside home due to changes in the marriage age and small family norms. Before the marriageable age there is a peak in women employment and in recent times there is a significant second peak between the age group 30-40 after which the decline in women's work participation is very steep. Averaging these participation rates, there results an overall proportion of the gainfully occupied among women working age group viz. 15-55 which is typically in the region of two thirds of the total women labour force.

Equal Pay for Equal Work : With such a volume of women workers, why does their career power fall below that of male workers? Many reasons may be attributed to this. They are paid less because many jobs are demarcated as male and female tasks and the latter are supposed to be less strenuous and less important among the processes of work. Employers deli gently sustain this demarcation to take advantage of cheap labour. Equally valid is the preference of females to join certain occupations, which unintentionally reinforce the cheapness of such labour.

A fundamental principle in Labour Economics and also in Indian Constitutional theory is equal pay for equal work, irrespective of sex. This is given statutory support all over the world. All the same, whenever and wherever possible, a situation of de facto unequal pay is maintained by classifying particular tasks as female tasks and placing them at a lower wage category than male tasks which require a similar degree of qualification or strain. The vested interest of employers and the deep-rooted prejudice of the employees tend to reinforce each other and there is little resistance to the sharp distinction between male and female labour. The sex of the employer makes no difference in the vested interests, while the prejudices against female workers are reinforced by the male household members. Particularly, this practice is widespread in the third world economics where the family bondage and hierarchy have not been disturbed by the modernising influence of the twentieth century. There are earnings differentials for equal work. The male and female earnings vary between 40% to 80% of the male earning for the same work.

Rates for Males and Females : The male and female labour force rate (LFR) has undergone marked changes in the last sixty years bringing to light the sharp contrast between the male and female activity differences. The 1961 Census reported a labour force of 190.0m. The female labour force rate for all ages was 28.02 in all areas and 31.05 and 11.25 respectively for rural and urban areas. The respective male labour force rates were 57.69, 18.62 and 54.16 respectively.

The LFR trends for men show an upward increase whereas for the females there are significant gaps and disparities. There is a fall in the total rates between 1971 and 1981 in all areas except that in rural areas. In the case of females LFR has increased from 12.13 in 1971 to 14.44 in 1981 excluding the marginal workers and to 22.69 in 1991. Ambannawar has made certain demographic projections. With the 1981 Census Report and provisional results of the 1991 Census Report available now we find that most of his assumptions as stated below are valid and not off the mark.

(i) The population is likely to grow at a medium rate from 547 million in 1971 to 682 million in 1981 to 1002 million in 2001.

(ii) Urban population would reach 291 million in 2001 i.e. will change from present 20% of the total population to nearly 30%.

(iii) LFR in the age group 10-14 will decline to zero by 2001 with progress in education.

(iv) Similarly, in the age group 15-19, LFR will decline by 50% in rural areas and 75% in urban areas and 60% for all by 2011 owing to expansion in education.

(v) LFR for females in the age group 15-19 will remain constant since a large population of girls in this group do not participate in schooling or economic activity.

(vi) In the age group 20-24, LFR will decline by 10% for males due to urbanisation and for females there would be no change and

(vii) LFR between 25-59 will remain the same but will decline in the age group of 60+. Based on the above assumptions the growth of labour in India is estimated as follows by Ambannavar. The estimated projection for 1990 and 2001 are meaningful.

Causes for Differential Labour Force Rates : The demographic causes for the differential LFR for males and females are broadly classified as arising from age structure of the population, urbanisation and education. Between 1921 and 1961 the male LFR has changed by 50% due to changes in age structure and 12% due to increased urbanisation. These are 37% and 7% respectively for females. Education has been and will be the main factor influencing such a change.

The factors that influence LFR among women are complex

and less understood. Ambannavar surmised that these tend to fall in the initial stages of development. However, the recent Censuses have a different tale to tell altogether and whatever increase we notice in female LFR it is not development oriented. Female work participation rate varies considerably among different age groups. Though there are wide differences between male and female work participation rates the age-wise skewness appears to be the same for both sexes. There has been a sharp inversion in the rural areas between 1971 to 1981. The urban female work participation is largest among the age group of 30-50 whereas in the rural areas participation rate is more or less equal in all age groups between 15 to 60. This is mainly because of the lack of educational facilities in rural areas.

A study on female LFR has to make an examination of the problem in an age-wise disaggregation of the total female labour force to distinguish between actual workers, potential workers and movement of one age group into another in the time spectrum. The highly aggregated data which have been collected without specific focus on female employment seriously limit the scope of any study on women. Information on the unorganised sector is nil and that on the organised sector as subdivided into public and private sectors it is seldom that data reflect women's contribution in these fields.

Employment and Education : Providing employment in an economic set up depends upon the capacity of production process to generate new jobs. Every individual enters the working age group with or without education. Based upon such educational attainments or specific training qualifications the prospects of the employment market differ for the individuals. A systematized educational system keeps the young out of the labour market. Non-schooling pushes this age group into the labour market. There is no gainsaying the fact that it is the level of literacy and the progress of education that dictate to a large extent the performance of the labour market in the past, present and future.

The linkage between employment and education is such that demands are made by each on the other. Economics of manpower requirements demands education, skill formation and training for employment purposes and the output of the education system viz. the school leavers at all levels and those with higher education demand employment and await employment opportunities. When such opportunities are fewer this demand is not only intensified into unemployment problem but is also a challenge to the educational system. In short, social, economic and demographic factors are so closely inter-related, that change in one or more, invariably involves all of them. The emphasis on human resource development cannot be over-stressed.

While the employment- education linkage appears to be more significant for males than females in all the developing countries. There is a large gap between male and female literacy levels in India and other developing countries. This is the result of the dogmatic view that women are not likely to be breadwinners of the family. Their socio-economic status does not depend upon their professional occupations or earning capacity and women's careers are presumably only of shorter duration.

All those assumptions are being disproved and there are abundant data in all countries to prove that there exists a strong positive correlation between the educational level and the employment rate of women. The educational attainments of women above the secondary education level are more or less the same in most countries of the world. Higher education being at the apex of the educational pyramid, nowhere it has been more than 50% of the total enrolled except Israel.

In higher education for women, Israel ranks first of all the countries of the world with 51% women among all students in higher education and the second country USA is far behind with 40%. India ranks the last with only one woman for every five men in higher education. Within two decades there were large changes in the relative position of the countries of the world, India still limping behind.

Women's labour force is sharply divided into (i) uneducated and illiterate women and (ii) educated women workers. The mobility from the former to the latter is possible only through attaining certain educational levels. There is, therefore, a division into blue colour and white collar women, and apart from the common problems of working conditions, there are distinct work characteristics and handicaps for each group.

The educated women has broad intellectual horizons with a stable and mature personality and develops "a deep and lasting commitment to many experiences at many levels". She can seek solutions to problems and has a "sense of personal obligation to contribute something to society". For the rare privilege of the education, she has had, she should accept herself as an active participant in nation building and not rest contended as an onlooker. Those women have a very special responsibility over the unskilled, uneducated and disadvantage in Indian society.

This is an ideal picture of an educated women. Whether they live up to these expectations is an embarrassing question. For a stable nature, personality accomplishment and capacity to solve problems within their own orbit, less literate are not different from their educated sisters. The society, family and environment are their teachers and if only many of the so-called illiterate women have had the privilege of even a short course of education they would beat hallow most of the educated and sophisticated women. Such indeed is the impression we get of a few who with a helping hand have made great impact.

Education of Women

The literacy level of Indian women is very low and it differs between regions. Since Independence, there has been considerable progress in education and particular attention is given to women's education. From a literacy rate of 8% in 1950, it increased in the seventies to 19% and even this low level is twice what it was nearly thirty years ago in 1920's.

The Educational Survey of 1954-55 sounded a cheerful note. The wide and disquieting disparity in the literacy levels between men and women was being gradually narrowed down. Still the male female literacy ratio stood at 5:1. Indian women are 32 years behind the literacy level of Indian men. The decade 1951-1961 registered the highest growth of 12.3% in school enrolment and the enrolment in IX - XI was the largest with 23.3%. In the succeeding two decades the growth has declined to 9.8% and 4.0% and the sharpest decline was in the enrolment in I - V classes. This implies that enrolment in primary school is reaching the maximum with less scope for more enrolment.

At the collegiate level the increase in enrolment appears to have made a considerable increase from 40,000 to 81,67,000 amounting an increase of 20 times. As a percentage of total students, however, women in higher education have registered only a small increase of 4.7% between 1950-51 and 1981-82.

The gap between social status is more or less synonymous with that between educational levels. The parental attitude which discriminated against daughter's education has changed to a great extent and the imperative need for raising women's literacy levels is well understood by all in the society, scholars, parents and the state. However, among the 330.59 m women population in India there are only 78.94 m women who can read and write. Just above one fifth. This number of illiterate women exceeds the entire population of many countries in the world. Those in higher education is about 2 million which is a bare 2.0% of the literate women, and those who reach the highest levels in education at the University level is about 0.8%

The literacy level in India has improved rather slowly to the level of 36% with 46.74% for males and 24.88% for females (1987). The massive literacy programmes are still to make an impact in Indian society. There are interstate variations in literacy levels and Tamil Nadu ranks among the top three States in literacy rate Kerala 69.17%, Maharashtra 47.3% and Tamil Nadu 45.78%. In women's literacy rate the general performance is still worse; for every literate woman (i.e. who knows to read and write) there are three illiterates.

Kerala tops in the literacy rate for women as well with 64.48% followed by Maharashtra 35.08% and Punjab 34.14%. Tamil Nadu comes very closely behind with 34.12% literacy rate. Education is largely a State responsibility and Tamil Nadu has made vast strides in the provision of social infrastructure like education, health and allied services. In the States of Bihar and Rajasthan the literacy rates are very low with 13.58% and 11.32% respectively. General policy objective with regard to women's education requires determined efforts to raise the literacy level to at least the all India level of 36% and to keep pace with the male literacy level thereafter.

The inequality in the distribution of education among men and women is further accentuated when the rural urban disparities are added to this. While the rural-urban population ratio is 2:1, in Tamil Nadu the ratio of literacy level of rural urban population is 1:2. In the case of all India figures with 3.3:1 ratio for rural-urban population, there is more accentuated inverse relation in the literacy level for the same. There are glaring disparities in male female literacy levels both in rural and urban areas. The male-female literacy ratio is 2:1 in rural areas whereas in urban centres it is a little narrowed down to 1.3:1. These generalizations apart, there are certain districts in Tamil Nadu with very low levels of literacy compared to other districts. Dharmapuri is the lowest with 15.48% and other equally backward districts are Pudukottai (19.34%) and South Arcot (19.12%).

All said and done about education, much of it appears to have no specific or unique application and orientation in employment, for want of data a comparison with the 1981 figures is not possible. But except for marginal changes, we do not except a major impact of education on volume and structure of employment in India. As we move up the educational ladder, in both urban and rural areas the employment rate rises. A rise in education above a certain level reduces the incidence of unemployment.

The lower category of literates are less employable compared to the higher level i.e. the higher level educated push out the lower level educated. But the same process does not work as we move further down the educational levels. The educated are not willing to accept jobs meant for illiterates or low level of educated. As in the two Censuses of 1961 and 1971, we there is an uptrend of unemployment at all levels in 1981 Census as well. Unemployment among the educated is more than the unemployment of the illiterate in both urban and rural areas. Poverty and necessity forces the poor and illiterate among them to accept low paid and part-time jobs. The apparent result of this analysis is that education has not equipped women for the labour market.

With regard to the output level of educations system, the challenges to India are two fold. There is imminent need to raise the level as well as standards of education implying the quantity -quality aspects of this most essential public good. Special efforts are already afoot to give a socially relevant and employment oriented educational system in India wherein technical and vocational lines require a higher priority than the present system with the result that the majority of young people who leave the educational system have no specific occupational qualification. Though this is perceived in developed countries as well, in India it is much more pronounced and perpetuated.

It does not require empirical proof to establish the fact that unemployment is highest among the least qualified and unskilled youth whether literate or illiterate. An extension of the period of education to include job orientation and training will relieve the employment market from the large inflows into it and the turn out of the educational system will be much more employable than at present. The additional costs of extended education vis-a-vis the individual and social costs of maintaining unemployed youth will be much lower and if not considerable. The long-run impact of this policy is bound to be to the advantage of the society and economy.

Both for efficiency in the allocation of resources and for balanced economic development, educational policy making should be geared to the employment objectives. Employment opportunity in an economy is largely a question of the capacity of the production system to generate new jobs. Education system has to move in consonance with the economic manpower policies to succeed in the provision of fuller employment. The malady that is gnawing the educational system is the fact that the large vulnerable sections of unemployed youth have 'experience' difficulties and the blame is not only on the existing pattern of education and training but as well on employment recruitment and utilisation of skills.

In the present pattern of utilisation, there is continued existence of unskilled jobs on the one hand and the demand for skilled and highly skilled manpower on the other, in many activities. The picture of the overall pattern of employment by educational level is not clear. Most new employment opportunities in India are in the secondary and tertiary sectors. Though the over-riding factor in the allocation of outlay in the various sectors, a coordinated effort is called for to knit the production structure and educational system through manpower planning which has to be dynamic enough to adjust to the changing times. Our objective is the transition from education to working life with the lowest additional training costs and the full utilisation of education and training facilities.

Women workforce dictated by rigid social values, is smaller than that of the male labour force and special attention is required. Employment for women is a socio-economic objective. The education that gives a social status to women should complement the employ ability to confer an economic status. With growing unemployment, female workers are the worst sufferers. The meagre improvement in literacy has not resulted in job skills and competence of women to compete in the labour market. Women's education should be adapted to skill orientation largely for rural employment in the non-traditional sectors. It is even doubtful whether employ ability is a criterion for the status of women. 80% of the rural working women are employed as main or marginal workers and yet their status is indeterminate.

On Growth Path

Several contributory factors have helped to give an impetus to women's education in India. They are

(i) the rise in the age of marriage for both sexes,

(ii) growing tendency among the educated young men who want to marry educated women so as to fit into their social life,

(iii) parents' increasing awareness to educate daughters to make them self-supporting, and

(iv) keen desire on the part of girls to be educated to have status, assurance and independence. The overall impact of all these is the stage wise and sex wise growth of school and college enrolment.

The increasing trend of women's education is a universal pattern and Indian performance is way behind that of the advanced countries and even some of the developing countries of the Third World. Without the foundation there cannot be a superstructure. Only one in ten who have enrolled in the I standard reach up to the XII standard." At the end of schooling in India there is 90% drop out rate. Thus very few could reach higher education levels. There were 7 million girls in high schools in 1981 while those in higher education were 8.17 lakhs. There is no significant relationship between school leavers and college entrants. In 1989-90 women in higher education were 12.51 lakhs constituting 31.7% of total enrolment. The educational pyramid for girls and women has very low gradients accounting for the small fraction of skilled women power in India.

The progress of women's education however, is quite encouraging in view of the past performance. Women illiterates still form the bulk of Indian women. There is a 20% increase in this category. Women with middle level education have increased two-fold between 1971 and 1981. Though a small number of women are in the higher education category when compared with the 1971 figure there is an increase of 300% in 1981. Though each level of education is a radical shift upwards, the shape of the educational pyramid has not changed considerably. This lack of balance is reflected in the distribution of women in various occupations. Those at the base of the pyramid enter into lowpaid low-status occupations and a good percentage of those at the top of the pyramid opt out of the labour market. Therefore, the composition of the labour force has very little linkage with the level of education.

Absence of the Occupational Application : Much of education in India has no specific application in employment. The output of education should not only rise steadily but its structural change should be in conformity with the manpower needs of the economy. In advanced countries, there is a rapid increase and change in the structure of the educational outflow with a very rapid increase in professional, technical and vocational training. Law, natural sciences and medicare together accounted for 13% of women students graduating in the US in 1960-61, 40% in Italy and 53% in France. In the erstwhile Soviet Union at a time well over 2/3 and later 1/2 of all medical students and 36% of engineers were women."Even in those countries it is felt that a reduction in the number of persons leaving the educational system without specific occupational qualification will be a long and difficult process." The need for improvement in curricula to facilitate entry into employment market is all the more important in the Indian context, and the New Education Policy, now well debated and contemplated, focuses on this gap between education and employment.

In the distribution of women enrolled in highest education in India, the lack of occupational orientation is evident and glaring. In the year 1981-82, 55.7% of all enrolled women in higher education were in Arts, 12.8% in Commerce, 20.2% in Science, 3.6% in Medicine and 0.72% in Engineering. In the late eighties there is a vast change in these figures. The higher women enrolment was in the faculty of Education (52.4) followed by Arts (43.2%) Science (32.6%), Medicine (31.7%), Commerce (20.5%) Others (42.3%). It is heartening to note that in the faculty of Engineering and Technology women enrolment as a percentage of total enrolment has increased from 3.8 in 1980-81 to 46 in 1988-89. But in absolute terms they number only 1.81 lakhs (men and women) only for the entire country". Dearth of facilities for vocational education and priority usually given to young men in vocational training leave very little for women to benefit from. Very few women get any vocational training at all.

There is a vicious circle developing in countries like India. Girls and women are presumed to need no special training. They are thought to be eligible only for those jobs which require little qualification and training. Hence, in many cases young women escape by keeping away from the labour market and do domestic chores. The result is the perpetuation of the traditional pattern of poor families - low educational status and low income. This vicious circle has to be broken and no single strategy is effective enough. An educational strategy with reformed curricula and training for employment, improvement and adjustment of the contents of education and training, extension of the period of education and training will be steps in the right direction to link education with employment in the economy.

If education is to have an impact on employment and economic development, it has to be integrated into rural development process.

Vocationalisation of rural schooling for efficient farming and teaching of fundamentals of hygiene and nutrition, basic accounting and simple organizational methods are to be included in school teaching. Particular emphasis in educational approach is necessary to utilise the unused and underused women power for reaping higher rewards for their labour.

Wage Differentials : Egalitarianism is acclaimed as universal value, and the constitutions of many countries have given statutory support to this principle. The International Labour Organization (ILO) has passed the Equal Pay Convention and equal rights legislative measures in various countries are aplenty. However, the principle of "equal pay for equal work" is very difficult to establish in many occupations. Professions which were traditionally taken up by women have a low pay structure and could only be improved by infiltration of men into those occupations like teaching, nursing and social work. But high occupations carry the same remuneration irrespective of sex. But these are much less within the reach of women than men. It should not be denied that most women's work is different in kind from men's, irrespective of the fact it is done by women. It is also true that where men and women do work of the same description, some disabilities are attributed to women employees viz. disinclination to do longer hours of work, and travel long distances for work.

These make them less preferred by the employers. From the supply side, women employment tends to be typically discontinuous and women themselves are reluctant to assume responsibility because of their family priorities. The newly emerging career pattern of women with ability to give nearly 30 years of continued service is a recent development which is yet to change the employers' attitude. Productivity differences cannot adequately account for the actual differences in male-female earnings gap.

By and large, customary attitudes and valuations and particularly the assumptions that women's productivity is lower in jobs, and women's contribution to the family income is only secondary, are the underlying reasons for the socially accepted practice of women being at a lower wage level than men. When the kind of jobs that men and women do are distinct and different, then the above said factors accentuate the differentials. A number of studies and discussions have been undertaken on this theme but there is hardly any agreement on the cause-effect relationship and identification of crucial differentiating variables and in the methodology and statistical techniques adopted for analysis.

The factors responsible for earnings differences between male and female workers can be brought broadly under four headings:

(i) the level of human capital accumulation,

(ii) productivity of the workers,

(iii) degree of control over resources, and

(iv) the prevalence of sex segregation. The first two lie within the supply and demand forces in the labour market the third pertains to the managerial structure of the firm whereas the fourth represents a social attitude, the rationality of which is an issue of debate. A brief account of studies relating to male female earnings gap is given to show that education is a very significant factor in equalizing the pay differences.

This view reflects the human capital approach adopted by

Donald Trieman and Heidi Hartman in 1981. Their survey of several studies reveals that differences in levels of education and training explain the variance from 0% to 44%. (Variance is the square of standard deviation which is a widely used measure of dispersion in statistical analysis.) This is quite a wide range and has to be carefully examined. Methodologically the individual studies differ from one another on many accounts viz. data used, inclusion of explanatory variables, statistical methods used and the conceptual differences with regard to the dependent variables. The highest variance estimation of 44% is obtained by Mary Corcoran and Gueg Duncan (1979) followed by 41% for Jacob Mincer and Solomon Polachck (1974). The above mentioned authors use a proxy for actual labour market experience and occupational training and a different proxy for experience. Ronald Oaxaco (1973) gets an estimate of 20%. Estimates of other studies range from 0 to 18%. It is evident that falling within a range of 0% to 44% none of those studies could explain even half of the earnings gap.

Focussing on work experience, training and educational achievements these studies follow a human capital approach to pay differentials. They confirm that human capital brings rewards for both men and women and difference in earnings are caused by differences in the quality of human capital accumulated (e.g.) years of schooling and experience.

Human Capital Theory : Earnings differences are also based upon the setting in which the human capital is employed. The influence of a dual market theory in explaining the difference is quite evident. Thomas N. Daymont and Paul J. Andrisoni have demonstrated that differences in preferences of tastes and the schooling and preparation for various types of work attained before labour market entry account for a substantial portion of the earnings gap between males and females. Based on a study of college graduates, they conclude that men and women prepare themselves differently for the world of work by choosing quite different fields of study in the college.

They emphatically point out that the elimination of discrimination would not lead to equality in earnings at least for the current entrants to college unless there are greater-similarities between men and women in their preferences and preparation for the labour market. Enrolment data on higher education show a universal trend in women's preference for teaching and nursing and only in very recent times increasing number of women show preference to non-traditional employment areas like business, law, computer science and engineering. It has to be stressed that women's current preferences and preparation for labour market result in part from a perception by them of the past labour market discrimination.

Productivity Differentials : There is a long held misconception that women and children are to be classified together in labour market analysis since their productivity is considerably low. The commonality between them is the low wage. The differential productivity of males and females is largely a question of the measure of productivity. The major part of labour put in by the male earns market wages whereas a major part of labour of women is in the non-market sector of the household. The labour of the full time housewife is counted as zero input in the labour market. Though she receives no wages she does contribute to her spouse's productivity. This is the "unmeasured support sector" of the economy which when appropriately captured in a "measured sector", a true picture of women's labour productivity will emerge. Even in the labour market a majority of women is in the low paying jobs which are mostly supporting jobs for male workers, and the productivity of the latter is dependent on the support sector provided by women whether paid for it or not.

Extending this argument further, the low productivity, and hence, lower payment for women can be explained in terms of the lack of the support system for female workers. It is also worth noting that a change in the support system will alter the productivity levels of males, and therefore, a change of the present pattern of sex division of labour will bring about undesirable results. This is purely born out of the mistaken view that larger economic contribution of women is at the peril of the household management and development of children.

The widely cherished hypothesis that increased entry of women into the labour market has lowered labour productivity should not go unchallenged. To prove the lowering of productivity, negative productively coefficients are assigned to women. This reinforces statistical discrimination and using these information shortcuts, sex discrimination is perpetuated. The so called low productivity depends significantly on how productivity is measured. In consistent definition of inputs, omission of the household sector, anomalies in labour market changes and inaccurate measurements of productivity with diversity of time and magnitude in labour market trends at a macro level, all contribute to show a comparative low productivity of women's labour justifying the earnings gap prevalent in the economies. Measurement anomalies relate to age, race and sex issues. They are

(i) an asymmetric treatment of capital and labour utilization,

(ii) Labour Market distortions such as wage discrimination, occupational segregation, segmented Markets or other forms of market distortions which affect wage patterns as indicators of productivity.

Control over Resources : The third determinant of earnings differentials is the degree of control over resources. This control may be over job-related resources like budget, work of others in a supervisory capacity, organisational policies and monetary resources. They imply authority of the position, supervisory authority, discretion and freedom of action. These characteristics along with structural determinants have important 'Wages

Effect' over and above the 'Effects of Human Capital'. With equal human capital endowments there arises wage differences if one is the supervisor and the other the supervised. How exactly to distinguish between the two is a moot question! The responsibility and control over resources come by experience and is certainly a component of human capital.

The fourth determinant resulting in earning differences between males and females in the sex division and sex segregation. Women tend to be employed in occupations for which firms pay less. When men's and women's earnings are compared within the same establishment as well as within detailed job classification, most of the earnings differences disappear.

The Differentiation

For most part men and women are not in the same detailed job classification and not in the same establishments. A more pertinent issue is why female occupations pay less than male occupations. Sex segregation argument does not help in determining the differentials when similar work is done by workers in different jobs and different firms. This issue has considerable practical importance. Occupational differences rather than characteristics of women's work should settle this issue. The present-day norms of equal pay for equal work, has done very little to close the earning gap. A more workable norm could be "more effective pay for comparable work".

Women's entry into the labour force is not a new phenomenon in India. The large number of women workers, the lack of opportunities for work and the segregation of women to certain classified jobs arising from the lower levels of training and education of women, account for the low earnings capacity and their unequal contribution to national income. Alongside these overall macro-economic observations and inferences regarding the existence and continuation of income and wage differences between male and female workers, it is necessary to have exhaustive studies of every sector of the economy to analyse the realities of the situation. Wage differences are there between males and males, regions and regions between industries and industries and between different states of India. The significance of wage differences in each case is as important as that of male - female differences. As yet very few attempts are made to have an in-depth study of matters relating to women employment. A highly disaggregated study of each occupation is called for to test the inferences drawn from macro observations.

From the Census data a list of occupational categories could be drawn and the relative participation of men and women identified. An account of the wage structure of each of the occupations and male-female wage differences prevailing in the occupations, the number of women workers in every classified job in each occupation, what minimum qualification requirements are essential for such occupations, the conditions of work including the disabilities and facilities present etc. will present an effective data base to draw inferences on this sensitive issue. But information on such vital issues are either not available or highly inadequate.

Demand and Supply Factors Fundamental to Wage Differences : Agriculture gives employment for the largest number of women in India. Within agriculture certain specified jobs are in women's domain. This is a historically obtained pattern and the lack of mobility for women to move across the various agricultural activities is largely dictated by social customs based on a certain division of labour giving due consideration to feminine limitations of a physical nature. With the rural economies turning into market economies the transformation could not leave behind the male-female hierarchy in agriculture. But as long as the differences in social status are entrenched in the Indian soil there could be but marginal changes brought about by economic and political changes.

In all cases, however, demand and supply forces, are fundamental to the prevailing occupational and wage patterns. Agriculture being a seasonal industry the interplay of supply and demand forces is dominant. In the various States in India, rural wages are prescribed and the difference maintained assiduously for the same type of job done by men and women. Though the Minimum Wages Act (1948) made it mandatory to fix minimum wages to labourers and review the same periodically not much has been done in this direction. The National Labour Commission also noted the continuation of wage differentials between men and women particularly in agriculture.

In all states in India wages are raised from time to time but the gap between male-female earnings continue unabridged. Unfortunately there are no studies to assess the situation in US totality. As in agriculture in construction industry which employs a large number of females workers, female-male earnings difference is more than 50%. Women are paid lower than men for handling the same type of job on the ground that they are unable to lift the same quantity of load as men and that they are slower than male workers. In Tamil Nadu, the male worker is called the big worker "(Periyal) and the female worker the small worker (chithal). The male big worker in due course of lime with more work experience becomes a mistry and mason whereas the female small worker remains a small worker! And as if to spite the economic society which continues to call her "small worker", irrespective of experience, she does limited work, takes long lunch hours to feed her children or to carry food to her husband. Low wages seem to have this compensation. Specific work characteristics of occupations limit movement for higher jobs. In the city civic body-the Corporation of Madras-sanitary services are the meanest jobs with lowest payment. But men sweepers get promoted to supervisory positions; women sweepers remain in the same category. The male-female disparities in earnings continue to be glaring as revealed by the NSSO and the Rural Labour Enquiry Reports. From the Wage Table prepared by the NSSO following inferences emerge:

(i) The earnings of the casual female labourers are highly depressed and are more pronounced than that of male casual labourers in both urban and rural areas. Between regular wage/salaries and casual female workers the latter earn one third of the former.

(ii) Male female differences in earnings are more pronounced in rural than in urban areas.

(iii) Among casual wage labourers female earnings are less than half of the male earnings. In rural areas these averages are Rs. 4.50 for females and Rs.10.30 for males. The corresponding male-female wages in urban areas are Rs.15.00 and Rs.10.00.

(iv) The wage differentials between males and females increase with age and after 60 the average wage falls sharply and this adds to the existing sharp differences with the result the women labourer above sixty, who for many reasons have to eke out a living by working are the most unfortunate in India. All piece rate workers, males and females are exploited by the corporate sector. For identical work wages vary. The case of self-employed is no better. As observed frequently "it is difficult to understand why and how the difference exists and why workers accept it." The answer is either accept it or starve! It is evident, therefore, that the constitutional guarantee that no citizen shall on ground of sex be ineligible for any employment or office under the State, stands corrected by social values and practices. In fulfilment of the above dictum all the services are by law thrown open to women. The strength of competition for all services lies in education and training. If they lack this, women remain segregated and pushed to lower jobs.

Employment Maximisation : Employment level and its follow up of income level of an economy indicate the potential economic welfare level of the nation. Several Five Year Plans have gone into operation in India. But the unemployment problem looks large. At the initial days of planning in India there was no political will to make employment maximisation as a priority strategy. Conflicting motives of growth, regional balance and agriculture - industry balance have superseded the employment motive.

More recently legal protection was given to women against exploitation in lower grades of occupation. The Government of India has accepted the convention of "Equal Value" adopted by the ILO. The Union Pay Commission used this principle as the basis for its recommendations and it is found in the Directive Principles of State Policy. The quest for technological maturity per se has left the employment generation as a secondary objective. The recent plan efforts are targeted for high levels of economic growth. Economic growth in aggregative terms has limited objective from the more important viewpoint of welfare and employment.

Mostly, the planning concepts, models, exercises and programmes run in terms of overall economic growth. Relating growth with poverty and employment is a recent realisation of planners. The enormous backlog of unemployment in India bears testimony to the failure of Indian planning. Our experience has only shown that "economic growth is not a sufficient condition" for betterment of employment status of a developing country. Growth exercise as practiced here belongs to an 'enclave variety' concentrating in certain sectors of the economy which does not in itself lead to employment. Income generation for relatively poorer sections of society and a sizeable section of the population are yet to be realised from the development process.

Adaptive Changes Essential for Increasing Participation Rate for Women : The late twentieth century has seen vast strides in the development of women in all parts of the world, particularly in the field of economic development. Women have been drawn into the mainstream of economic activity. With a marked change in their work force participation, concomitant questions of equality of opportunities, equal pay for equal work, exploitation of and discrimination against women labour are themes hotly debated and researched upon. The principle of equality of payment is accepted and implemented in the government and government sponsored sectors everywhere. The same is not true of women employment conditions in private enterprises and unorganised sectors. Even in many of the advanced countries, this still remains an issue. The keynote of the UN Declaration on the *Elimination of Discrimination* against Women could only arouse interest in women employment problems but could not serve as a guarantee for equality of incomes.

There is no denial of the fact that women's dependence leads to exploitation and denial of social justice. All great men including Karl Marx and Mahatma Gandhi were vehement against the rigid distinction between male and female employment roles in society. Full participation by men and women is a requirement for society's development. There are major changes in the rights and responsibilities of women. Rising age of marriage, smaller families, urbanisation, migration, rising costs and standards of living-all these call for greater participation of women in decision making and they have to meet these challenges by equipping themselves with education, training and involvement. Women themselves have to get over the conservative view of confining to rigidly defined limits and sex casting, and men should cast away the fear of unemployment due to entry of women. Today, practically there is no bar to women employment. They fill a variety of posts and positions barring very few vocations like the police, army and shipping. They are given statutory protection in all respects. Yet the majority of them lapse 'back into the old routine" " and the enveloped stalemate is rather heavy to lift. The cultural mileu of India is distinct.

'Women's coming out to work' in India is different from that of their counterparts in western countries. There are no accompanying adaptive changes. Working women have to perform professional as well as familial roles without the necessary complementary changes in their roles relations with other members of the family. The consequence is that employed women and especially married women are victims (or capable of making others victims) of conflicting role expectations from profession and domestic sides. There are ways to meet this challenge. One is to modify the work role to suit family role performance.

This facility is possible mostly in the unorganised sector of employment (e.g.) in agriculture and construction industry, women's work is somewhat flexible to care for family responsibilities. This is not, however possible in factory work and other occupations. Alternatively, coping facilities could be built to increase the effectiveness of family role performance. These facilities include home help, living in a joint family, household gadgets and coordination and understanding among the family members. Particularly, during the infancy of the children, the coping capacity is at the lowest and without entry possibilities into the labour market. There is a heavy wastage of women labour power. A good expedience could be part-time employment for women which will reduce the role conflict to the minimum. Reference could be made to the recommendation of the National Committee on Women in this regard viz.

(i) Extension of Maternity Benefits Act 1961 to all industries and agriculture and inclusion of anti-retrenchment clause in the Act,

(ii) Provision of Creches and other child care facilities

(iii) For extended working time, provision for transport and security.

(iv) Extension of Employees' State Insurance Scheme to all areas

(v) Equalization of wages

(vi) Integrated development of training and employment

(vii) Part-time employment opportunities

(viii) Employment information.

(ix) Provision of re-entry and

(x) Enforcement of laws protecting women workers.

Egalitarianism Practised in the Breach : The socio-economic legislation in India, pertaining to women promises equality for men and women in all aspects of life. Yet the society is hierarchical and status-oriented. The virtues of egalitarianism are practised in the breach. In every civilization, pursuit of justice is instinctive and is attained through the legal system. But the substantive rules are the products of the political process and are not adequate to meet the needs of society. The net result is that rate of development of law making lags behind the demands of social change.

Article 114 of the *Constitution of India* ensures quality before law, and equal wages for equal work. But fewer women get equal wages than men in the unorganised sector. Ratifying the ILO Convention No. 100, the Equal Remuneration Act (1976) has been passed, but is observed only in its breach. These several enactments have in fact backfired and have proved detrimental to women employment. The acts have been considered obstacles to women employment, on the basis that it is not possible to give several benefits to women which would put up the "real cost of labour".

No doubt employment opportunities for women have become more varied and wide. There is, therefore, immediate need for a shift of emphasis from protective legislation to legal guarantees. The various legal provisions for equality of pay have resulted in discrimination against employing women labour altogether. To avoid maternity leave facility, and provision of facilities for women labourers, employers are altogether avoiding women employment. Moving from legal safeguards to plan implementation in India, women continue to be low priority. Education, Health, and Welfare are considered low priorities in successive plan outlines. The proportional allocations for women's programme have been steadily declining.

The future is more open for women than at any time in the past. Science and technology has liberated women from building their lives around biological rhythms. They have control over birth and reproduction. But there are other questions at the deepest levels. The basic structure of society remaining unadaptable to modern views on women and work, reconciling home and career will remain a problem.

is her frailty. The intending murderer does not expect the same resistance from her as from man. Therefore, any leave or relaxation in Qisas will enhance oppression and tyranny and taking her life shall become an easy job.

These details reveal that there is consensus of the ummah or at least the four well known imams of Fiqh and the majority of the jurists are unanimous on the issue that a woman shall be put to death for taking the life of a man and vice versa. Now the question that remains is whether the punishment shall be enforced even if the murderer and the murdered are both women. The answer to this query is clear enough. When a man can be put to death for the murder of a woman why a woman cannot be put to death for the murder of a woman. The Quran is explicit about it:

> And woman shall be put to death for woman.[78]
> —Al Quran II : 178

So there is no contention on this point among the jurists that a female murderer can be put to death for taking the life of another woman. The statement of the Quran is general and the Hanafite Fiqh has also reasoned on its basis that a free woman murdering a slave girl shall also pay for it with her life.

Social Justice

Let us now take up the punishment for the physical injuries to a woman. It also takes the same forms discussed earlier under loss of life. A woman shall pay for her crime against man. Man shall be put to death for the murder of a woman. A woman shall be liable to punishment for any crime against a woman.

The following Quranic verse has ordained Qisas :

> We ordained therein for them 'Life for Life, eye for eye, nose for nose, ear for ear, tooth for tooth, and wounds equal for equal.' But if any one remits the

6

Women Professionals

Workers Venues

Economic literature which considers unemployment and poverty as synonymous fails to distinguish between unemployment as cause and poverty as effect. The Keynesian thought took notice of effective demand and employment causally, but did not comprehend sequential, and several contemporaneous causes. In reality, however, the distinction is vital and as Nurkse has so well demonstrated, capital formation in a developing economy like ours is more important than is realised in India. A good part of educated unemployment and women unemployment arises on account of inadequate cooperative factors.

Neither production nor prices, income and not even population contribute to the continuing failures of the Indian economy to the extent non-utilised human factors cause this pathological severity. Except for stray programmes in Seventh Five Year Plan onwards, i.e. since 1985, the Union and State Governments have had no employment policy worth its name.

Great administrators like the former Prime Minister, late Mrs. Indira Gandhi, conceded the fact, that "this is a lifetime operation and no great dent can be created". Nevertheless in both socialist China and capitalist U.S.A. full employment has been a realisable objective. Unemployed persons are explosive political material in our country. Yet women unemployment in India is a distinct phenomenon in itself and requires careful analysis. Even though they do not seem to be on the path of revolution, the deliberate non-use of their skills is revolting to our conscience.

Theoretically unemployment is the difference between the quantity of labour effectively supplied and the level of employment. $u = ls - l$ where u is unemployment, *ls* - effective supply of labour and *l* - level of employment. The tricky concept of underemployment though real, baffles measurement and hence the focus is mainly on unemployment which is apparently more readily measurable than the other concepts.

Labour services are heterogeneous. There are N different labour markets for N different types of labour which are distinguished either by quality or by location. Each type of labour is homogenous but even this cannot be pressed far to assume that in each labour market the wage currently paid is uniform. With such rigid assumptions, the behaviour of the rate of change of average wage and aggregate unemployment rate could be analysed following Philips curve treatment.

The analysis requires derivation of relations between each of these observed variables and an aggregate measure of excess demand by summing up the structural relations between the rate of wage change and excess demand, and between unemployment and excess demand in each of the N labour markets. Besides, the form of the non-market distribution of excess demand is also essential in the determination of aggregate unemployment rate.

Assuming homogenous labour and uniform wage in each

market, a simple and unambiguous measure of unemployment can be derived. Unemployment of the i th type of labour is $ui = l^s i - l_i$. The rate of unemployment for the i th type of labour is $Ui \frac{ui}{li} = \frac{l^s i - li}{l^s i}$

The relation between unemployment and excess demand for jobs involves the nature of restrictions on actual transactions in each market where exchange may be voluntary and exhaust all possibilities which are mutually advantageous at the current wage. Aggregate unemployment is determined by summing up unemployment of all labour markets. The overall unemployment rate is a weighted average of the unemployment rate in each labour market and the weights are the share of each market in the total labour force.

Excess demand may be increasing or decreasing in individual markets in response to wage adjustments and exogenous market disturbances. Excess demand of markets can change without altering the dispersion of excess demand. Positive unemployment denotes jobs less than job seekers and its counterpart is a positive number of unfilled vacancies. The existence of structural imbalance implies that aggregate employment is less than both the aggregate labour supply and aggregate labour demand.

A unit of measurement of employment is a difficult concept. Labour service can be graduated into man hours or days per week. Duration of work, however, has correlation with the level of wage by itself. Similarly, a unit of unemployment is equally a complicated concept where the main determinant is work and not its duration. Depending upon the economic climate, different approaches are used in the analysis of unemployment. In the Indian context, three types of unemployment are identified by the National Sample Survey. Based on the reference period of one year, one week or one day they are respectively called

(i) visible chronic unemployment,

(ii) weekly status unemployment, and

(iii) daily status unemployment. The first mentioned unemployment results when the labour force participant has not worked even for a fraction of the reference period. The NSS has also evolved a standard person year unemployment concept. Considering the nature of rural employment in India, 270 days are equated with a full year work. One unit of female labour is equated to half unit of male labour. Based on these two norms employed person days are aggregated into standardised person year employment and unemployment.

There appears to be no rationale behind the formula of one female equals half a male as followed by the NSS. A female labourer may be doing a different work from that of a male labourer but she does not work for half the time to claim the full wages. Female labour force participation has come to stay and is not a marginal phenomenon. Instead of the harsh aggregation of male and female employment into a meaningless standard person year employment, the two could have been left as distinct figures for the two sexes separately. This will serve as an effective policy variable. On the other hand, the NSS method of standardising leads to gross underestimation of the female work-force and perpetuation of sex discrimination in the labour market.

Estimates of Unemployment : Apart from that of the NSS, there were several other attempts to quantify the volume of unemployment in India. In the early seventies, the Dantwala Committee wound up its operations after conceding its inability to measure the volume of unemployment. With due caution, the Bhagavathi Committee (1973) did not go into the volume of unemployment but merely made a proposal for absorbing four million people requiring an outlay of Rs.2000 crores. Other estimates put the total outlay at Rs.800 to Rs.1000 crores per annum to provide gainful employment for 30% of the rural population and this by itself is proof of the dimensions of the problem of unemployment in India. The National Income Committee reiterated the need for regular statistics relating to employment in respect of all sectors not yet covered.

The semi-arid tropics of the developing countries have a relative abundance of labour in proportion to capital and land. Statistics on this 'apparent abundance' are available in terms of national or regional annual averages. Even those data are not reliable particularly for the rural areas. Problems of seasonal unemployment are most acute in rural areas. It is necessary to derive more accurate measures and a better understanding of the demand and supply parameters of labour markets particularly in India where 70% of the labour force is classified as agricultural workers.

The Data Base **:** The data base on employment and unemployment in India is very unsatisfactory. The Government of India Act, 1935 classified employment as a provincial subject and *Constitution of India* has placed 'social security and social insurance, employment and unemployment' in the VII Schedule, List III, namely, concurrent list - item 23.

Under the Employment Market Information Programme (EMIP) for the State Governments, Employment Exchanges provide the major source material for employment and unemployment statistics in India. All establishments in public sector and non-agricultural establishments in private sector, employing 25 persons and above on a compulsory basis and 10 and above on a voluntary basis are covered by these employment exchanges.

However, the two major gaps in information arise from

(i) the unorganised sector which accommodates the majority of the labour force and which is characterised by seasonal employment, and

(ii) disguised unemployment which is outside the ambit of the programme. Also the employment exchange data suffer from limitations because of voluntary enrolment system and hence in-comprehensive in coverage and inaccurate in the live registers. Those who have secured jobs remain in the live register for a long time. These data provide only a rough indicator of the unemployment situation. The Indian census provides massive data but only once in ten years; they are not adequate to meet the requirements of day-to-day administrative work and planning.

The Five Year Plan documents especially in the last two-VII and VIII Five Year Plans take cognizance of the enormity of the unemployment problem in India. Unemployment rates are apt to be depressed owing to the dominance of self employment in the agrarian sector and majority of workforce engaged in the unorganised sector employment. The measure of unemployment in terms of open unemployment is inadequate.

The National Sample Survey Organisation (NSSO) provides estimates of unemployment in its quinquennial surveys using three different concepts viz. usual status (US - working, or seeking work, or available for work for a longer time in the reference year). Current Weekly Status (CWS -worked for even an hour during the week but seeking and available for work) and Current Daily Status (CDS - total person days of unemployment of all persons in the labour force during the week). In 1987-88 these rates were respectively 3.77, 4.80 and 6.09 per cent. In absolute terms the respective figures were 11.53 m, 14.35m, and 65.08m person days.

The Characteristics : Employment generating capacities of different sectors of the economy are different and the agricultural sector has the largest employment generation in India. But the pressure of rural illiterate population and the inherent seasonality of agriculture, overpower this sector; unemployment and under-employment are the result. Women labourers are less equal and less competent competitors in the rural sector and naturally rural unemployment rate is higher for women than men. The secondary priority given to women's work from both demand and supply aspects of the rural economy makes rural women unemployment invisible and unaccounted.

Employment Generation

The generation of employment opportunities in the organised sector is relatively higher in urban than in rural areas. Large towns rather than small towns and villages have higher potential for absorption in the organised sector. This is due to agglomeration economics and is indicated by the elasticity of total employment to basic employment. (Basic employment is employment in mining, quarrying, manufacturing, and livestock sectors). This elasticity was 0.81 in class I towns, 0.33 in class II towns and 0.41 in class III towns.

A distinct problem in the case of Indian women is the voluntary unemployment among women and particularly among educated women. Despite shortage of trained doctors, there were 1000 doctors unemployed voluntarily in 1971. The largest number of unemployed were among the degree holders in arts and humanities. They make up 96% of the total unemployed women among university degree holders, according to 1971 figures. 53% of this employment was voluntary and the corresponding figure for men was only 9%. About 18% of the unemployed women holding technical or engineering degree are not keen on jobs: 9% of those with vocational training choose to remain unemployed. 55% of those with degrees in arts and humanities and 50% of those with general science degrees do not seek work. This social wastage is occurring at an exorbitantly high social cost.

Social Cost : From an economic point of view this voluntariness of women unemployment has varied implications. With low levels of employment opportunities women opting out of the employment sector reduces unemployment problem to a remarkable extent. But from the human resource development point of view, education and training that they have had is a social cost which gets a zero return. The levels of development of the economy does not warrant wastages of scarce educational resources on 50% of the educated women in India. Educational expenditure has to be largely investment outlay and not consumption expenditure particularly in view of the large state expenditure on education and training.

Unemployment does not harm everyone uniformly. It strikes mostly the weak, poor and the under-privileged. "It strikes from underneath at those at the bottom of our society." A disproportionate share of unemployment has been borne by the unskilled. There are fewer jobs available for the unskilled. The old, the very young, the disabled, those in depressed areas and declining industries, and particularly, women who stand last in the queue are vulnerable to unemployment. This is reinforced by the acceptance of certain inequalities in the distribution of employment. It is justified if it is a simple lack of demand for labour. On the other hand, unemployment is not to be rationalised as an "inevitable exhaust of our economic engine". Unemployment indicates a social process powered by the poor and ineffective values we hold and the choices we make.

To a large extent, women unemployment in India is to be understood in this context and not to be considered on par with male unemployment problem. Supporting evidence for this is readily available from Indian experience in recent years. Economic growth has not ensured that its benefits will trickle down to the poorest and the weakest. Policies to promote employment and reduce unemployment have not led to any improvement in female employment.

In this modern era, it is still not considered relevant to consider female employment as a separate and specific category in view of the fact that women constitute one-third of the labour force and their share of unemployment is 40% of the total work force and is higher than their share in the labour force. The *raison d'etre.* of differences between male and female employment need not be elaborated upon. Since women are unequal beneficiaries of economic development, there is need to consider female unemployment separately to formulate appropriate and effective employment policies.

VARIOUS METHODS

The Report of the Dantwala Committee, the several Rounds of the National Sample Survey, the Census Reports and other individual studies have led to some understanding of the extent and nature of women unemployment problem in India arising from the basic structural process at work in the economy.

The first employment and unemployment data for India was collected in the 9th Round of the N.S.S. during May to August 1955. The total population of 382.4m was divided into urban population of 66.3m and rural population 316m. The labour force contained 42.5% of the total population, 44.2% in rural and 34.5% in urban areas. The unemployment rate was very low at 0.29% for rural and 1.99% for urban population and it was 0.59% for India as a whole. Within the labour force, the unemployment rate was around 6.7% (6.1% urban and 0.66% rural).

Though this condition very well qualified for a full employment economy by all standards the large difference between rural and urban employment ruled out any place for complacency and satisfaction. Unemployment was almost 10 times greater in urban areas. No break up of male-female figures are available. However, from the labour force figures of 1951, as constituted by 90% of males and 36% of females in the age-group 15-64, certain rough derivations could be made to say that one third of unemployment was women unemployment.

The earlier 8th Round of the N.S.S. gave the breakdown of unemployment with educational levels as follows: Urban unemployment was made up of 21.6% illiterate, 60.23% literate but below metric and 17.99% educated. The illiterate unemployment rate was nominal at 3.46% of the labour force. Thus the unemployment problem from the start has been that of educated and urban unemployment problem and the subsequent surveys only reiterated the aggravating and increasing dimensions of educated unemployment. The educational level for women was considerably lower in the early fifties and the educated unemployment of women or for that matter, employment of women was a non-issue in the early days of Independence.

Low Priority : The information available from the various sources does not fully reflect the real unemployment trends in India. But whatever is available could serve as proxy for the same. The trend is clear. As we move up the educational ladder in both urban and rural areas the unemployment rate rises. More matriculates are unemployed compared to graduates; post-graduate more employed than graduates. The practice of higher level educated pushing out of employment the lower levels is apparent in India. However, the same process does not work as we move down the educational ladder. The educated would wait and be unemployed rather than accept jobs open for low levels of education. The changes in unemployment levels by education for a ten year period reflect the changing trends in educated unemployment pattern in India. Female unemployment which is higher than total unemployment shows the low priority of women employment in India.

Incidence of Unemployment : The incidence of unemployment is particularly heavy among females and within ten years there is more than a doubling of unemployment rates in all categories. On the basis of daily status, 25% in urban areas and 33% in rural areas are unemployed in India. The 27th

Round of the N.S.S. had a clear emphasis on unemployment and gave three estimates of unemployment:

(i) chronic unemployment (measured in number of persons)

(ii) weekly unemployment (measured in number of persons) and

(iii) unemployment including underemployment (measured in person days or person years). In the 1971 labour force of 230.5m, chronic unemployment was 3.6m. (This figure is based on 1972-73 National Sample Survey rates). The daily status unemployment rate for 1972-73 was 8.34% and its equivalent in person years was 18.57 m.

Assuming the labour force participation rate to be the same as in 1972-73, the fourth Five Year Plan estimated the labour force in 1978 as 265.3m with the adding of 6m per annum. The number of chronic unemployment persons in 1978 was estimated as 4.4m.

According to usual status approach, unemployment by March 1980 was estimated at 11.4 m. persons in the age group 15 and above. Weekly status unemployment puts the same figure at 11.6m. and the average daily unemployment as 19.8m. We hold that at least 30 to 40% of this magnitude is women unemployment in India. The 43rd Round of the NSS put the unemployment of females at 488 per thousand person for all Indian cities, 488 in urban India and 177 in rural India for the year 1987-88. Female employment by current daily status for the above mentioned categories were 101, 110 and 207 respectively." An inter-state comparison of unemployment in states gives certain striking results.

There occurs a high incidence of unemployment and underemployment with high wage rates (Kerala, Punjab and Haryana), as well as low wage rates (Bihar). Low incidence of underemployment co-exist with high wage rates in the Punjab and Haryana. Economic development generates high rates of labour absorption even at relatively high wage rates and at the same time high rates of employment are sustained by downward wage flexibility as in Madhya Pradesh, Uttar Pradesh and Rajasthan.

In spite of increasing scope for employing women in urban areas the incidence of unemployment of women in urban areas is high. This high incidence does not imply labour market discrimination which is but nominal. Nature and location of work opportunities do not meet the location specific work demands of female workers. Agriculture and household industry offer the facility of time and location for female workers and hence their concentration in those sectors. This is equally applicable to work preferences of females in urban areas as well, and particularly in the illiterate and unskilled women. Only 12% of the female labourers are willing to work outside their locality. (25th Round of N.S.S.). The major cause of female unemployment in India is restricted to mobility of women.

Visible and Invisible Employment : There are essential differences between unemployment problems in the industrialised western countries and India, a semi industrialised state. Western unemployment is in the background of labour shortage, long continuous periods of employment with intensity of effort, high extent of urbanisation, educational level and efficiency of the system of information, transmission and communication. In the Indian case, conceptualization and analysis of employment and unemployment based on the western notion are inappropriate. Free mobility of labourers between regions and occupations is restricted due to many reasons characteristic of the Indian economy.

India is a continent of vast differences and homogeneity is seldom found in living conditions, language, geography, culture, land ownership rights, educational levels, employ ability and employment opportunities. Self employment forms a high proportion of enterprises and persons and self-employment conceals unemployment and underemployment.

The unemployment problem is basically the consequence of the slow growth of employment opportunities in India. Between 1960 and 1968 productivity grew at an annual rate of 3%, employment at the rate of 5% and wage bill by more than 10% . One eighth of the capital outlay had to be spent on housing. The net result of these was the inability of the economy to generate worthwhile surplus to reinvest and to increase employment opportunities.

Existing data on employment of women fail to expose invisible unemployment. Even this inadequate data reveal increase in the rate of unemployment among rural women over the years particularly after 1966-67. Visible employment of women hides the stark reality that massive numbers of women are displaced from employment at an alarming rate not only in agriculture but also in the formal and informal industry sectors in rural and urban areas. The marginal increase in the number of women in the service sector is more than offset by the decline in employment opportunities in agriculture, industry and traditional services. Even this increase in employment in service industries is in poverty-oriented occupations like personal and domestic services generated by the increase in population in urban areas.

The new employment opportunities in modern industry and services have absorbed women mainly from the middle class because of education and training essential for entry into such occupations. The commercial sector, in which women played a significant role in the traditional economy has virtually become inaccessible to them with the increasing complexity of the market system. Added to this alienation by the economic forces, the social system adds to the non utilisation of women labour in our country. The prejudice against employment of married women is a special and crucial problem. This is an imposed household value system and is complemented by the ban and bias against married women in employment market.

***Problem of the Educated* :** Educated unemployment is a special problem in the Indian setting. A survey conducted by the Indian Institute of Public Opinion in 1972 indicated that one in four of literate youth between 18-24 years of age were unemployed. This gives for the whole country a literate youth unemployment figure of 7 million. On this assumption the total unemployed (literate and illiterate) aged under 24 was not likely to be less than 15 million and all unemployed (all ages and working less than thirty days in a year) not less than thirty million. This is grave enough as a base. The labour force growth is assumed to be 6 millions per year and jobs are available to the extent of only 2 million a year.

The backlog, therefore, of a 4 million is added every year. In the several plan periods the backlog of unemployment has been rising at enormous rates and so is the despair and frustration among the unemployed and particularly among the educated. On both counts female workers are affected in very large numbers. In 1987, there were 167.35 lakhs of educated unemployed from the registers of employment exchange. Among the educated unemployed the proportion of matriculates is falling and that of graduates and post-graduates is rising . It has risen from 9.5% in 1961 to 17% in 1987. Registration of unemployed shows that matriculation is not a terminal stage in the Indian educational system and that there is a tendency towards over education leading to a paradoxical manpower situation. The growth rates of educated job seekers are 12.4, 17.0 and 16.3 among the matriculates, higher secondary educated and graduates and post-graduates respectively.

Though agriculture offers part-time jobs for many more the educated employed can obtain only a few. The placement rate of employment exchanges is only a fourth of the new job seekers registered. An analysis of women unemployment is not available except for the total, and that for women have to be derived or assumed. Moreover, the data are in terms of stock of labour and not flow of man hours. Women's labour participation is either underestimated or ignored. Indian 'unemployment statistics" is, therefore, a reflection of the failure of the market to clear labour supply and the result of incomplete or non-available information on the part of job seekers regarding relevant alternatives they face.

The educated unemployed growth problem rests on the question of waiting period before entering a job. It is observed that in other developing countries as well waiting time for school leavers is less than that of college graduates. A list of skills and areas of job-oriented courses available to girls and women is furnished. However it is to be noted that not only admissions into these courses are restricted to women candidates and the number of women's polytechnics are very few considering the large number of school leavers.

Skills/Employment Areas Available for Women at the Higher Secondary Vocational and Training Levels in the Chennai Metropolitan Development area (Mmda)

1. Accounts - Theory and Practical; auditing - practical theory 2. Advanced Welding 3. AMIE Civil 4. AMIE Electrical 5. AMIE Mechanical 6. Aircraft Maintenance 7. Air-conditioning and Refrigeration 8. Auditing and Accountancy 9. Audio Mechanism 10. Bakery and Confectionery 11. Banking 12. Book binding, Album making and Files making 13. Balasevika Training Course 14. Batik craft course A and B levels 15. B. Pharmacy 16. B.Sc. Nursing 17. Business Management 18. Business Management for Small Industries 19. Canning and Food preservation 20. Certificate Course in film acting 21. Certificate in Laboratory Technology 22. Child care and Nutrition 23. Commerce, Accountancy, Office Administration with Management Principles and Techniques 24. Commercial services 25. Compositors' work 26. Computer Programming in

BASIC, COBOL, FORTRAN Languages 27. Cookery course for House-wives 28. Cooperative Management 29. Creche- cum-pre-school Helper's training 30. Data Processing concepts 31. DCE Civil 32. DEE Electrical 33. Dietetics, nutrition and food preservation 34. Dress Designing and making 35. Draughtsman (Civil) 36. Dental Hygienists 37. Draughtsman (Mechanical) 38. Diploma in public health nursing 39. Designing controls for information system 40. Diploma in Business Administration 41. Diploma in Music 42. Diploma in Painting 43. Diploma in Pharmacy Course 44. Diploma in Tailoring 45. Diploma in Computer Programming, word processing and analysis 46. Embroidery and Needle Work 47. Envelopes making 48. Footwear Advanced Course 49. General Nursing 50. General Mechanic Electronics 51. Hand Composing and Proof Reading 52. Hotel Reception and Book keeping 53. Heat Treatment 54. Health workers (female) Training 55. Homecraft course 56. Industrial Hydraulics and Pneumatic controls 57. I B M card punch operator 58. Industrial Chemistry 59. Medical Record Technicians 60. Metallurgy and Engineering Inspection 61. Mechanic-General Electronics 62. Mechanic Radio and Television 63. Maintenance and repair of domestic appliances 64. Material Testing - Engineering 65. Machine Tool maintenance 66. Marketing and Salesmanship 67. Nursing 68. Needlework, Dress making and Embroidery 69. Office Secretaryship with Accountancy 70. Printing 71. Pupil Nursing course 72. Production Technology and Operators Course 73. Proof Readers Work 74. Personal Secretary Course 75. Pre-school Teachers Training course 76. Post Diploma and Diploma Course in Dance 77. Photography 78. Post Diploma and Diploma Course in painting 79. Post Diploma in Advanced Cobol 80. Radio and Television Engineering maintenance and Repairs 81. Restaurant 82. Surveyor 83. Sewing prefabricating and closing footwear 84. Sandal making and finishing 85. Television Technology 86. The Fortran IV Language 87. Telex Operator 88. Teacher Training course 89. Telephone

Operator 90. Tool Room Operators Course 91. Tool and Die making 92. Watch clock maker 93. Wireless Operator.

Education - Employment linkages do not show uniform pattern in different countries of the world. If we graph the rate of unemployment among those completed successfully higher levels of education against the other levels (low and high) we find that at a certain level more education improves the chances of employment and at a different level more education make people less employable and the resultant is an inverted U shape denoting that the rate of unemployment for secondary school leavers exceeds that of primary school leavers and it declines again for University graduates.

In India educated unemployment is a burning issue. Young and educated "tolerate continuous unemployment" for long spells of time. It is more by choice than compulsion because they refuse to offer their services for a lower occupations where their expected earnings are below their reservation price. This type of unemployment arises from waiting for the right job and is quite reasonable because of the strong correlation between the level of initial start and subsequent promotion in their career.

During their waiting time their families sustain them and, therefore, persons chronically unemployed are necessarily above the poverty line. Family income tends to be higher than average for families to which most unemployed workers belong." The intensity of waiting time for employment by male and female youth in India is not the same. Vocation is primary to the males and is still considered secondary and less prior to female who belong to middle and higher income groups.

Upemployment and Poverty

Chronic poverty forces poor to accept whatever work

available regardless of the rate of remuneration. Men and women of this group cannot afford unemployment for long. This phenomenon is present in more intense form in the case of poor women in India. Economic necessity overrides social customs and women are driven to work outside home. The pull factors are social rigidity, family responsibility, inadequate education and training; the main push factor is poverty and hence, the economic necessity is to seek employment of whatever nature.

Manpower planning is non-existent in India at the macro level. Special Census of 1971 shows that more than 20% of science graduates and 14% of engineering graduates in India were unemployed. In 1976 there were over 18,400 unemployed engineers in India. Anticipating increased demand for this category of manpower in the country there was considerable expansion in educational facilities during the past decades. But the development plans have failed to generate an adequate demand for this critical category of manpower and is evidence to the built-in imbalance in our system and the absence of interaction between industry and education.

Economic Analysis of Domestic Work : Domestic work is a catcall residual category covering "many kinds of work involved in transforming, stretching and augmenting a predominantly male income so that it becomes a living for the family". It is necessary to analyse domestic work and the socio-economic composition of those primarily engaged in it. The generally held view of low labour force participation of the poorest women and the most affluent women should stand empirical verification. The reason for and policy implications of these low participations are totally different. Two important questions relating to the behaviour by two extreme groups of women are:

(i) How does the preoccupation with domestic work insulate women from outside employment, and does it signify the family's economic and social status?

(ii) To what extent the time spent on domestic work is really unemployment?

In general the richest and high caste women do not seek employment. Women of the middle peasant class are not averse to occasional wage employment. The poorest low caste women regularly seek paid work for supporting the family. However, in the case of the last two classes of women, poverty, education and living costs, to a great extent cut across the social hierarchy and include or push them to the labour market. Though precise estimation is not possible, the correlation between occupation with domestic work and socio-economic status cannot be ignored. Applying Amartya Sen's treatment of employment in terms of the income, production and recognition aspects to domestic work of women, we find that the first aspect of income or valuation of domestic work is non-existent in the Indian context.

In recent times its significance is realised only to the extent of stating that it cannot be valued. To return to the typical example from Alfred Marshall that when the man marries his cook, the national income is reduced and there is one less in the employment statistics, economists, great and small have given scant attention to this aspect of women's time allocation and their inhibition with value oriented economic system has led them nowhere.

The second aspect of production through employment is a severe testing ground for women's domestic work. But this work does not contribute to the Gross National Product. The third test of recognition of work hits the whole issue of domestic work of women. Like social work, domestic work is also honoured and held valuable but not recognized as "being engaged in something worthwhile".

Approaching this issue from the side of unemployment it is essential to consider the behaviour patterns of women in "their own assessment of their position". Household work might convince women in a certain context that she is fully employed and in another that she is 'wasting' her time. Women's behaviour pattern and attitude to work and her own valuation of it, are largely based on how she herself recognises her own state to be, which amounts to be the resultant of social conditioning. To qualify for the employment status, one has to 'seek work' and this distinguishes women workers from kitchen happy housewives' and other 'satisfied' members of the non-working population.

Darwinian Principle : Development in the Indian context may be examined in the light of the popular belief that women are equally discriminated and exploited against in their economic role as they are in their social role. We may review the two diverse schools of thought on the sex differences in earnings viz. that of the sophisticated social Darwinian school which attributes them to difference in biological, genetic, anthropological analysis and that of the human capital school according to which differences are accounted for in terms of the existence of vicious circles in the division of labour between men and women in the household work and that in the labour market.

Family members with lower potential market value allocate relatively more time to household work because the opportunity cost for them in the labour market is low. Both theories seem to fit well in the Indian context. Wage fixation for labour and particularly women labour have followed the former theory and this historically obtained wage differentials are perpetuated by the latter human capital approach. The illiterate, untrained, particularly low paid women are found to be more efficient and cost effective in housework and the allocation of women's time between housework and labour market is made flexible more in accordance with her household responsibilities than the low wage levels.

Gary. S. Backer, who has contributed to the human capital theory of sex differentials in earnings, puts the causes of women's failure to achieve economic parity in labour markets as their disproportionate commitment to unpaid work within the family unit. For women, household and labour markets are competing sectors while for men they are complementary sectors. Sex differences in any society has to be understood in this cultural context of complementarity and competition between the two sectors of the economy. As women move into higher status occupations, the degree of complementarity increases giving time to intensifying role conflicts. The fact that sex differences in earnings disappear in higher status occupation does not make one conclude that for these women housework is not competing with labour market. Part of the housework can be purchased and therefore indirectly is still the women's responsibility.

Theories of economic development teach us that migratory characteristic of a population is a contributory factor for progress and development. Census reports reveal considerable migration in our population. In the one-third of population who are enumerated outside their place of birth, women are preponderant over men. But this migration does not contribute to development since much of this is marriage and associational migration. Female migration which is more than double that of male migration is a cultural factor consisting mostly of rural migration. Urban environment appears to be hostile to rural women migrants. This cultural factor adds to the limitation of the woman worker who is apt to be a less firm-specific human capital and the cost minimising employers make use of this characteristic to charge discriminatory prices for women labour.

In spite of charters and enactments, it is quite difficult to establish the principle of equal pay for work of equal value. Professions traditionally preferred by women have a low pay structure. In high professions remuneration is related to the post irrespective of sex. However, it is much more difficult for women to compete with men for high level position. The entrenched male prejudices continue unabated, the discontinuity of most women's careers and the reluctancy of many women to assume positions of responsibility owing to priority given to family are all responsible for disparity of achievement between sexes. The new employment pattern with women's careers extending upto retirement is a recent development and is yet to change employers' attitude.

The pay differentials between men and women could be examined from different angles. Most work women do as in agriculture and other unorganised sectors is different in kind and where men and women do the work of the same description, certain disabilities attaching to women as employees as to discontinuity or interruption, make them worth less to the employer wherever statutory protection is not given to women's employment. For most occupations in the organised sector there is no difference in payment of men and women. Customary attitudes and valuation, social prejudices against women's work and the long held assumption that women's productivity and efficiency are lower in all jobs are factors responsible for the sex differences in the payment of work. Unorganised nature of employment, the seasonal nature of demand for labour as in agricultural operations, lack of organisation and lack of regulatory conditions add to the retention of the *status quo*.

Exchange Entitlement : There arises the question -Are the 80% of women population who do not enter the labour market an economic liability? Indian data show that more than three-fourth of this voluntarily unemployed women in the age-group 15-59 report their main activity as household duty. Let us argue for an alternative to household sector. There are comparable market prices for most of household services, cooking, washing, cleaning, hospitality, medicare, child care, nursing, baby sitting, tutoring, shopping and a host of household chores. Changing pattern of the use of domestic works in advanced countries involve priced finished and semi finished goods which are consumed and processed further for domestic use. The use of processed food is yet to take roots in the Indian system of living. One could, therefore, impute money values to the unremunerated household work of the majority of women of our country and entitle them as contributors to the national product. If the functional classification of the household as a consuming unit holds true elsewhere in other advanced countries, a good part of household work finds a money value in India as well.

Analysing the causes of the most acute of human deprivations of drought and famine, the modern theory's emphasis is on the inadequate Exchange Entitlement. Prof. Amartya Sen argues that the Bengal Famine of 1945 was caused by the inadequacy of monetary purchasing power. This theory has been applied even to the more gruesome Chennai Famine of 1876-78 in an earlier study by Prof. V. Shanmugasundaram. These theoretical findings could be appiied to women studies to account for the deprivation, malnutrition, neglect and not infrequent deaths due to maternity during the last several centuries of Indian womanhood. The answer to two questions :

(i) why are the women poor?

(ii) why do they find themselves poorer? could be sought in terms of the economic pathology attributable to the scarcity of exchange media and inaccessibility of it in non-monetary spheres.

Pure economic theories could not be pursued too far. In cases like this cultural economics takes a side seat of pure economics of money. Are there not goods which cannot be sold and bought except at fancy prices, any works of art? Are there not human values which transcend traders' transaction motives and their money weapon? Surely these are goods and services like children and kinsmen, love and affection, long term goodwill and short term compassion and the tender care of women at home.

Studying the most monetised of world economies and their economists thereof who are worshipped and thoughtlessly quoted by some pseudo scholars who are often men - we have somehow come to realise that even the 100% monetized economies like that of the American economy can better be understood, in terms of three pronged economic analysis (i) political economy, (ii) social economy, and (iii) cultural economy. The first two have served economics for a fairly long time and the third is now making a clean sweep of the over-worked monetary and market analysis. There is need to develop as facets of Applied Welfare Economics specialities like Cultural Economics, Health Economics, Environmental Economics and Socio-Legal Economics to make sure that institutional, and related human values are not lost in socio-economic calculus.

It is ridiculous to calculate the cost of the child in an economy where very long term values and attachments do not give scope for proxies to fix prices nor do enduring marriages based on sacrament rather than contractual arrangements brook the insolence of commodity markets. The cost of the child or the cost of marriages may fill volumes in new, highbred and also highly monetized economies of the west but, not as yet in traditional societies of India, China or Japan which between them provide scope for relevant socio-economic theorization for well over half the humanity.

Cultural Composition of Entitlement : Culture involves all the material and non-material products of human activity. It exhibits human achievements in terms of language and literature, artifacts, ideas, ideals and techniques. A cultural group is a union of persons who have a common material and social heritage, common beliefs, habits, activities and interest and who live in the same social environment, whether urban or rural, foreign or native, civilized or primitive. In general any social group which maintains social cohesion and expresses and attains common interests in its own unique manner is a cultural group.

In a large area, say city or country, there are many sub-cultural groups. Any cultural group has some social organization, some prescription for law and order, some traditions in the pursuit of various life activities, some norms and patterns in carrying on an associated existence, some form of social control to which members of the group are subjected and which most members recognize and acknowledge. In fine, the culture of a group fairly completely encompasses the activities, the thinking, and feeling of its members. Cultural uniqueness does not preclude multiplicity of standards, varying in extent and intensity with age groupings. "Men are creatures of culture rather than knowledge *per se,* creatures of habit rather than, reason, and what the individuals learn at home and in the streets has much more influence on his behaviour than the facts that he has been told in the schoolroom".

With respect to women's employment we could venture to suggest a normative theory of value, *a la* Cultural and Applied Welfare Economics sans pure economic theory. A Cultural Composition of Exchange Entitlement (C.C.E.E.) rather than mere Exchange Entitlement (E.E.) which pervade the minds of novitiate even if it cannot enter the thoughts of others for reasons of conformism as easy option. Let us consider two economic situations and try them in terms of E.E. and C.C.E.E. Teaching has been a traditional occupation of some of the social and cultural groups; some have been teachers for generations, and we know that it is a rare honour to be taught by them. Qualities like social grace, courtesy, consideration and concern apart, depth of knowledge, command of a wide range of learning and capacity to communicate and to think with a scholar are not easily available purely under the terms of Exchange Entitlement.

What is true of teaching may apply *mutatis mutandis* to highly skilled service and commodity sectors as well as household services which are mellowed by feminine qualities. When specifically applied to women, this is an aspect of theory for which we must widely seek franchise outside household. Women workers are preferred to men in many departments like teaching, electronics, medicare etc. because under given C.C.E.E. women are less prone to insubordination and distraction or even labour unrest.

The positive aspects of this, if not recognized respected and valued, women work force would also turn out to be mercenary and less devoted. The cultural component of the social system could not be diminished in the tradition-bound social system in India. As yet much of the women force has not entered the modern factory system and there is scope for economic programming to harmonies the honour and dignity of women through Cultural Composition of Exchange Entitlement System.

Direct and Indirect Costs : Alongside the innumerable benefits, modern industrial urban society has concomitant social costs and insecurities. Unemployment is one such bane of modern economies. Employment is a blessing. Many pertinent queries relate to the volume, identity and distribution of unemployment in a society.

Even from the narrow economic point of view, we are concerned not only as to what are the real and money costs of unemployment but also to what extent and in what ways these costs are met by the individuals, family, communities, employers and the whole society. To what extent has unemployment reinforced the stratification of our caste-bound and class-bound society? And are we sincere in our attack against unemployment? To add to the general misery, should the social system and economic sanctions work against the economic and social emancipation of majority of women in the entire world? Such questions have no ready answers but are often repeated in the interest of our commitment to welfare of the weak and under privileged.

In fact a large proportion of the unemployed has been

unemployed for long periods and women in particular for longer periods. Compared with other countries, the unemployed in India have relatively longer spells of unemployment. And when the unemployed are unemployable or work shy as it is mainly the case with women, it is at a substantial social cost. The direct and indirect social costs of the enormous backlog of unemployment represent frustration, anger, unhappiness and violence in the lives of individuals and families. The less ignorant they are, more are the social consequences as in the case of educated unemployed. They form a disadvantaged group of formidable dimensions and the social security schemes in the form of unemployment allowance do not touch even the fringe of the problem, even if they are feasible financial propositions in view of the low profile of the Indian economy.

The Goals

The Seventh Five Year Plan (1985-90) gives considerable importance to the Socio-Economic Programme for women and discusses the varied aspects of women in India in a separate chapter. Taking note of the distinctly low levels of literacy and health of Indian women, it concedes that some of the new technologies have displaced women from many traditional activities and the limited job opportunities available to them in modern occupations and trades have led to a declining trend in women employment.

The long term objective of the Seventh Plan with regard to women is to raise their economic and social status in order to bring them into the mainstream of national development. The planning strategy would be an integrated multi-disciplinary approach, covering employment, education, health, nutrition, application of science and technology and other related aspects in the areas of interest to women. Income and Employment generating schemes in the rural areas like the IRDP, DWCRA, NREP, RLEGP, TRYSEM, etc would be strengthened and modified to reach the target groups taking particular note of the recently emerging phenomenon of the 'single' parent rural family arising from the large scale migration of men seeking employment outside their villages. In the industrial sectors, the Seventh Plan, envisages that Entrepreneurial Development Programme (EDP). Industrial Estates, Process Cum Product Development Centres (PPCC) Small Industries Services Institutes (SISI), District Industries Centres (DIC), and National Small Industries Corporation (NSIC) would identify and target women beneficiaries for promotion of skilled employment for them. Particular stress is on the Khadi and Village Industries sectors where the percentage share of additional employment of 2,06 million persons will come to women.

The Eighth Five Year has not given an exclusive chapter on Women Development. There is no particular focus on women employment either. The Plan envisages employment to grow at the rate of 2.6% per annum which will provide 8 million jobs in the first two years of the Plan and 9 millions job in the last three years. But these estimates appear to be based on overestimated employment elasticities in different sectors of the economy. In other words the overall assessment of employment objectives is highly exaggerated and lack realistic basis for its formulation. The tall claim of the eighth Five Years Plan to generate adequate employment by 2000 AD appears to be mere lip service without adequate policy insights. Women employment finds no special focus in the plan framework.

Policy Imperatives : The very livelihood is at stake for the unemployed and they suffer loss of earnings and the whole range of benefits and rights. Even in developed countries the levels of unemployment show increasing trends and greater duration thus making it essential to measure the social cost and economic impact of joblessness on those experiencing it and the drain to the society. The need to study the burden over time and its effect on particularly vulnerable groups in the poor and developing countries cannot be further emphasised. However, detailed analysis of short term and chronic unemployment is exceedingly limited except for a few attempts. Worswick rightly condemns the current method of measuring unemployment with its technical and economic dimensions without an accompanying measure of the social impact and significance. The misery and inequality cannot find their compensation in the unemployment allowance and grants. Economists have traditionally fought shy of questions of this kind. Except for their analysis of welfare in abstract, their reluctance to get to grips with any applied welfare question in detail is very glaring.

There is a general practice of considering women only as a target group for social welfare schemes and not as contributors to productivity and progress. Indian development plans have overlooked the need to strengthen women's productive roles. It is not far from truth when we say that throughout the plan programme in India there is a "general tendency to direct services designed for economic development mainly to men".

Programme for women are but marginal in Indian economic development activities. The benefits of development are not equally shared by men and women. This is particularly true of rural population. The effect of developmental efforts has been a progressive reduction in the size of female labour force together with a widening of male-female wage differentials. In the increasing unemployment situation in India, women are worst sufferers than male workers. The increase in the literacy levels of women is not resulting in improved skills and competence of women to survive in the labour market.

Women's reluctance to seek work outside their homes, though very much weakened in recent years, still stands in their way. Realising that majority of women will continue to be full time home makers, the Education Commission observed that women's world should not be limited to that relationship alone. In line with the cultural background and in view of the need to reinforce the existing strong family ties in the household, the Report called for a harmonious adjustment between women's economic interest within and outside their home.

In low income countries educational expansion is not easy. Education is both the responsibility of the States and the Union Government. Even after making all possible budgetary provisions it was found that at least three possible sources could be explored to finance education:

(i) aid from abroad

(ii) direct transfers from private sector in labour, cash or kind and

(iii) taxes at different levels. Till recently foreign aid was in the form of fellowships, whereas now "offshore" aid in the form of local building and equipment costs are also contemplated. With better tax administration states could raise additional resources for education. It has been said that "one form of aid which the advanced countries can most usefully give them (less developed countries) is to help overhaul their tax structures and to train tax administrators". On the lines of reasoning of this great authority on Public Finance, late Lady Hicks, whose love of India especially Tamil Nadu, the present author had known in person for several decades - may we add that fiscal measures to help women employment could be tax rebate incentives and

(i) for addition to women labour force, and

(ii) for training women skilled occupations.

Physical capital vs. human capital in planning present a contrast in India. The role of human capital in economic development is not yet fully recognised in the Indian context. India is an ethnically heterogeneous society and at an early stage of economic development. Prof. P.T. Bauer rightly argues, that "development literature accepts much too uncritically the role of investment expenditure as an engine of growth. Instead of money and physical capital alone being the bedrock of development, we have to recognise the equally important role of human capital.

Women and Human Resources

Even here there is scope for error arising out of undue emphasis on any one factor, including human resources. As is observed the importance of human resource need not be exaggerated ignoring the importance of physical capital. All the same the very low level of literacy itself is proof of the low cognizance of human capital factor in Indian economic development. Human resources include entrepreunorial ability, skilled manpower, state of administration and national character.

Prof. Jewkes is an uncompromising critic of the very concept of planning. He points to the utter neglect of women in Indian economic planning almost for three decades and indicates that even if they are key points to be noted planners were not good at identifying the more important points for action. The intellectual error pertain to certain key points at which governments can bring pressure to bear and thereby determine economic growth.

To provide the supportive mechanism for progress of employment of women, implementation of the various legal enactments like the Equal Remuneration (Act 1976) and the Mines Act of 1952 could be strengthened and thereby the interests of women would be adequately protected. Particular emphasis is on the study and identification of factors that hinder women employment. The possibilities for creating part-time employment for women would also be explored under the current plan.

Self-employment and Home Based Work : The Union Planning Commission, the Industries Department, Union and

State Governments and other agencies support programmes of cottage and small scale industries employing processes which will not remove women far away from their households. Particularly attempts to promote self-employment among women are appropriate. Though in the early stages such attempts failed to generate employment due to lack of managerial training, credit facility and raw material supply, there is an increasing measure of success in this direction. Special emphasis could be on agro-based industries. A coordinated rural development plan and establishment of agro-based centres will link rural-urban development and generate large employment opportunities for men and women.

Women do not get necessary training for many kinds of organised sector work. Vocational training facilities for women have been neglected and industrial training facilities are very insignificant. There were only 4% of women trainees out of 356 in the Industrial Training Institute in 1977 and the proportion of women in total number of apprenticeship training in June 1977 was only 2.5%.

An effective approach for fuller utilisation of women-power resources in India could be in terms of planning for part time work for women on a wider scale. Most women prefer work that will allow them time and emotional energy to look after their families. Rather than exploiting this weakness by discriminating against women in employment and barring their entry into certain professions, qualified and professional as well as trained and semi-skilled women can fit in their work on part time basis. There is unfortunately a Mug's Law according to which the more desperately you need part-time work, the more you have to pay for it in terms of low pay, low job protection, low responsibility, low chances of promotion and low security. Facilities for part-time work at higher levels of employment will certainly draw out the near 50% of educated women who are voluntarily unemployed.

There are professions in which part-time work can be

easily introduced without much inconvenience. Teaching in schools and colleges, social service, nursing, journalism and similar jobs can be adapted for flexible timing of women workers. The Commission on Women's Education had made similar recommendations to extend part-time work for women. A survey of employment opportunities for part-time work accompanied by the establishment of placement services was also recommended by the Commission. In certain service institutions like schools, colleges and hospitals, work in multiple shifts could be organised for increased productivity and employment. The close relationship between the status of women, and economic independence cannot be denied. The full integration of women in development will take place only when the human resources that women represent are no longer wasted. Women unemployment problem is to be viewed in this perspective to devise appropriate strategies for its effective reduction.

Meeting Human Needs : The simple theory is that poverty is a received phenomenon and its solution can only be by a change, and a reversal of the received situation. Isolated policies crash land. A simple equation which relates HR and HN takes care of absolute poverty by related work leisure preferences. All other technological and organisational issues fail into a consistency pattern. Human resources especially hitherto unsued educated women employment potential could be harnessed to generate many goods, especially agricultural and industrial products and services for meeting basic human needs like food, clothing and shelter for the half starved, ill-clad and houseless people of India. The Indian economy is socialistic according to the "Preamble" to the Constitution. Nevertheless, the basic needs of the people have not yet been met, and inequality between classes is wide, and between men and women wider still.

The Significance : The significance of this study is that it identifies a gap in the theory of economic literature on employment. By employment whether it is in the writings of early works of Adam Smith or in the writings of Physiocrats, Alfred Marshall, A.C. Pigou, J.M. Keynes, W. Beveridege, or J.E. Meade or A.P. Lerner there is little specific reference to women employment. Alfred Marshall gives a classic example which is widely quoted that when a man marries his cook, national income estimate is reduced. But what had Alfred Marshall to say when he married Pally Marshall a co-author of his book, a teacher in her own right and active to the last days as hostess to many economists and in charge of Marshall Library in Cambridge? Is she not a self- employed economist, and hence is it not the fault of the national income statistician who underestimates her contribution?

The conceptual clarification of employment, paid, unpaid, or underpaid, is one of the themes of discussion in this study. Large quantities of materials from the Census Reports, N.S.S. and other official reports are available and to our surprise male-female categorization is confined to birth and death and age structure. These are basic biological data. What we miss from the economists' point of view are employment statistics. While highlighting these inadequacies, piecing together available data is a task germane to this study. In poor countries, there are many in absolute poverty or misery due to unemployment and low income. Women, and children are helpless without work which could earn them income. To picturise and hypothesise these situations have been our tasks.

According to Prof. J.E. Meade full employment means that

(i) the person concerned in the work force *seeks* employment,

(ii) is *capable* of employment, and

(iii) is in fact *socially permitted* to be employed. If these criteria are enforced most of the women may not be reckoned in the work force. Further those who are under training/education are again persons not in the labour market. These are arguments well known to economists in the works of A.C. Pigou, J.M. Keynes, W. Beveridge and Joan Robinson.

In this exercise it could be noted that in the next decade the policy of near 100% literacy and training programme could take care of the sizaeble portion of women labour now outside labour force but potentially demanding employment. Secondly, cultural institutions governing choice of employment, categories and places of work which also voluntarily remove a large chuck from women labour market now, will be less powerful. If those changes do not take place, statistically we would come to the same conclusion as the Dantwala Committee did for the overall labour force, on Meade's definition, that there is no unemployment in pure economic theory. We are concerned with applied Welfare Economics, and reform of cultural institutions.

Convenient assumptions, and concepts of *laissez faire* economics seem to cloud reasoning. We seek women employment from the macro-economic perspective of increasing the production of goods and services, augmenting real national income and towards this end we decry the non-utilisation of women work force in sufficiently articulate and significantly large measure. The present day Cooks may graduate to Clerkship, and later to Chartered Accountancy. The underpaid woman agricultural worker could well be a manager of a cooperative farm or a soil chemist.

With given participation rates and employment opportunities, wage levels and employment opportunities do not seem to square either with the micro economic marginalist firm analysis or with macro-economic appraisal of growth. So far as women employment is concerned, underpaid, uncertain and temporary, are the terms applicable to women employment phenomena. In the abundance of literature on Poverty, Growth and Income Distribution, one gets very few glimpses of the conditions of women employment.

A lady carrying a pot of water on her head is a photograph accompanied by the promise of rural water supply. Water, every human being needs - man, woman or child. The issue that is missed is the nature of women employment which is caricatured by a large pot on a slender female head-taking for granted that this is a kind of work assigned to women, forgetting that a pipeline could bring water (clear, pure and abundant), whereas women could be designers of waterline systems or chemists to take care of purification and prevention of pollution. Sympathy for women may be well intentioned. But this is not enough. Substitution of water pots by protected water supply is necessary but not sufficient to create alternative women employment, unless women are skilled and their skills are used.

Occupational pattern and wage differentials, causes of unemployment and kinds of employment, and new avenues for employment are thematic sections of earlier chapters to assess the significance and potentialities for women employment. This work on some of the significant facets of the phenomenon of employment of women has its base on institutional theory of women. From cradle onwards women all over the world are made to feel different, and indeed are reared to sustain and strengthen the institution of home. Four walls of a room, or a count of the heads within a house are not enough to make a home - doubtless the best attribute of received culture. The cry of exploitation of women and in turn the clamour of women for participation in market-oriented employment- income cycle are inescapable signals for change in contemporary times.

We have delineated in the previous chapters, relationship between women and home, the occupational choices for women, the characteristics of interdependence between female labour supply and the institution of marriage. There are certain eternal values which distinguish the animals in the forests from the more evolved homosapiens. Sociological and political values were shaped and reshaped after thousands of years of human experience and hence tradition has yielded place to modernity, wherever, and to whichever extent, logic of civilized community living has justified. Social morality consists in that pattern of individual and family conduct which if practised would make the individuals happy, without making the society unhappy. The economic position of women in developing countries what with illiteracy, ignorance and poverty haunting them is seen by us in the backdrop of gradual evolution from historical staticity to evolved modernity.

The factor labour is said to be non-homogeneous. Women labour seems to be even more non-homogeneous. Their motivations for work is as feeble as the wages offered to them are meagre. A conceptualisation of women worker in the employment sphere is essential and an attempt is made to study the different contexts in which the woman participates in the national economy, struggling as she does to take on new supportive roles, notwithstanding, hazards in the way of removal of barriers to female employment.

The six chapters which sequentially studied the institutional theory of women employment, trends in developed and developing economies in respect of women employment, the occupational conditions and emerging patterns of women employment, the linkages between earnings and labour force participation rates, the picture as it emerges from the field study and specific micro-case studies -can all be pooled together in a policy perspective for full employment of women in India. This covers in a broad spectrum the intricacies of finding and rewarding increasing levels of women employment in India.

The chronic nature of unemployment in India relates to both men and women and one should be brave indeed in the existing social and political framework to argue for full employment here and now. The Seventh Five Year Plan covering 1985-1990, has gone on record that the supply of employment opportunities will be larger than the demand for it.

Idle human resources, more than any other malady, has perpetuated "poverty - low productivity - inequality syndrome. Any effort to break this, even though feebly, is worthy of appreciation. Through the nineties the imperative of larger employment prospects have been the overall objective be it the Eighth Five Year Plan, the resolutions of the All India Congress (Ruling Party) Conference presided over by Mr. P.V. Narasimha Rao in March 1993 or the election manifestoes of major political parties in India. The question from women studies point of view, is whether there is sufficient political will and an articulate understanding of the realities which are perpetuating chronic unemployment.

One can conveniently assume that the proper place of women is the home, and proceed to the next stage of reasoning that women are either not willing or that they are not capable of employment. This is a contention consistently refuted with facts that are available, and economic reasoning that is based on sound theories of social sciences. That more employment opportunities for men and women could be provided and among the takers of new employment opportunities, women should have more than their historical share, are arguments advanced for future policy making and implementation.

There are many fallacies of reasoning and errors of facts as regards women employment. It is said that urban participation rates for women are low. The field study gives evidence in this work, to disprove this contention. Selected micro case studies show how cruel and uncultured, how gruesome and calamitous are the lives of individual women under the threat of starvation, unemployment, low income and institutionalised cruelties like dowry extraction and humiliation of human personality.

Women and children suffer poverty and to a great extent this can be mitigated by employment and income. It is no part of claim in this work that men have no disabilities. This is a man's world but can also be argued that it was made in historic times of remote past with good intentions to make the lives of women happy. The hell too, it is said, is paved with good intentions. Good intentions are essential causes; good effects are the real test of causation. There are numerous careers, women could launch as may be seen listed in a Section above. In many countries the right to work has become a constitutionally recognized norm.

The Indian Constitution which has incorporated the duties of citizens in the 1975 amendment, also promises in its original form equality of opportunities for men and women, irrespective of religion or caste. The preamble of the Indian Constitution was considered by Sir Earnest Barker as the most outstanding in the world. As if to paint the lily, or add fragrance to the rose, the preamble has also been widened in 1975 to incorporate the terms "socialist" and "secular". Decades in the life of a nation are brief spells of time, and we have waited for nearly four decades in a situation of massive unemployment of men, and more so, of women.

But despair is not warranted. Despite, decades of underemployment, India which could not manufacture a bicycle at the dawn of Independence, today rolls out ten-tonner heavy vehicles for the world market. Women who were mostly illiterate in the past are becoming literate and skilled. Many of them fill the offices of the nationalised banks, and enrich the corridors of power at the highest levels in Indian Union, and State Governments and international administration in the United Nations and World Bank. And as outstanding woman of the twentieth century late Mrs. Indira Gandhi the late Prime Minister was hailed as the Empress of Asia by the renowned global journal *The Economist* of London. One would say they are exceptions; but exceptions prove the rule. A great humorist of the House of Commons Sir A.P. Herbert (b.1890) in a poem brings out the manifold skills and potentialities of a woman. He says:

> "I am not a jealous women, but I *CAN'T* see what he sees in her, I can't see *WHAT* he sees in her, I can't see what he *SEES* in her."

The underlined terms *can't, what, sees* make all the difference between what is reality in respect of woman employment what we are willing to see or believe. Women are an enigma; so indeed are men. Economic philosophy governing human beings is complex and closer to what Mathew Arnold would have us believe.

"We, in some unknown power's employ, Move on a rigorous line: Can neither, when we will, enjoy, Nor, when we will, resign".

To make the complexities of physical life simple, physicists like Sir, C.V.Raman or Dr. Albert Einstein produced the theory of light or of the Universe. To link food and population there is T.R. Malthus, and to see through the maze of unemployment in an industrial capitalist society there are Karl Marx and J.M. Keynes, though they have opposite theories or to peer through the monetary machinations, there is Milton Friedman. And yet even the feeble voice of institutionalists like T. Veblen or Gunnar Myrdal in defence of the poor in his *Poverty of Nations* or the articulate economic philosophy of Joan Robinson pleading for a more egalitarian society, does not seem to reach the powers that be. Employment of women is an economic necessity, but not yet a reality. Full employment of women, is but a dream today. May it be a reality tomorrow.

BIBLIOGRAPHY

Ahamed Shohail : *Women in Profession — a Comparative Study of Hindu and Muslim Women*, Royal Publishers, New Delhi, 1996.

Ahmad, Anis : *Woman and Social Justice*, Royal Publishers, New Delhi, 1997.

Altekar, A.S. : *The Position of Women in Hindu Civilization*, Motilal Banarsidas, Varanasi, 1962.

Anand, U.K. : *Working Women and Retirement*, Anmol Publications, New Delhi, 2001.

Anita, Arya : *Indian Women*, Gyan Books Pvt. Ltd., New Delhi, 2000.

Anshen, R.N. : *The Family— its Functions and Destiny*, Harper & Row, New York, 1959.

Asthana, P. : *Women's Movement in India*, Vikas Publishing House, Delhi, 1974.

Badel, Auguste : *Women— Past, Present and Future*, Bone and Liveright, New York, 1918.

Balakrishnan A. : *Problems of Rural Landless Women Labourers*, Gyan Books Pvt. Ltd., New Delhi, 2004.

Beteille, Andre : *Position of Women in India Society*, Publication Division, Government of India, Delhi, 1975.

Bhatnagar, Sudha : *Scheduled Caste Women*, Rawat Pub., Jaipur, 1997.

Chaudhury, K.N. : *Economy and Society*, OUP, London, 1979.

Cohn, B.S. : *Structural Change in Indian Rural Society*, MacMillan, London, 1969.

Das, Ram Mohan : *Women in Manu's Philosophy*, ASB Pub., Jalandhar, 1993.

Deckard, B.S. : *The Women's Movement*, Harper and Row, New York, 1979.

Durkheim, E. : *The Division o f Labour in Society*, MacMillan, London, 1933.

Esther Boserup : *Women's Role in Economic Development*, Chicago, 1976.

Everett, J.M. : *Women and Social Change in India*, Heritage Pub., New York, 1979.

Fromm, E. : *Man for Himself*, Holt Rinehart and Winston, New York, 1964.

Gorwaney, N. : *Self Image and Social Change— a Study of Female Students*, Sterling Publishers, Delhi, 1977.

Gupta, Sunit : *Role of Women in the 21st Century*, Anmol Publications, New Delhi, 2000.

Jaya, A. : *Women's Studies— an Engineering Academic Discipline*, Gyan Books Pvt. Ltd., New Delhi, 1993.

Jayal, Shakambari : *The Status of Women in Epics*, Motilal Banarsidas, Delhi, 1966.

Kalarani, A. : *Role Coriflict in Working Women*, Chitra Pub., New Delhi, 1976.

Kumar, Ashok : *Women in Contemporary Indian Society*, Anmol Publications, New Delhi, 1993.

Lakshmikumari, M. : *The Role of Women in Society*, Sterling Publishers Pvt. Ltd., New Delhi, 1997.

MacIver, A. : *The Society*, MacMillan, London, 1952.

Mahta, Basant : *Role of Banks in Women Development*, Discovery Publishing House, New Delhi, 2003.

Mandal, Amal : *Women in Panchayati Raj Institutions*, Kanishka Publishers, New Delhi, 2002.

Meena, A. : *Dalit Women — Fear and Discrimination*, Gyan Books Pvt. Ltd., New Delhi, 2004.

Mehta, Rama : *Socio Legal Status of Women in India*, Metropolitan Book Co., Delhi, 1982.

Minault, Gail : *Secluded Scholars, Women's Education and Muslim Social Reform in Cobaial India*, Oxford Univ. Press, Delhi, 1998.

Mitra, Joyati : *Women and Society —Equality and Empowerment*, Kanishka Publishers, New Delhi, 1997.

Moore, W.E. : *Man, Time and Society*, John Wiley and Sons, New York, 1963.

Mukherjee, Asha : *Conditioning and Empowerment of Women*, Gyan Books Pvt. Ltd., New Delhi, 2003.

Mukherjee, Doel : *Status on Crime Against Women in Different Countries*, Gyan Books Pvt. Ltd., New Delhi, 2004.

Narasaiah, M. L. : *Women, Children and Poverty*, Discovery Publishing House, New Delhi, 2001.

Neera, Maithreyi, Krishnaraj : *Women an Society in India*, Ajanta Publication, New Delhi, 1987.

Pandey, A.B. : *Society and Government in Medieval India*, Central Book Depot, Allahabad, 1965.

Prasad, R. : *Social Reforms: An Analysis of Indian Society*, Y.K. Publishers, Agra, 1990.

Ramesh Saini M. Kalpana : *Status of Women in Rural Societies*, Gyan Books Pvt. Ltd., New Delhi, 2002.

Ranganathan, Sarala : *Women and Social Order — a Profile of Major Indicators and Determinants*, Kanishka Publishers, New Delhi, 1998.

Rao, Y. V. Lakshmana : *Communication and Development in Indian Society*, University of Minnesota Press, Minneapolis, 1998.

Reddi, G.Narayana, and Reddi Soma Narayan : *Women and Child Development: Some Contemporary Issues,* Chugh Publications, Allahabad, 1987.

Rehana, G. : *Women in Indian Society— a Reader* Sage Publications, New Delhi, 1988.

Sabyasachi, B. : *Development of Women's Education in India,* Kanishka Publishers, New Delhi, 2001.

Sarada, D. : *Family Life Education for Adolescent Girls,* Discovery Publishing House, New Delhi, 1999.

Saxena Kiran : *Women and Politics,* Gyan Books Pvt. Ltd., New Delhi, 2000.

Selznick, P. : *Law, Society, and Industrial Justice,* Russell Sage, New York, 1969.

Shaikh, M.H. : *Women under Different Social and Religious Law,* Seema Pub., New Delhi, 1976.

Shirwadkar Swati : *Women and Socio-Cultural Changes,* Gyan Books Pvt. Ltd., New Delhi, 1998.

Singh, Indu Prakash : *Indian Women: The Captured Beings,* Intellectual Publishing House, New Delhi, 1990.

Skolnick, J. H. : *Justice Without Trial: Law Enforcement in Democratic Society,* John Wiley, New York, 1967.

Tara, A. : *India's Woman Position,* S. Chand & Company Pvt. Ltd., Delhi, 1976.

Thapar, R. : *Status of Women Employees in Government,* Mittal Publishers, New Delhi, 1990.

Usha, A. : *Indian Women Education and Development,* The Indian Publications, Ambala, 1995.

Uthapna, J. : *Indian Women Freedom Fighters,* Manohar Publications, New Delhi, 1986.

Verba, S. : *Status of Rural Women,* Akarshan Publishing House, Mumbai, 2002.

Vibhuti, P. : *Women Challenges of the New Millennium,* Gyan Books Pvt. Ltd., New Delhi, 2002.

Weber, Max : *The Position of Women in Migrant Bastis in Delhi,* New Delhi, 1976.

Whyte, H. : *Women and Career,* Tata Institute of Social Sciences, Bombay, 1963.

William, Z. : *Women in Contemporary India and South Asia,* Manohar Pub., Delhi, 1980.

Wilson, J. : *Women's Equality in India,* Discovery Publishing House, New Delhi, 2000.

Winch, P. : *Culture and Society in India,* Popular Prakashan, Bombay, 1967.

Zaidi, M. : *Women in Hindu Society,* Jyotsana Prakashan, Delhi, 1982.

Zeitlin, M. : *Women in Contemporary India,* Manohar Books Service, New Delhi, 1975.

Index

D

E

F

G

H

I

❑❑❑